Doing Business In Ghana

John E. Spillan • Domfeh Obed King

Doing Business In Ghana

Challenges and Opportunities

palgrave
macmillan

John E. Spillan
University of North Carolina at Pembroke
Pinehurst, North Carolina, USA

Domfeh Obed King
Kumasi, Ghana

ISBN 978-3-319-54770-1 ISBN 978-3-319-54771-8 (eBook)
DOI 10.1007/978-3-319-54771-8

Library of Congress Control Number: 2017937941

Printed on acid-free paper

This Palgrave Macmillan imprint is published by Springer Nature
The registered company is Springer International Publishing AG
The registered company address is: Gewerbestrasse 11, 6330 Cham, Switzerland

Contents

List of Figures

List of Tables

CHAPTER 1

Introduction to Doing Business in Ghana

1.1 Introduction

Globalization has changed the way business is conducted around the world. Changes in the exchange of ideas, information and technology, and the political process have served in many cases to improve and expand the market systems in Ghana. As such, the potential opportunities for business investment in the region have blossomed. While several areas of Ghana demonstrate great opportunities, such possibilities have not uniformly occurred throughout the country. The Ghanaian regions embracing the challenges posed by the globalized economy are providing different business opportunities and different developmental models.

For managers to do business in Ghana, they need to select which region, city, and location is best suited for marketing their products or services. Business opportunities in Ghana have different potential depending on the size of the economy, gross domestic product (GDP) growth, political and governmental systems, the openness of the economy, and their friendliness toward investors. In addition, the levels of penetration or per-capita consumption on each industry, sector, or product/service category need to be understood.

Where is Ghana?

J.E. Spillan, D.O. King, *Doing Business In Ghana*,
DOI 10.1007/978-3-319-54771-8_1

As one can see, Ghana is a small country in sub-Saharan Africa (Fig. 1.1). This larger map of Africa shows Ghana tucked in the Gulf of Guinea. Africa is a large continent with 54 countries and a population nearing 1 billion people. Ghana is a small but thriving country on a large continent with lots of opportunities and challenges.

Fig. 1.1 Map of Ghana

Source: Central Intelligence Agency: Regional and World Maps: Africa Map. (n.d.). Retrieved October 26, 2016, from https://www.cia.gov/library/publications/the-world-factbook/docs/refmaps.html

The map presented here is a closer look at where Ghana is exactly located. While it is a small country, it has a very active business environment with great access to seaports and many opportunities to grow and develop.

1.2 The Thrust of the Book

This book aims to provide a thorough perspective on the realities of doing business in Ghana. Detailed information about the economic, social, technological, and cultural dimensions of the society will be discussed. Recommendations and suggestions regarding the paths a businessperson can pursue in seeking a business venture in Ghana will be provided. Additionally, this book will provide academics with a good understanding of the major issues affecting business development in Ghana.

Ghana is an important country in sub-Saharan Africa, whose business opportunities and ability to create entrepreneurs have not been given much attention. This book gives the reader a snapshot of one country in Africa that has demonstrated significant potential for long-term success. Ghana is one of the showcase African countries illustrating how the free market can operate in a developing country.

Ghana has many positive attributes. The prevailing peaceful political atmosphere, the rich traditions and culture, the calm, hospitable attitude of its citizens, and the enormous resources nature have endowed the country offer huge opportunities for prospective entrepreneurs. Additionally, its citizens have a real passion for engaging in business for their individual survival and for the sake of the country's long-term stability and prosperity. Comparatively, Ghana has the strongest competitive edge among other countries in the region.

This book will help readers determine which Ghanaian region and which Ghanaian markets are more likely to prosper and thereby offer better business opportunities for the foreseeable future. Managers, students, scholars, future leaders, and other types of business people will be provided with in-depth first-hand information to help them make informed decisions and choices as to whether to engage in business in Africa, and Ghana specifically.

1.3 The Structure of the Book

This book is composed of nine chapters. It begins with an introduction and overview of the state of Ghanaian business, why it is important to study business in Ghana, and who will benefit from the details that are presented in this discussion. From this introduction the authors discuss the business environment, the history of doing business in Ghana, the cultural issues affecting business activities in Ghana, the political and economic climate there, how to establish a business in Ghana, the marketing process in this African country, and finally what speculation on future trends and opportunities there are in this land of plenty.

1.4 Background

Ghana is a region worthy of further consideration by both academics and practitioners. Apart from being the first country to gain its independence among countries in the West African sub-region, it has known and enjoyed uninterrupted political peace and stability since gaining its independence in 1957. Ghana has benefitted from approximately 36 years of general peace for the most part, with 21 years of smooth and continuous democratic political transitions since the fourth republic in 1993. There were five successful coups during this period that changed the leadership of the country. These coups (attempted, plotted, and alleged) occurred over a period of 38 years from 1966 to 2004 (see Table 1.1). In almost all cases new leadership was installed to manage the country. Specifically, the coups were as follows:

> While Ghana has had its issues with political change, it's deepened democratic credentials and geographical position close to the center of the globe, Ghana is considered to be a beacon of hope for Africa.

The Ghanaian economy has a formal economy as well as a traditional, informal economy of peddlers and itinerant vendors. The Accra-Tema metropolitan area is the most populous in the country, with about 3.5 million people, and it remains a hub for major trading activities. The development of a stable, multiparty democratic system, and a commitment to market reforms, has been attracting investors and promoting private sector growth (U.S. Department of State, 2011). Although Ghana's industrial sector is still emerging, it is more developed than its counterparts in the sub-region. This is due in part to the fact that the adoption of

Table 1.1 Summary of coups in Ghana – 1966–2004

Country	*Month*	*Day*	*Year*	*Success*	*Leaders*	*Deaths*
Ghana	2	24	1966	Successful	Gen. Ankrah	27
Ghana	4	17	1967	Attempted	Lt. Arthur	4
Ghana	1	13	1972	Successful	Lt. Col Acheampong	0
Ghana	5		1977	Attempted	Lt. Col Minyila	0
Ghana	7	5	1978	Successful	Gen. Akuffo	0
Ghana	5	15	1979	Attempted	Flt. Lt Rawlings	1
Ghana	6	4	1979	Successful	Jerry Rawlings	13
Ghana	12	31	1981	Successful	Allies of Rawlings	50
Ghana	11	23	1982	Attempted	Allies of Sgt Akata-Pore	0
Ghana	6	19	1983	Attempted	Lt. Col Dennis	26
Ghana	3	23	1984	Alleged	Unspecified	5
Ghana	11	6	2004	Plotted	Members of Disbanded Infantry	0

Source: Annex 2b. Coups d'Etat in Africa, 1946–2004. p. 3. http://www.systemicpeace.org/Africa.

quality management programs has promoted increased technical proficiency and productivity in Ghana (Fening et al, 2008).

Mining, manufacturing, construction, and electricity account for about 30% of Ghana's GDP. The country is well endowed with natural resources with a per-capita GDP about twice of that of its neighbors. Ghana's primary minerals and other national resources include gold, diamond, manganese ore, bauxite, and timber. Cocoa provides about a third of the nation's export revenues. Other prominent exports include palm oil, shea butter, coconuts, and coffee. Support from foreign governments and nongovernmental organizations (NGOs) have promoted export growth in the production of other agricultural products such as pineapples, pepper, and cashews. Petroleum exploration and related industries have received considerable attention since a 2007 discovery of large deposits of oil off the Ghanaian coast (BBC News, 2007). As a result, Ghana is fast becoming one of the major oil producers in the region.

Ghana is a country with many opportunities. Some of the benefits relate to it being an open society that has English as its official language. This attribute offers easy communication with the rest of the world and minimizes many of the complexities that exist in understanding international economic and business discussions. Some other attractive factors include:

- Ghana is a member of the World Trade Organization (WTO);
- Ghana has a competitive labor force;
- Ghana has a stable political environment;
- Ghana has a continuous infrastructure development program that is constantly improving roads and supply chain capabilities so as to be world class;
- Ghana has continuous privatization of important sectors of the economy.

All of these features are critical to business development and successful business operations. They have become very important attractions for businesses interested in working in Africa (Advantages of Doing Business in Ghana, 2015).

Globalization has changed the way business is conducted around the world, and Ghana has benefited from these changes. The exchange of ideas, information, and technology, as well as political change, has served in many cases to improve and expand the market systems in Ghana. As such, the potential opportunities for business investment in the region have blossomed. While several parts of Ghana demonstrate great opportunities, not all parts have presented these opportunities uniformly. The Ghanaian regions that present challenges posed by the globalized economy also provide different business opportunities and different developmental models. This book will help readers determine which Ghanaian regions and which Ghanaian markets are more likely to prosper, and thereby offer better business suggestions for the imminent future. Ghana is, by virtue of these facts, a region worthy of further consideration by both academics and practitioners.

1.5 History of Business in Ghana

Ghana has been a business-oriented country as early as the thirteenth century. Business activities were part of Ghana's early development. In the thirteenth century, Ghana was considered to be a promising opportunity for the countries that ventured there. Rich in gold and other valuable natural resources, Ghana became an important attraction to the West. The first European contact with Ghanaian citizens occurred in 1470 and continued for centuries. The Portuguese and the British occupied and controlled various parts of Ghana and its surrounding areas throughout this time (Business Ghana, 2012). Because of its great quantities of gold, Ghana was labeled the Gold Coast. The British and Portuguese built forts and other installations in order to export and protect gold and other resources to their mother countries and around the world. Once trade activity was established, the French, the Dutch, the Swedes, and the Danes also began to establish themselves in these parts, taking part in the lucrative trade opportunities that the Gold Coast offered. A variety of conflicts and encounters between the Europeans and the Ghanaian tribes occurred, putting pressure on the Europeans to pay fees for their stay in Ghana (Business Ghana, 2012).

As time passed, the world trade business shifted from commodity resources, such as gold and cocoa, to the slave trade. The demand for labor on American and European plantations provided a sure market for the exportation of slaves. One of the key factors that led to the ability to trade human capital was the importation of firearms. These instruments gave the people doing business the force and the power to gather slaves and require them to obey the rules associated with slave exportation.

Social structures and economic changes occurred between the beginning of Europeans' arrival and the eighteenth century. The British became the dominant European players in Ghanaian society. A man named George Maclean provided the initial foundation for British control in 1830. His role was to protect British interests and make sure that the slave trade would continue (Business Ghana, 2012).

During the British occupation, various institutions were put in place that made sure stability and control was permanent. For example, the first Supreme Court was founded in 1853. British rule and dominance did not go unchallenged. Various tribes that resided in different parts of Ghana began to voice their concerns and desire for independence (Business Ghana, 2012). These tribes moved toward establishing their own governments, wherein tribal leaders began to set up their own constitutions and political structures. The Ghanaian tribes made progress by creating federations and consolidation of their members. This gave them the power and opportunity to make policies that would affect the future direction of the country. From 1902 to 1951, the British controlled Ghana. Their colonization was all encompassing. It constituted economic, social, and political development (Business Ghana, 2012).

Ghana's economic strength came from two areas, namely agriculture – the cocoa bean – and gold. As these resources became more abundant and useful for sale and trade in the world market, more suitable infrastructure needed to be developed in order to get these goods to market. While transportation was needed for market growth, education also became a very important aspect of society. Tribal leaders knew that without education, future progress was not possible. The early part of the twentieth century – 1913–1922 – saw the burgeoning of formal schools and funding for schools. As these social structures emerged, other vital institutions were created. In 1921, hospitals and medical facilities became an important element of society. The establishment and construction of these entities became a priority, as leaders realized that they were to be an essential foundation if economic and business development were to become a reality. Over time, into the late 1930s, these new necessary institutions were expanded and made more sophisticated (Business Ghana, 2012).

1.6 Self-Rule

As Ghana became more economically and socially developed, its people's desire for independence grew more intense. General elections were held in 1951, which became the catalyst for Ghana's struggle for independence in 1957. More economic development began to emerge after Ghana won its independence. New roads, bridges, railways, and other infrastructure elements were built to provide the mechanisms to support and invigorate business development. Kwame Nkrumah, a progressive, became the first prime minister after Ghana's declaration of independence. Nkrumah became a strong, popular, and driving force politically and economically. His philosophy and initiatives set the foundation for full independence and for the free market to develop and flourish.

Some Important Development Dates in Ghana's History:
1482 – Portuguese settlers arrive and begin trading in gold, ivory, and timber.
1500s – Slave trade: Slavery overtakes gold as the main export in the region.
1600s – Dutch, English, Danish, and Swedish settlers arrive; slave trade becomes highly organized.
1642 – The Portuguese relinquish their territory to the Dutch and leave the Gold Coast.
1807 – British dominance: British ban on slave trade from the Gold Coast becomes effective.
1874 – The Gold Coast is officially proclaimed a British crown colony.
1957 – Independence: Ghana becomes first black African colony to declare independence.
1964–1992 – Military rule: Succession of destabilizing coups, Ghana is predominantly a one-party state.
1992 – New constitution, multiparty system is restored.
2010 – Economic woes: Offshore oil production starts, fueling Africa's fast-growing economy. Public deficit spirals.
(*Source*: BBC, News –Ghana country profile, January 6, 2016-via Global edge, UM).

1.7 Why Study Ghana

Ghana is one of the most stable countries in sub-Saharan Africa. Ghana is attractive to and active with small- and medium-sized enterprises. The oil boom has been a major positive force for investors and has drawn the attention of many who would like to expand their market to developing countries. Essentially, five major areas have sparked the interest of worldwide investment entities. These five are listed below:

a. Manufacturing – pipeline manufacturing is gaining attention. Again, the oil and natural gas boom has ignited excitement about manufacturing opportunities. Ghana has a lot of manufacturing potential because of its natural resources, its ports, and its workforce capabilities, even including talk of manufacturing automobiles. As such, Ghana presents promise in manufacturing and industrial development.
b. Telecommunications – the advent of the cell phone and the introduction of user-friendly phones has exploded in the last several years. Acquisition of mobile phones has surpassed projections multifold. The market continues to grow among all sectors of the Ghanaian economy. Potential investors can take advantage of this growing market from a variety of angles.
c. Financial Services – this is a growing area of economic development. Financial services in Ghana have improved significantly and offer major opportunities for individual and corporate investment. Since the economy has grown, there has been major expansion in financial services.
d. Real Estate Investment – this sector has major potential. If managers in this area can move forward in increasing the efficiency and effectiveness of their organizations, both residential and commercial real estate investment in Ghana can offer great opportunities.
e. Services – there is a large need among the Ghanaian population for a variety of services, such as education, medicine, and information and technology services are in demand and would benefit from serious investment by interested and capable enterprises. Huge business opportunities exist in this sector of the economy.
f. Tourism and Hospitality – here is a growing area. Since Ghana is a very stable, English speaking country, it presents a chance for people and organizations interested to visit Africa, especially Ghana. This area of the economy is ripe for investment and business development.

One can easily observe that business opportunities in Ghana are broad and deep. Those who are willing to explore, take risks, and invest money can, in most cases, achieve a substantial return on their investment. Solid business analysis and planning is the key to achieving these goals.

1.8 Who Will Benefit

Is there a future for business development through Foreign Direct Investment (FDI) and entrepreneurship? There is no question that FDI and entrepreneurship can thrive if the correct approach to business development is presented in Ghana. As mentioned above, numerous business opportunities exist, but initiative and ambition will be required of the Ghanaian people to move forward in a positive business development direction. The benefits for the individual Ghanaian and the country of Ghana as a whole are enormous; however, initiative and perseverance will be necessary for these opportunities to become a reality.

1.9 Discussion

Entrepreneurs, business developers, and existing business organizations are always looking for opportunities to expand their markets, create growth, and enhance profit centers. Ghana is an attractive country because the factors of endowment are plentiful, the economic environment is suitable, and the political situation is stable. This is a rarity among developing nations. Having all of these factors favorable to investment offers motives to investors and business developers to explore in Ghana. As previously mentioned, six major areas of business development (manufacturing, telecommunication, financial services, real estate investment, services and tourism, and hospitality) are immediately available to potential investors. For business managers to not recognize the great business opportunities in Ghana would be very neglectful of its potential. Few developing countries have the number of business opportunities immediately available as Ghana does. Ghana wants to move forward economically. Its leaders have recognized its potential; yet have also realized its limitations at this point in its development. Nevertheless, they want to progress and be as focused on development as possible. The recent discovery of oil and natural gas has heightened the enthusiasm for business development and given both Ghanaian citizens and leaders the hope that continued development is a real possibility. Poverty, however, is still a major problem in Ghana. People continue to work for very limited wages, which do not allow them sufficient income to have decent housing or living conditions. This is in part why the pursuit of economic development and business development is a priority for the Ghanaian people. It is attainable, but will take time and diligent effort among all sectors of the society. The future for Ghana is bright, and commitment by its leaders and its people will determine the way forward.

1.10 Conclusion

Ghana is a country rich in resources, history, and culture. Its people have come a long way since becoming an independent nation in 1957, and it has seen many economic ups and downs. At times, there seemed to be little hope of future achievement. To the credit of the Ghanaian people and its leadership, they have made remarkable progress. Ghana is globally recognized as one of the Gems of Africa. With its stable economy, its industrious work force, its rich endowment, and its political leadership, Ghana has set a course that offers great potential for its citizens of all ages and investors from all over the world. As it works toward improving its business and political environment, it needs to steady its course and recognize that as the country reaches its individual economic goals, it provides opportunities for its present and future citizenry. The main concern is Ghana needs to be alert to be losing its progressive momentum. Keeping its eyes on the prize is a critical activity, which can and will be done. If history is any judge, the Ghanaian people will move forward and achieve their business development goals.

References

Annex.2b. "Coups d'Etat in Africa, 1946–2004." p. 3. http://www.systemicpeace.org/Africa.

Advantages of Doing Business in Ghana. 2015. http://www.ghanaembassy.org/index.php?page=advantages-for-doing-business-in-ghana. Accessed January 2016.

BBC News. 2007. "Ghana will be an African Tiger." http://news.bbc.co.uk/2/hi/africa/6766527.stm.

Business Ghana. 2012. http://www.businessghana.com/site/. Accessed January 2016.

Fening, F. A., Pesakovic, G., and Amaria, P. 2008. "Relationship between Quality Management Practices and the Performance of Small and Medium Size Enterprises (SMEs) in Ghana." *International Journal of Quality & Reliability Management* 25(7): 694–708.

U.S. State Department. (2011). "Ghana Constraints Analysis Partnership for Growth." https://www.gtai.de/GTAI/Content/DE/Trade/Fachdaten/PRO/2015/08/Anlagen/PRO201508245004.pdf?v=1.

CHAPTER 2

Current Business Environment

2.1 Introduction

A snapshot of Ghana shows it as a Western African country neighbored by Burkina Faso, Cote d'Ivoire, Togo, and the Gulf of Guinea. Lake Volta, the largest artificial lake in the world, is entirely in Ghana. The country practices a constitutional democratic system of government, with a president as the head of government and head of state. The country is also multiparty state with two dominant parties, known as New Patriotic Party (NPP, being the strongest opposition) and the National Democratic Congress (NDC, the ruling party). Ghana is a member of the Economic Community of West African States (ECOWAS) and the African Union (AU), with a mixed economic system that includes some private financial freedom, combined with weak centralized economic planning and government regulation.

With its lower middle-income status, Ghana has an estimated population of 26,786,598 million and an annual growth rate of 2.35 (globaledge.com 2015). The country's land area of 239,000 sq. km is endowed with human, oil, agricultural, and mineral resources, and is West Africa's second largest economy, after Nigeria, as well as Africa's twelfth largest. In addition to uninterrupted national peace, political stability, and respectable governance, oil in commercial quantities has recently been discovered. Oil and gas production in Ghana commenced in 2010 and provided

J.E. Spillan, D.O. King, *Doing Business In Ghana*,
DOI 10.1007/978-3-319-54771-8_2

an astronomical 14.0% increase to GDP growth when combined with the revenue from the export of cocoa and gold in 2011.

This chapter focuses on the current business environment in Ghana, demonstrating the major trends in business activities, describing proper business ventures, explaining globalization and its effects on the market structure and business opportunities, as well as providing information about the trade blocs – the European Union (EU) and AU – with which Ghana participates. The chapter ends by drawing conclusions from all of the issues discussed.

2.1.1 Current Business Environment of Ghana

Two forces support the economy of Ghana: the informal and formal sectors. The informal sector is also known as the private sector, and there are about 90% of the businesses dominating this sector. The majority of the enterprises in the private sector are Small-Scale and Medium-Scale Enterprises (SMEs), employing no more than 20 people in each firm. Ghana's main employer in its national economy is the private sector, which primarily generates exports. Agriculture is the dominant player in this sector. Even though its performance in relation to GDP growth has declined, it employs about 56% of the labor force. This is a little over half of Ghana's entire labor force. To build a stronger economy and to ensure a thriving business environment, Ghana's government has been relentless in its efforts to provide the resources and incentives to achieve its goals. Because of this persistent attention to making itself a desired location for investment, Ghana has, at least twice, performed among the top ten global reformers' according to the World Bank "Doing Business" team. This country, with lower risks but higher returns, is considered to be one of the best destinations for investment in Africa (Ernst and Young 2013; World Bank Group Doing Business 2015), rated as "B," with a good investment environment (according to globaledge.com). Private sector development continues to face numerous challenges, including infrastructural weaknesses, difficult public administration, complicated land tenure systems, and weakly developed financial systems with some less capitalized financial institutions. Other challenges include the high interest rates and high nonperforming loans driven by the government of Ghana arrears, as well as weak human capital and poor access to technology nationwide, including within agribusiness. The Public–Private Partnership (PPP) regulatory framework is being developed by the government of Ghana not only to inspire confidence in the business environment but also to control fiscal commitments. In other words, the government has been trying to seek ways to improve SMEs' access to the capital market.

2.1.2 *Major Trends of Business Activities in Ghana*

Over the years as a lower middle-income economy, with a relatively slower structural transformation process, Ghana has been developing three business sectors that focus on economic sustainability and growth. The business sectors that form the engine of economic growth of Ghana can be categorized under three sectors: agriculture, industry, and service. It must be noted that each of these sectors have many varied smaller businesses whose activities support the major sector's growth as well as the overall economy.

Since 2010, the Ghanaian economy has witnessed unstable trends in terms of overall GDP growth. The 2016 budget statement revealed the GDP growth rates of Ghana's economy from 2010 to 2015. In 2010, the economy recorded a 7.9% GDP growth rate, but grew to 14% GDP in 2011. The economic growth in 2011 was due to the inclusion of oil production in the last quarter of the same year. In 2012, GDP decreased to 9.3% and steadily declined from 7.3 in 2013 to 4.0 in 2014. Currently, the 2016 budget statement and economic policy showed an expected slight increase to 4.1% growth of GDP from 4.0% in 2015, as revised in 2014. The 2015 GDP reflected a percentage growth.

Figure 2.1 shows the annual trends in GDP growth trends from a chronological point of view. It appears that 2011 and 2012 were very robust growth years. The structure of Ghana's economy is statistically presented in Fig. 2.2.

The preceding graph shows the sectors of the economy and their percentage of growth from a chronological point of view.

2.2 Ghana's Strength

Ghana is endowed with many opportunities that contribute to support the economy and create a stable business, social, and political environment. Below are some of the economic opportunities of the country.

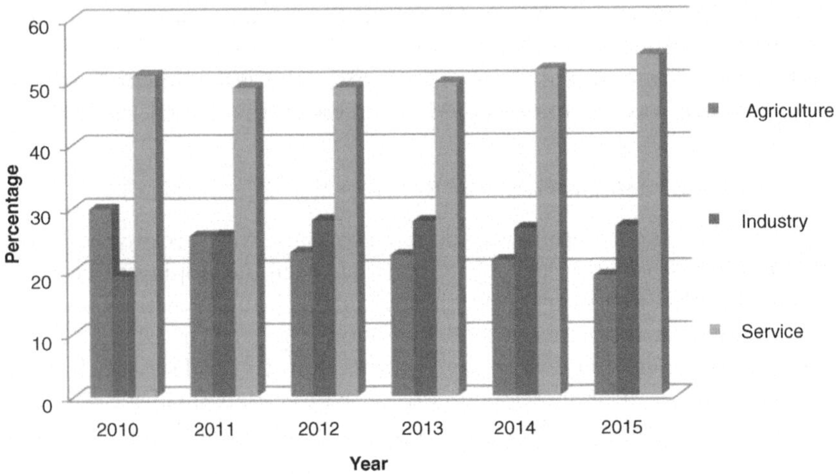

Fig. 2.1 Trends in Economic Structure

Source: Trend of annual real GDP growth 2010–2015, Revised, provisional 2016 The Budget Statement and Economic Policy and GSS, Central Intelligence Agency – The World Factbook

2.2.1 Oil and Gas

Ghana became an oil producing country on December 15, 2010, after oil was discovered in commercial quantities in 2008. Oil deposits in Ghana are modest, estimated to be 490 million barrels; compare that number to Nigeria's 37,200 million barrels and Angola's 9,500 million barrels. Oil production in Ghana rose to about 80,000 barrels per day (bpd) in 2011 and is estimated to peak at 120 thousand bpd (again, compare to Nigeria's average 2 million bpd). Though more drilling tests are being done, the oil potential in Ghana is relatively and comparatively better than it has in the past. The export of crude oil became the second largest export earner for Ghana in 2011, generating $2.6 billion. Oil export could have potentially surpassed the export contribution of gold to Ghana's economy when production peaked in 2011 (4.5 billion). In 2014, the oil sector was estimated to directly employ around 60 employees and potentially increase to 1,860 employees. The oil industry has been responsible for recruiting highly specialized and

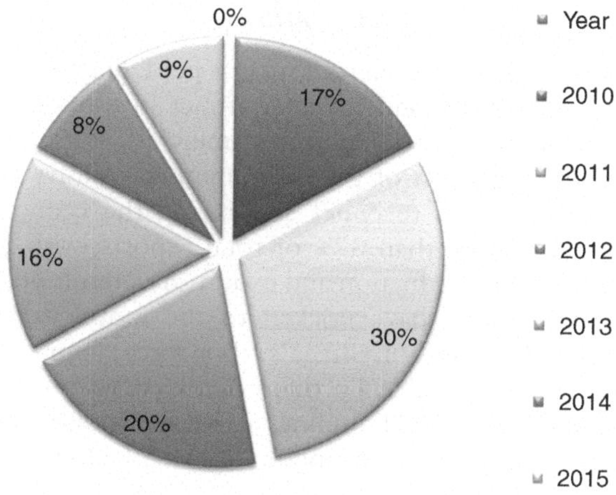

Fig. 2.2 Trends in GDP Growth

Source: GSS: Revised* Budget statement of 2016, Provisional**

skilled personnel, who are not of Ghanaian descent, into the country. These workers enjoy highly paid jobs. To address this labor gap, the government of Ghana has started providing education and skill development, by offering technical skill training for Ghanaian citizens. The government has also enacted an oil and gas local content bill, and has also upgraded certain mining universities to introduce degrees in oil and gas. Offshore gas reserves have also been discovered in commercial quantities in the Western region. The quantity of oil is estimated to peak at 120 million cubic feet a day, which would yield revenue of $120 million a year with its accompanying energy production. (The Africa Competitive Report, 2013)

2.2.2 *Forests Endowment*

Reports indicate that in 2010, Ghana exported timber products worth $180 million. Forty-seven percent of the exports were made to other African countries, 21% to Europe, and 17% to the Far East. More importantly, appropriate measures need to be put in place to prevent deforestation and ensure sustainable use of the forest resources in order to remain a significant export.

2.2.3 Mining

Mineral deposits in the Ghanaian soil, such as gold, diamonds, manganese ore, limestone, silica sand, and bauxite, attract investment, making the country a major producer and exporter of minerals. With the extraction, production, and exportation of gold, the mining industry has gradually seen growth for years, its revenues supporting the economy. Mineral exports account for more than 37% of total exports, with gold making up 90% of total mineral production and export. As a result of its significant growth, foreign investors have flocked to the industry. The minerals industry only absorbs 0.69% of Ghana's labor force despite its significant contributions to national GDP. Furthermore, it is faced with major challenges emanating from illegal mining activities (locally referred to as "galamsey"), instability in the supply and cost of electricity, and high taxes (Mikva, 2015).

2.2.4 Political and Institutional Stability Benefits

Ghana has gained confidence in the eyes of the international and local economic communities through its political peace and stability over the years, making it an attractive zone for FDI in Africa. According to Africa Business Panel 2011, Ghana was ranked the fourth best destination in Africa for international investment, after South Africa, Nigeria, and Kenya. In the 2011 World's Investment Report of the UN Conference on Trade and Development, Ghana was not only rated the seventh largest beneficiary of FDI inflows in Africa but also the third largest also in sub-Saharan Africa. The FDI inflows to Ghana were estimated at about $2.5 billion, up from 1.7 billion in 2009, with oil and mining as the prominent drivers of the economy. Currently, the FDI inflows are pegged at $3,227 million (2013, globaledge.com). Considering the fact that a greater percentage of FDI is directed toward the extractive industries, the government of Ghana should make sure that enough resources go to priority areas like agriculture, agribusiness development, and manufacturing to reap the most from the benefits of FDI.

2.2.5 Domestic and Regional Markets

One of the fastest growing regions, West Africa was expected to grow at 6.9% GDP in 2012. Tapping into this similar potential, Ghana can ensure a similar rise in its growth rate if the ever-expanding regional markets can be easily and widely accessed. Taking advantage of these domestic and regional markets requires improvement measures, including development in macroeconomic management, enhancement in regional financial market integration, implementation of policies that address weaknesses in domestic and regional infrastructure, and applying regulations that create bottlenecks to the provision of a free and integrated regional market for goods and services. (Ventures, 2012).

2.2.6 *Potential Remittances*

Ghana receives a lot of remittances from citizens who live outside their own country. These remittances not only provide a good source of finance but also contribute to national growth. The government of Ghana should make good use of remittances in terms of taxes, fees, and other sources of revenue, culminating in a steady source for raking in funds for national development.

2.2.7 *Manufacturing Sector Opportunities*

In terms of manufacturing, Ghana is gradually developing, growing, and expanding. The key industries in the manufacturing sector include aluminum smelting, cement, hollowware, plastics, pharmaceuticals, textiles, and wood processing. Though a greater percentage of the products in this sector are meant for local consumption, some are exported to nearby countries in the West African regional market. The sector is not, however, without certain challenges, such as high costs for production, raw materials, and utilities, as well as unhealthy import competition, especially from China. Overall, the sector has the potential for growth in the long term. Growth is expected to be influenced by industries like agri-business, with further assistance from infrastructural development. To help growth, the government should strive to create an enabling business environment and demonstrate its commitment through sector reform programs that reduce transaction costs.

2.2.8 *Regional Integration Opportunities*

Trade between Ghana and other African countries, as well as exports to Brazil, Russia, India, China, and South Africa (BRICS countries), has been increasing. On the contrary, imports are comparatively higher. Ghana must take advantage of the benefits stemming from deepening economic relations with member countries of BRICS. This means that the opportunities and challenges of these relations in trade and finance must be given proper management, in the interest of all parties involved.

2.2.9 *Corruption Minimization*

Corruption in Ghana is less rampant than in most of the countries in its West African subregion. According to the Transparency International Global Corruption Perceptions Index (2014), Ghana was ranked the 61st out of 175, which was a slight improvement from 2013. A homegrown corruption element, known as "sakawa" and similar to Nigeria's "419," is common in Ghana. This is always a threat to investors – some individuals even defraud their victims under the disguise of being public officials through social media. The government of Ghana has put measures in place to address corruption, but it is still a problem. Certain laws concerning public financial administration and procurement have been amended. The Commission for Human Rights and Administrative Justice was established under the 1992 Constitution to investigate, among other things, alleged and suspected corruption and misappropriation of public funds by officials. An anti-corruption institution known as the Serious Fraud Office (SFO) was established in 1998 to investigate corrupt practices in both private and public sector institutions. In 2010, SFO was renamed as the Economic and Organized Crime Office, with additional functions to start prosecution and to recover the proceeds gained from criminal activities. The passage of a "Whistle Blower Bill" in 2006 was intended to encourage Ghanaian citizens to willingly leak information on corrupt activities to the appropriate agencies (Global Corruption Perception Index, 2014).

2.3 Challenges and Weaknesses

While Ghana is a promising investment destination, it still faces many challenges. The government continues to work hard to reduce the following difficulties:

2.3.1 *Inadequate Skilled Labor*

Ghana has numerous job vacancies that have not been filled by qualified graduates. Though majority of the Ghanaian populace is educated, graduates from the universities, polytechnics, and other colleges do not have the required skills for the available job opportunities. This is due to the fact that the institutions do not organize programs tailored to meet the challenges of the country's industries. Academic institutions should mount productive academic programs and create reasonable links with the industries in Ghana. The government should give needed support to improve science, technology, and vocational education, so its own citizens can meet the requirements for jobs in sectors such as manufacturing, Information and Communication Technology (ICT), oil and gas, agro-industry, agriculture, and project management.

2.3.2 *Difficulty in Obtaining Land Titles*

Although the existing legal framework recognizes and provides ways to enforce property rights, the procedure to obtain a clear title over land is often difficult, complicated, and lengthy. The land tenure system in Ghana is a difficult obstacle that might dissuade investors.

2.3.3 *Absence of Intellectual Property Rights*

Lack of protection of intellectual property rights, including computer software and pharmaceuticals, is a major threat to the country. Recent worldwide incidents of computer hacking have motivated managers and government officials to find methods that can protect intellectual property in many sectors of society. Ghana is not an exception. Ghanaian managers and government administrators need to be vigilant and risk aversive in making sure that the intellectual property rights and operations are fully protected from any threat that may occur. Proper planning will be a great step in the right direction for achieving this goal.

2.3.4 *Bottlenecks in Establishing Business*

The process for establishing a business in Ghana is lengthy, complex, and requires compliance with the regulations and procedures for at least five government agencies. Ghana's local content regulations in the oil and gas sector entered into force in November 2013. Additionally, obtaining a Tax Identification Number (TIN) for business registration is very cumbersome.

Other challenges Ghana faces include the current increase in public debt, which is the result of poor management and over spending on the part of the government, weak public banks, and international market interference in commodity pricing.

2.4 Description Business Ventures in Ghana

There are countless businesses operating in various formal and informal ways in Ghana. These business activities partly or fully contribute to the sustainability of the economy. Each of the businesses that exist in Ghana can be classified under one of the three sectors as: agricultural, industry, and service. These sectors and their business activities support and sustain the economy of Ghana. The individual sectors and their performance to the GDP are thoroughly examined below:

2.4.1 The Agricultural Sector of Ghana

The economy of Ghana is heavily dominated by agriculture, with primary products as the main commodities for export. The sector employs a little above half of Ghana's labor force (about 56%) even though its performance on GDP growth is declining.

The Ministry of Food and Agriculture is the main agency responsible for regulating the affairs of the agricultural sector. As the main driver of Ghana's economy, the sector contributed 22.4% in 2013, 21.5% in 2014, and 19.0% in 2015 to the national GDP (*Source:* GSS 2016 budget statement). The sector is blessed with vast forest resources, and agricultural land capacity spreads over 13.6 million hectares (ha), out of which only 7.8 million ha has been cultivated, with 5.8 ha million still available. This forms about 65.1% of the total land area, including inland waters (*Source:* ADB & ADF 2012). Businesses in the agricultural sector comprise all forms of farming activities, such as crops, cocoa production, livestock, fishing, forestry, and logging. The main items produced in this sector can be categorized into several groups: industrial crops, starchy and cereals (cassava, cocoyam, yam, maize, rice, millet, legume, and plantain), vegetables and fruits (pineapple, citrus, banana, cashew, pawpaw, mango, tomato, pepper, okra, eggplant, onion, and Asian vegetables), livestock, and fish. This sector is also rich in timber production.

Agricultural Sector Investment Incentives and Opportunities
As a net importer of food currently, Ghana annually imports rice, which is worth more than $450 million, not excluding other amounts spent on importing chicken, meat, and dairy products. Furthermore, Ghana is lacking in its processing of dairy products as well as in its supply of equipment, for example, to establish hatcheries for day-old chicks. As such, there is a vast area of investment opportunity in crop and livestock production available on the local market. Again, rapid urban growth, with its accompanying per capita income rise, is tied with an increase in local demands for staple foods.

Agricultural Sector Tax Benefits and Exemptions Investment
In Ghana, a three-year tax exemption from the date business commences is given to companies that process raw materials such as raw crops, fish, or livestock into edible canned or other packaged products in commercial quantities. Companies that produce cocoa by-products from cocoa waste enjoy a five-year tax freedom from the time of the start of business, and cocoa farmers enjoy tax-free income from the sale of cocoa products. Not only is there a five-year tax holiday for agro-processing businesses established after 2004, but these enterprises also enjoy location-based tax benefits. Ghana's tax laws give exemptions to imported plants, equipment, and machinery.

Agro-processing Opportunities
There are opportunities available for investment in the agro-processing sector; some of which include adding value and reducing losses after harvest, promoting stability of prices, and increasing demand for domestic agricultural products.

Examples of such instances are the processing of cocoa beans into cocoa products and fruit into fruit juice, etc. Again, available opportunities also exist in the provision of agricultural materials, which include improved seed breeds; agro-chemicals (fertilizers, pesticides, fungicides, herbicides); veterinary medicines, vaccines and chemicals; animal feeds and feed ingredients; and many more.

Agricultural Sector's Floricultural Segment
Ghana's climate and topography are suitable for growing exotic flowers. Plant species, including helicon, caribea, celosia, curcuma, gladioli, hibiscus, roses, ornamental palms, and fern, do well under nonartificial conditions. Floriculture not only promises a solid investment opportunity in

Ghana but also response to increased demand in domestic, regional, and EU markets.

Agricultural Sector Challenges

The agricultural sector faces several challenges. Such obstacles include Ghana's land tenure system; poor access to loan facilities; unstable weather conditions and its associated problems, such as perennial bushfires and flooding; lack of agriculture equipment and chemicals; poor access to technology and Internet; infrastructural challenges (lack of access to good roads and transportation); an insufficient number of agriculture extension officers; and lack of training for farmers. There is also another challenge relating to the threat from the activities of nomadic cattle bearers known as Fulani men.

2.4.2 The Distribution, Technology, and Services

Post-production services such as transport and packaging are always needed for companies to deliver their products. This means that investment opportunities are available in the distribution field. Further, opportunities exist in the provision of standards training and certification, skill development for management and market-oriented businesses, market intelligence research, development of agricultural, and finance and insurance.

More investment opportunities are available in agricultural technologies and services, which include hiring tractors, harrows, combined harvesters, ploughs, etc. The storage industry is another profitable venture for investment. Insufficient storage facilities threaten the agricultural production industry, causing high losses and low returns for farmers and processors during post-harvest time. Investors can also develop irrigable lands. Ghana has 346,000 ha of potential irrigable land; however, only 10,000 ha have been developed (Keller, 2004).

The Cross-Border Trading

Ghana's government has upgraded the infrastructural status at the Tema Port to ensure smooth and easy cross-border businesses. With this, Ghana is opened to both regional and international trade.

The Access to Credit

Credit facilities to support businesses in Ghana have recently been enhanced. License was given to a private credit bureau, which started operations in 2010, to see to all credit issues. A centralized collateral registry has been established to strengthen access to credit.

2.5 The Service Sector

The services sector is the largest contributor to Ghana's GDP. In 2012, it contributed close to GH¢33.963 million, about 50% of the GDP. During the third quarter of 2013, the services sector recorded a contribution of 50.6% of GDP (i.e., GH¢39,714 million). The services sector is estimated to provide about 30% of Ghana's employment, second to agriculture. Transportation, storage, public administration, trade, hotels, financial services, and insurance are among the leading service subsectors that contribute toward the GDP. Ghana has a large and growing service sector that encompasses many parts of the public sector, as well as a wide range of private activities (construction, finance, trade). The services sector serves demand, mainly arising from resource-based extractive industries, remittances, and international partners' development assistance (Terkper, 2016). The following are some businesses in the service sector.

2.5.1 Banking and Finance

The banking and financial service industry in Ghana is relatively robust. The Bank of Ghana (BoG), the central bank, has a legal mandate to regulate all operations of the sector. The sector comprises a broad spectrum of organizations that manage money. The industry is grouped under three canopies: banking and finance (consisting of nonbanking financial services and foreign exchange bureaus), insurance, and financial markets/ capital markets. The financial service sector made a 10% contribution to the total growth rate of the service sector in Ghana in third quarter of 2013. There is strong governmental support for the development of the financial sector. The government approved the Financial Sector Strategic Plan (FINSSP) in 2003. The institutions that operate in the sector include both foreign and local major banks, rural and community banks, savings and loans companies, and other finance and leasing industries. As part of a 2015 vision of strategic objectives to push Ghana into middle-income status, there has been massive financial sector restructuring and transformation. Before 2003, the Central Bank implemented the use of a three-pillar banking model and licensed all banks either as development, merchant, or commercial baking. In February 2003, the Central Bank brought Universal Banking to reality, permitting the banks to operate as commercial, development, merchant, or investment banking without acquiring a separate business permit. This move has not only created an even playing field but has also opened up the floodgates for healthy competition, product innovation, and entry. The following are the number of banks and nonfinancial institutions at the close of 2012: 26 universal banks, 136 rural and economic banks, 145 nonbank financial institutions, 333 foreign exchange bureaus, 43 insurance companies (life and nonlife), 2 reinsurance, and 54 insurance brokers (PWC 2014 & KPNG). The banking sector has several factors that are required to make it operate effectively. They are as follows:

Minimum Capital Requirements
The banking sector requires industry investors to meet the minimum start-up financial requirements, listed below: commercial banks should have at least GH¢60 million (GH¢120 million proposed); nonbank financial institutions, GH¢7 million (GH¢15 million proposed); microfinance (deposit taking), GH¢500,000; and microfinance (non-deposit taking), GH¢300,000. Additional capital contributions may be required depending on the number of branches established by the institution. The BoG hopes that start-up capital will assist industry players not only in funding big projects to ensure development of the private sector but also to use as a cushioning for absorbing unexpected losses that may arise during normal business operations (Kusi, 2013).

Systems of Banking and Payment
The payment system for banking services in Ghana has had dramatic improvement since 1997 with the introduction of Magnetic Ink Character Recognition cheques to speed up cheque processing and clearance (PWC 2014).

Ghana Interbank Payment and Settlement System (GhIPSS)
GhIPSS is a subsidiary body owned completely by the BoG. After its incorporation in May 2007, it was given the sole responsibility and mandate of implementation and management of all payment system facilities for banks and nonbank financial companies in Ghana. Currently, GhIPSS is responsible for the management of the National Switch and Biometric Smart Card Payment System, Cheque Codeline Clearing, Ghana Automated Clearing House (ACH), Real-Time Gross Settlement System

(RTGS), Central Securities Depository (CSD). CSD supervision of the system by GhIPSS enhances automated banking settlement and payment transactions, as well as electronic clearing of cheques and transfers between banks. All banks in Ghana are expected to directly or indirectly sign on to become members of GhIPSS. The implication is that all banks are required to be members of the national switch and smartcard, ACH, RTGS, etc. *Source:* PWC 2014; KPMG 2013 doing biz in Ghana.

Capital Markets

Over the past decade, there has been increased investor confidence in Ghana's capital market. There are about 27 companies, 10 brokerage firms, 5 mutual funds, and 1 unit trust firms listed on the Ghana Stock Exchange (GSE) currently. The Securities and Exchange Commission has put a smooth participatory platform in place for all parties in order to protect investor interests.

Demutualization

The need to expedite action to demutualize the GSE is a result of the present structural challenges confronting GSE, a nonprofit institution. Therefore, the purpose of demutualization is geared toward creating a platform for stronger diversity of ownership. This will help ensure improved public participation in the management of the Exchange and continue to remain competitive and responsive to the needs of market players. In 2009, the strategic plan for demutualizing the GSE was finalized and the report was sent to the GSE for review.

Other Relevant Matters

Numerous bills have been passed in the parliament, while others are in their progressive stage. These bills include the Anti-Money Laundering Bill, the Credit Union Bill, the Insurance Bill, and the current Insolvency Bill (Bankruptcy law). Again, work is in progress concerning borrowers and lenders, as well as Non-Bank Financial Intermediaries bills that were seeking approval and passage in 2008. There will be a massive transformation in the financial service sector when these reforms are implemented. An offshore banking license to Barclays Bank was the result of the Banking Amendment Act being passed in 2007. With the current resourcefulness of the GSE, the required Automated Transfer System, the Electronic Clearing/Settlement, and the Depository system that was activated in 2008, dealers have access, using secure Internet facilities, to investments in stock exchanges. The automation of the trading platform offers many prospects for enhancing liquidity on the market, as well as for improving trading on the Exchange. Additionally, the automation system, as well as GSE's move to develop a program that will help lure SMEs to list on the Exchange, is expected to enhance the bond market, which is gradually gathering momentum (Kusi, 2013).

Foreign Currency Dealings
Part of the measures taken to manage the depreciation of the Ghanaian cedi (Ghc) against foreign currency used in trade, the BoG has, in accordance with the Foreign Exchange Act of 2006 (Act 723), issued a directive to the general public placing a requirement that all domestic business transactions (sale and purchase of goods and services) be done in the Ghc. Again, any businesses in the foreign exchange market should obtain licenses for operations from the BoG. This relates to any dealings in foreign currency, including purchase and sale of foreign currency, the receipt or payment foreign currency, lending and borrowing of foreign currency, and import and export of foreign currency.

Exchange Controls
Prior to 2006, Ghana used a stringent foreign exchange control regime under the erstwhile Exchange Control Act, passed in 1961 (Art 71). This legislation was withdrawn and replaced by the Foreign Exchange Act of 2006 (Act 723).

The latter has introduced a more flexible regime. Under the Foreign Exchange Act, authorized dealer banks now operate exchange controls, which were previously exercised by the BoG. These banks are only required to report their foreign exchange dealings to the BoG. Transfer of funds or dividends, and payments in foreign currency to or from Ghana between a Ghanaian and a foreigner, or between foreigners, must be made through legally mandated dealer banks. There are no exchange controls or currency regulations, as long as transactions are effected through these banks.

2.6 Challenges and Weaknesses in the Financial Sector

The financial sector faces challenges that emanate from the bottlenecks that are a result of obtaining licenses for operation, infrastructural deficiencies, and poor access to the Internet, among other weaknesses.

2.6.1 *Investment Opportunities and Incentives*

The demand for financial services is considerably high in Ghana; therefore, the sector requires growth to increase the number of companies in the banking sector to meet service needs. The financial service industries in Ghana have the opportunity to expand their customer service offerings by rendering their services not only to the domestic market but also extend them to the relatively less developed countries in the African subregion.

2.6.2 *Credit Reference Bureaus*

The Credit Reporting Act of 2007 (Act 726) makes provisions for a legal and regulatory approach for credit reporting for banks in Ghana. There are opportunities in Ghana for financial organizations to obtain licenses to operate credit reference bureaus. The existence of credit information is important for the development and maintenance of an efficient financial sector. The system of credit reporting in Ghana gives timely, realistic, and current information on the debt profiles and repayment histories of borrowers.

2.6.3 *Discovery of Oil*

Ever since Ghana discovered oil in commercial proportions, followed by its continuous exploration activities, there have been greater business opportunities for the banking sector. The banking and financial sectors have far greater opportunities to finance and insure various large-scale transactions that occur in the oil production sector (PWC 2014).

2.6.4 *Tax Exemptions*

Companies in the financial sector that are newly listed on the Stock Exchange are exempt from paying the 22% corporate tax in their first three years. On the contrary, these companies pay a tax rate of 25% after those three years. Again, there is a reduced income tax rate (20% instead of the 25% set standard) on income obtained from loans given to farming businesses; the same percentage is also fixed on income gained from loans given to leasing companies for acquiring assets for the lease.

2.6.5 *Ghana's Competitive Advantage in the Banking Sector*

The financial sector has several genuine competitive advantages. These include the fact that there are skilled professionals; improved academic, financial, and training institutions; increasing widespread ICT infrastructure to ensure competitive and efficient operations; proper regulation and supervision of financial institutions; and a relatively conducive legal and regulatory environment compared to some other West African countries in Ghana's proximity.

2.7 Service Sector (Tourism) Travel to Ghana

Ghana is easily accessible to visitors from various parts of the world. Its popularity has been gained from certain endowments like gold and cocoa; Ghana provides superior hospitality and tourist attractions when compared with some other African countries. The tourism industry is rapidly making the country an attractive destination for tourists in the subregion, and therefore ranked as the top foreign exchange earner compared with other sectors in the country. The Ministry of Tourism and the Ghana Tourist Board are the regulatory agencies charged with the responsibility of steering the affairs of the sector. The Ghana's government, through the Ministry of Tourism and the Ghana Tourist Board, has been taking measures to offer needed support and development to efficiently manage the industry and transform it into a good source of foreign exchange and revenue generation for the development of the country. The country prides itself on its numerous tourist attraction centers. These places of interest range from the friendly sandy beaches of the Atlantic coast, to rich tropical forest zones, and spectacular wildlife. Again, the country is endowed with several cultural attractions, which include handicrafts, traditional clothes (e.g., kente), local cuisines, and many beautiful festivals that are observed throughout the year. The historical European-built forts and state-of-the-art castles played a major role during the transatlantic slave trade. These artifacts now provide a major touristic site for the large and growing tourism industry that is beginning to blossom in Ghana. Other touristic activities that tourists can actively participate in are listed below.

2.7.1 *Festivals*

Festivals and durbars are observed annually in many areas of Ghana. These are done to recognize the many cultural heritages of the country's forefathers. Various rites and rituals are performed. The traditional elders of the ethnic groups concerned and their surrounding villages strictly attend the celebration. Some of these famous festivals include Akwasidae, celebrated by the Ashantis, Homowo, by the Gas, Hogbetsotso by the Ewes, Damba of the northerners, as well as Aboakyir by the people of Winneba.

2.7.2 *Forts and Castles*

These are located along the coastlines, constructed and used during the time of slave trade by traders from Europe, Portugal, Spain, Demark, Sweden, Holland, and Germany in the fifteenth century. Examples include Cape Coast and Elmina Castles, located in the Central region, as well as Christiansborg castle and forts in Accra. There have been many renovations on the castles and forts to make them available for the public to visit.

2.7.3 *Museums and Other Attractions*

Ghana has national museums that showcase exhibits reflecting the cultural heritage of the country. The National Theatre with its beautiful design, Independence Square, the Kwame Nkrumah Mausoleum, Accra International Conference Centre, Ghana Academy of Arts and Science, and the National Archives of Ghana are some attractions for tourists.

2.7.4 *Beaches and Lake Resorts*

Beaches and resorts on Ghana's coast offer colorful scenery and relaxing getaways. The public is allowed to access most beaches to enjoy the breeze and beautiful seascapes. Major beaches include Labadi Beach, Coco Beach and Kokrobite, in Accra; Elmina Beach, Anomabo Beach, Winneba Beach, and Gumoa Fete located in the Central region; and Busua Pleasure Beach, Princess Town Beach, and Miami Beach in the Western region. Other beaches in Ghana also include Keta Beach, in the Volta region, as well as Ada Beach in the Greater Accra region. Famous beach resorts in these areas are Coconut Beach Resort, Biriwa Beach Resort Next Door Beach Resort, White Sand Beach Resort, Tills No. 1 Beach Resort, and Ada Manta Paradise Beach Resort.

2.7.5 *Waterfalls*

Ghana's waterfalls are among its many magnificent natural wonders that draw tourists and nature lovers. Some of the waterfalls have a series of falls with lots of adjoin spaces, which are good ground for picnics. Some of these waterfalls only flow during specific seasons, such as Alambo and Likpe Todome in the Volta region. Some popular waterfalls in Ghana and their location can be seen in Table 2.1.

2.7.6 *National Parks and Gardens*

National parks and gardens, enriched with wildlife and exotic plants, are more examples of the natural beauty Ghana has to offer. The Kakum National Park has a canopy walkway that gives visitors a panoramic view of the tropical rainforest, the surrounding areas, and the wildlife there. Kakum National Park in Cape Coast, the Aburi Gardens on the Akwapim Ridge in the Eastern region, and the Mole National Park of Damango in the Northern region each provide a colorful experience of wildlife, such as elephants, antelopes, hartebeests, and buffalo. The central shores of the Volta Lake are home to Digya National Park, woodland that shelters elephants, buffalo, waterbuck, hartebeests, bush pigs, crocodiles, and five different monkey species.

Table 2.1 Some famous waterfalls in Ghana

Name of waterfalls	Location
Kintampo Waterfalls	Brong Ahafo Region
Fuller Falls	Brong Ahafo Region
Begoro Waterfalls	Eastern Region
Boti Falls	Eastern Region
Tagbo Falls	Volta Region
Fuller Falls	Brong Ahafo Region
Tsatsadu Falls	Volta Region
Wli Falls	Volta Region
Tsenku Waterfalls	Eastern Region

Source: Easy Track Ghana, Waterfalls of Ghana, www.easytrackghana.com/tour-ghana_waterfalls

2.7.7 *Other Places of Interest*

Additional noteworthy tourist centers include the Boabeng-Fiema Monkey Sanctuary in the Brong Ahafo region, with over 500 mona and 200 Geoffrey's pied Columbus monkeys living with the indigenous people. Tafi Monkey Sanctuary in the Volta region is another habit for wild but playfully mona and patas monkeys. Frequently visited places in the country also include the Larabanga Mosque in Tamale, the oldest in Ghana as well as in West Africa.

2.7.8 *Lodges and Hotels*

Ghana's tourist areas are not without comfortable accommodation, ranging from five star hotels to homestays. They are of high quality, meeting international standards. The best hotels are mostly located in the regional capitals, district capitals as well as some towns. The more luxurious hotels are at Osu Roman Ridge, Labadi and Central Accra, as well as close to the main airport. Similar facilities of or above international standards are around the popular beaches like Ada Foah, GomoaFetteh, Elmina, Axim, and Busua.

2.8 Tourist Sector Challenge and Opportunities

2.8.1 *Challenges*

Some of the challenges in the tourism industry include infrastructural deficiencies, public encroachment on tourist lands, poor management, bushfires, and other human and natural activities.

2.8.2 *Opportunities*

There are available opportunities to upgrade most of the tourist centers to international status to make them more attractive to visitors. This could be done by constructing more hotels, restaurants, and places that would accommodate tourists from various parts of the world. Tourists want activities that are relevant to the place they are visiting. As such, guided tour trips and various tourist activities would be helpful in selling the environment to the outside world.

2.9 ICT Sector and Its Attributes

2.9.1 Information and Communication Technology (ICT)

According to Ofori et al. (2013), the greatest transformation in the banking industry in Ghana was with the introduction of the government's development agenda, known as the "ICT for Accelerated Development (ICT4AD) policy" in 2003. The goal of this policy was to create ICT-led socioeconomic development in the country. Amazingly, Ghana was known to lead in ICT development and Internet adoption in the West African subregion as of 2003 (Zachary 2003; Adams & Lamptey 2009). The ICT industry consists of Internet Service Providers (ISPs), telecommunication companies, software manufacturers, ICT education providers, VSAT data operators, broadcast institutions, and Internet cafés, to name a few examples. The industry is regulated by the Ministry of Communications and the National Communications Authority (NCA). Compared to the 1.1% average in the sub-Saharan region, infrastructural development in Ghana's ICT is progressively better, making Ghana an attractive destination for business process outsourcing. The country was ranked the best destination in sub-Saharan Africa for ICT than Mauritius and Senegal. Overall, the country ranks 15th out of the 50 nations indicated by the 2009 A.T. Kearney Global Services Location Index.

In terms of infrastructure, the sector is supported by licensed gateway operators, SAT-3 Access, Private Licensed VSAT Systems, Fixed Wired Line Networks, Wireless Mobile Operators, Public Telephone Systems, Telecentres, Dedicated Transmission Networks, Public Distribution Networks (cable, TV, DSL, etc.), ISPs, Internet Backbone Connectivity across the nation, Public Access Points, and Broadcasting Systems. By creating a strategic initiative to improve the ICT sector, the Ministry of Communications is also assisting the establishment of Science and Technology Parks. Accra lies at the heart of the ICT industry, hosting the headquarters of the ICT companies, as well as their associated branches, infrastructure, and support companies. In 2012, the sector added 1.8% to the GDP. The Ghana Statistical Service recorded a 24.3% growth to GDP in 2013 and 38.4% growth in 2014, according to the 2016 provisional budget statement.

2.9.2 *Ghana's Initiatives on ICT*

Ghana's government has enacted several initiatives to promote rapid ICT development and growth. Among them is a national fiber optic network (VOLTACOM) developed by Ghana's electricity company, the Volta River Authority. ISPs and telecommunication companies in Ghana have invested heavily in ICT infrastructure. Ghana also runs a collaborative project with India called the Kofi Annan Center of Excellence in ICT. This center is responsible for developing the human resource capacity required for the ICT industry emerging in Ghana and the West African subregion. Mobile phone industries provide the necessary platforms for smooth access to ICT in Ghana through their Internet and cellular services. Cellular phone SIM subscribers in Ghana are in close proximity with the 25.1 million population. As of 2013, NCA data indicated that the total mobile voice subscription stood at 27.2 million while mobile data subscription was at 10.2 million (Amega-Selorm, Charles Internet Research, Telecommunications, 2016).

2.9.3 *Ongoing ICT Projects in Ghana*

Presently, Ghana is embarking on the e-Ghana project. The goal of this project is to improve ICT and create a PPP to ensure development and employment. An ICT park is being constructed at Tema on a 20-ha campus. The World Bank's International Development Association finances this program. The objective is to put up a technology village to serve as the hub of ICT in Ghana. Another commendable ICT project that Ghana launched in 2013 was the Hope City project. This project was to build Africa's tallest building with the capacity to employ over 50,000 citizens, and eventually house over 25,000. The city featured an IT university, residences, a health center, and social and sporting facilities. The ICT field has generated the interest of the government since it can lure new investors into Ghana. Ghana has shown strong commitment to upgrading its ICT infrastructure through proactive ICT policies and laudable initiatives.

2.9.4 *Market in the ICT Sector*

The ICT sector has had some of its subsectors licensed to undertake business activities beginning in December 2009. Such subsectors include telecommunications, with two fixed line operators and six mobile cellular operators. With these, the two fixed line operator together with five mobile cellular operators had the full operation. The market had 165 ISPs legally licensed to function, but only 29 were in operation. The sector also had 13 DTH satellite service providers with only 8 in business operation. Out of 179 data operators, 29 have at one time been or are currently in full operation in the country. 99 Public/corporate data operators were licensed in the given year, but only 25 are in active business. The sector also saw about 190 FM radio stations and 32 TV stations, with 84 and 13 in full operation, respectively (Amega-Selorm, 2016).

2.9.5 Market Trends

According to the African Business Panel's research, Ghana is projected to be a major ICT investment player in Africa in the next five years. Ghana was ranked fourth on the continent following South Africa, Nigeria, and Kenya. The ICT market continues to grow in all areas, especially with rapid mobile phone penetration. Access to Internet has also increased despite the high costs of connectivity. Internet usage has also increased despite the expense.

2.9.6 Investment Opportunities

The ICT sector in Ghana offers further investment opportunities. Service providers are needed to connect international voice calls to the local public network. The country requires ISPs to ensure easy Internet access to the public, particularly in rural areas, at an affordable cost. Broadcasting operators have the opportunity to develop radio and television broadcasting in the country. Furthermore, there are deficiencies in the ICT infrastructure and facilities across the length and breadth of the country that investors could develop. The country also needs investments in software provision and broadband network extension in order to provide access to computers for rural students. Businesses could also supply quality telecommunication equipment, ICT equipment, and office and network equipment. Other areas that need an investment boost are education and training in software development, networking, VSAT, telecommunication, IT engineering, business processing, outsourcing, back office operations (particularly for the financial services), broadband facilities and services, transaction processing. Also the manufacture, assembly and supply of computers and accessories, e-commerce, legal database services, and logistics management services are areas that offer investment opportunities.

2.9.7 The Real Estate Sector

The real estate sector has been growing as a result of continuous investment and rapid improvement of the economy. High demand for residential and industrial facilities has helped to build the economy. Enormous opportunities exist in Ghana in the field of construction and real estate development and management.

In Ghana, residential and commercial development dominates the property market. The residential market has had an estimated 85,000 transactions annually over the past 10 years. The second largest aspect of the market is in commercial property. This includes office accommodations and space for retail operations. The industrial sector is considerably smaller in size compared to the commercial market. On the contrary, recreation and civic or cultural property development are in effect absent, and therefore an opportunity for investment.

There is currently an estimate of one million housing unit deficits in Ghana. Dealing with this challenge, about 150,000 housing units will need to be provided annually for the next 20 years. To make this a reality, the government of Ghana is embarking on a housing program, building over 300,000 housing units over the next five years through the participation of the private sector in a PPP (African Development Bank & African Development Fund, 2012).

The rapid development and growth of the economy of Ghana, together with influx of foreign investors, has resulted in a tremendous expansion in the real estate market. There is a high increase in demand for different kinds of property because of the opportunities for industry players operating in Ghana, as well as for those who want to enter the industry. Development of residential houses, industrial and commercial buildings, shopping centers, hostels, hotels, and educational institutions are all potential investments for the real estate sector.

2.9.8 Real Estate Types

The composition of the real estate industry includes residential, commercial, industrial, and recreational property. Commercial property consists of hotels, office buildings, conference centers, and retail space. Currently, there is a dominance of residential and commercial property, with residential property taking the most active part. The commercial property market is larger than the industry property market, while recreational market properties are the smallest part. Private firms control most of the residential and commercial property markets, with over 90% of property investments.

2.9.9 *Residential Properties*

Traditionally, the government of Ghana has used a formal housing supply approach with the help of major housing companies, such as the State Housing Corporation (SHC), the Tema Development Corporation (TDC), and the Social Security and National Insurance Trust (SSNIT). SHC and SSNIT have centered on the provision of blocks of flats in the regional capitals such as Accra, Cape Coast, Takoradi, and Kumasi. TDC basically plays the role of site serving and assisting residential development. To improve the supply of houses, the government of Ghana has introduced various programs. One such program is the Affordable Housing Program, which was started in 2005 and aimed at building over 100,000 units of affordable housing all over the country through PPPs. The government's efforts to reduce the housing deficit are assisted by individual households and real estate property developers to meet increasing demand. The government of Ghana has signed a PPP agreement with HFC Bank Ltd for the next five years to provide about 200,000 housing units across the country for people in the low-income bracket.

2.9.10 *Affordable Housing Project*

The concentration of the population in the Accra–Tema metropolis is growing higher, resulting in the need for more housing units. Ghana Real Estate Developers Association (GREDA), the parent organization of a loose association of private estate builders, has taken strides to develop new housing estates in the country. The five main recognizable GREDA industries, accounting for about 75% of the association's residential property development, include Regimenuel Gray, Parakuo Estates, NTHC Properties Ltd, ACP Estates Ltd, and Manet Housing Company Ltd. The main objective of the government in the housing sector is linked with the creation of affordable housing for the people in the middle and lower income earning brackets. These people form the highest percentage of those in need of houses. The government's priority policy move is to scrap the five-year tax holiday and give it to investors in real estate development, currently limiting it to only investors who partner with the Ministry of Works and Housing to provide affordable houses.

2.9.11 Commercial Properties

Numerous residential property investors in sensitive areas of Accra are rebranding or changing their properties into commercial spaces. Sensitive commercial areas and streets in Accra consist of the Accra Central Business District, the Airport Commercial area, Asylum Down, Osu, Kwame Nkrumah Avenue, Kojo Thompson Road, Independence Avenue, Sprintex Road, Liberation Road, Ring Road Central, and Cantonments Road, also known as Oxford Street. Property demands in Takoradi (Western region) are high because of the discovery and exploration of oil and gas there. The investors in the oil and gas industry compete for the few spaces available for residences and offices.

2.9.12 Industrial Properties

The industrial property market has been slow to develop, mainly as a result of the decline in manufacturing, which is also linked to the rise in importing finished products into the country. The industrial property market comprises factories and warehouses for rent or sale. It is limited to the North and South industrial zones in Kaneshie, the Sprintex Industrial Area, and the Tema 22 Industrial Area.

2.9.13 Recreational Properties

Private investors who are interested in building recreational centers finance these complexes either as individuals or as entities. Several cultural properties to promote tourism are owned by the government of Ghana. Dominant amongst these are the Accra Art Center, the Center for National Culture, and the Kumasi Cultural Center.

2.9.14 Construction Finance

The stability of the economic atmosphere is responsible for easy access to debt financing for real estate development and construction in Ghana. There are no specific standards for lending conditions for interested individuals set by the financial institutions involved with financing construction. The terms of lending for the institution is based on the risks associated with the project to be developed, and application and development is considered on these merits. Barclays Ghana, the National Investment Bank, Amalgamated Bank, and HFC are some of the banks that offer construction financing in the country.

2.9.15 *Home Purchase Finance (Mortgage Market)*

Economic, political, and environmental stability in Ghana is also responsible for the progressive increase in the mortgage market in Ghana. Interest rates are currently stable, which has made the industry attractive to financial institutions and other local investors looking to engage in the mortgage market. There are funds available with competitive pricing to help Ghanaians obtain affordable, decent housing. The dominant mortgage market players include HFC and Ghana Home Loan. Other banks, such as Fidelity Bank, Barclays Bank, UBA, and Ecobank also offer such products, but in a lesser proportion.

2.9.16 *Investment incentives*

Real estate industries are entitled to a five-year corporate income tax exemption. This is connected to the construction of low-cost and affordable housing as approved by the Ministry of Works and Housing.

2.10 Ghana's Energy Sector

The energy sector is expected to play an important role in Ghana's development. During the post-colonial era, the energy sector was noted as a major driving force behind the economy's transformation from one largely sustained by subsistence farming to a fully industrialized one. This started with the construction of the hydro-electric dam at Akosombo, a major initiative by the then Convention People's Party (CPP) government, which opened up the economy, and the energy sector in particular, to the exploitation of the power-generating potential of the country. Later, other forms of energy have been tapped, including renewable, nuclear energy, and fossil fuels. The government's overall goal for the sector has been to develop and sustain an efficient and dependable energy sector that provides a secure, safe, and reliable supply of energy to meet Ghana's development needs in a competitive way. The country is interested in ensuring universal access, with a choice, to modern energy forms is available to all Ghanaians. The sector is also expected to significantly contribute to national revenue and economic growth, with the potential to transform Ghana into a net exporter of oil and power by 2013. Thus, Ghana's energy sector can be classified into power and petroleum subsectors (Power Africa, 2015).

2.10.1 The Current State of the Energy Sector

For nearly five years, Ghana has experienced a continuous energy problem. This situation has negatively affected the economy since 2012. Currently, the country is shedding about 500 MW of electricity daily because of an insufficient energy supply. The side effect of this power rationing is the rise in the cost of engaging in business activities, especially on the part of SMEs and industries such as mining, telecoms, and manufacturing. The energy problem rapidly decreased the growth of the GDP to 4.2% in 2014. Heavy downsizing of the workforce in many communities in Ghana has also been a result of this shortage. According to the Association of Ghana Industries' 2015 report, businesses may be forced to lay off employees. The Ghana Employers' Association revealed that about 113,000 employees had been retrenched by several businesses in 2015 as a result of the ongoing energy challenge and the associated increase in the cost of production (Power Africa, 2015).

2.11 Oil and Gas Upstream

2.11.1 Brief History of the Oil and Gas Industry in Ghana

Exploration for oil and gas in Ghana began in 1896. The Ghana National Petroleum Corporation (GNPC) had undertaken active research until 2000. Moving away from the research approach, the government of Ghana opened exploration opportunities to international oil industries and private investors in 2001. The discovery of oil in three places off the coast of the West Cape in 2007 was the result of the government's move away from research into investment. This was believed to have produced an 800 million barrel deposit in light crude oil with an increased potential of about 3 billion barrels. The oil and gas industry is expected to significantly improve the economy of Ghana in the future. The country began the commercial production of oil and gas in 2010 and has been reported publicly to produce an estimate of 120,000 barrels a day. Crude oil contributed an estimate of 6.8% to GDP (Kastning, na).

From 2002 to 2008, about 12 Petroleum Agreements (PAs) have been executed between the GNPC and different oil and gas companies. The acceleration in the growth of the industry led to the creation of the Petroleum Commission (PC), which shoulders the responsibility of regulating the licensing of companies that operate in the petroleum sector. Any investor who is interested in the petroleum business and would like to engage in PAs for a specific period is expected to apply to the ministry responsible for energy. Currently, the PC is tasked with the administration of the application process, involving reviewing, evaluating, and recommending the award to be allotted for the petroleum agreement.

On the contrary, the GNPC, in practice, perpetuates its involvement in reviewing and negotiating the terms of the drafts of the PAs. The benchmarks set for any application include the financial strength and technical track record of the applicant, the proposed business operation, and the budget and financial terms proposed by the applicant. When recommendations from the PC are received and the terms of the PA are negotiated, the agreement draft is forwarded to the cabinet for approval. Later, the parties involved and then sent to parliament to be ratified agree the agreement. Here, there is no mandated timeline for parliamentary approval.

2.11.2 *Investment in the Oil and Gas Sector in Ghana*

Local Content Requirements (Equal Participation of Ghanaian Investors)
The government of Ghana in 2013 approved petroleum regulations on local content and local participation. The regulations encourage Ghanaian citizens to participate in trades within the petroleum industry. Therefore, provisions in the regulations, under the supervision of the PA or the license holder, allow at least 5% equal participation of ownership by a Ghanaian company. In contrast, the minister in charge of energy has a mandate to withdraw this requirement. Similarly, non-Ghanaian service companies are required to ensure joint venture arrangements with native Ghanaian companies that provide them with equal participation of at least 10%.

Downstream Oil and Gas

Ensuring performance efficiency, growth, and stakeholder satisfaction, the National Petroleum Authority has the statutory mandate to regulate, oversee, and monitor the downstream petroleum industry in Ghana. The Tema Oil Refinery (TOR) Limited, founded in 1961 with start-up operations in 1963, is the only refinery agency in Ghana. Interestingly, TOR does not refine local crude oil despite the fact that local crude oil production began in 2010. The refining industry was designed to refine imported light crude oil. TOR reduces the amount of imported and refined petroleum products in the country in order to assist the economy. TOR has the capacity to refine 45,000 barrels per day. Numerous Oil Marketing Companies (OMCs) undertake businesses in Ghana, among them Royal Dutch Shell, Total, Ghana Oil, Allied Oil, Gulf Oil, and Star Oil.

Downstream Development

The government of Ghana intends to increase local refinery capacity to adequately address both local demand and export demand. Currently, TOR has the capacity to address about 60% of the local demand for refined petroleum. There is an urgent need to not only expand TOR's capacity, at least to an acceptable level, but also improve its business operations. An estimated investment of US$300 million is required to help improve TOR's capacity of operation to produce 100,000 barrels a day.

The Bulk Oil Storage and Transportation Company Limited has been infused with about US$683.5 million for its operations in the medium term up to 2015. This is to help ensure transportation of petroleum products in a larger quantity to the northern part of Ghana. The government also has plans to encourage OMCs in Ghana to increase the number of service stations of petroleum products to ensure easy access. Other factors the government is considering are premix fuel management is under review and the development of bio-fuel as an alternative transportation fuel.

Upstream Oil and Gas

The potential benefits to obtain from Ghana's oil and gas are phenomenal. Oil and gas are widespread across the shores of Ghana from Cape Three Points in the West, to Keta in the East. Additionally, the Voltaian Basin of the country is believed to be endowed with oil and gas. The Voltaian Basin will soon receive full attention for exploration. Recently, oil was discovered in an assessment of two blocks in the

Jubilee Field. The findings from this assessment indicate that it has potential recoverable oil reserves of about 800 million barrels of light crude oil, including an upside capacity of about 3 million barrels. The Jubilee Field has thus been programmed for development in segments in order to ensure that the gas reserves are properly managed. Production of oil began in 2011 with the aim of increasing the value of the resource. Tullow Oil, who is responsible for the operations of the Jubilee Field, made a production projection of 120 barrels daily onto early 2013. As of May 2012, the field had produced 33 million barrels of oil. Numerous investors have expressed interest in Ghana's oil and gas as a result of several recent discoveries and prospects in the industry. At the moment, a lot of companies wish to explore oil in Ghana's sedimentary basins. The government wants to fast track the process for blocks of acquisition in Ghana's sedimentary basin to improve and increase their oil and gas potential.

Establishing Petroleum Regulatory Authority
A draft of a bill to control the upstream petroleum industry is under review to minimize redundancy. The overall aim of this bill is to consolidate the activities of more regulatory agencies in the energy sector. A minimal amount of regulatory agencies are required to manage the sector to ensure proper efficiency and coordination to operate and enforce regulations.

Investments in the Energy Sector
Estimates indicate that about US$9.0 billion is needed to financially support the initiatives in the energy sector over the next five years. Oil and gas business activities need over US$5.5 billion. Even though Ghana's government continues to fund activities in the energy sector, a policy paradigm shift to make sure that institutions within this sector raise their own investment capital and avoid dependency on the government is necessary. Sector agencies such as the CRA, the Ghana Grid Company, the Electricity Company of Ghana, and the TOR have been asked by the government to raise financial support from commercial loans, the GSE, and other private sector financing agreements. Additionally, the GNPC is expected to, and must, raise US$161 million in shareholder financial support for the development of the Jubilee Field.

2.12 Electricity

2.12.1 Brief Background

Ghana continues to obtain a commendable amount of energy from wood fuel to power many households, making up about 70% of the energy consumption in the country. This level of consumption has triggered the provision of sustainable energy sources through efficient management, as well as the creation of alternative energy sources to wood charcoal. Electricity provides about 69% of the energy used to support the economy. Companies that generate and supply electricity employ a large number of Ghanaians. Ghana also earns foreign exchange revenuc by exporting electricity to neighboring countries such as Togo, Benin, and Burkina Faso. The electricity supply industry is not monopolized, but the responsibility for generation, transmission, and distribution of electricity is shared among agencies. In 2011, the amount of electricity generated hit 11,200 GWh, comprised 7561 GWh (67.5%) hydroelectric power and 3134 GWh (32%) thermal power. The Akosombo Dam and Kpong Power Plant generate hydropower in Ghana. A minimal percentage of power is obtained from photovoltaic (PV) solar. The government is largely responsible for the generation and distribution of electricity; on the contrary, Ghana's government has recently opened discussions with investors concerning the construction of power plants [Power Africa, Ghana Investment Brief (http://www.usaid.gov), 2015].

2.12.2 Generation of Power

The government of Ghana aims to achieve a target of 5000 MW of power generation capacity by the end of 2015. The objective is not only to increase electric power capacity to feed an increasing local demand for power supply but to also export to nearby countries in the region. The goal is to improve and modernize transmission and distribution systems, while at the same time increasing the extension of electricity to rural areas to help provide easy access by households and industries.

2.12.3 Hydropower

Ghana has made a quantum leap by increasing the potential of hydroelectric power to an estimate of about 4000 MW. In addition to the construction of the Bui Hydropower Project, aimed at producing

400 MW, a Memorandum of Understanding (MoU) has been signed between Ghana and Brazil to develop the Juale River and Pwalugu hydropower plants. These two projects are supposed to provide the country with the generation capacity of 87 and 48 MW, respectively, at the total cost of US$555 million. As part of the National Energy Commission of Ghana's strategic plan from 2006 through 2020, hydro dams for the expansion of power generation are being constructed. A 93 MW Hemang hydroelectric power dam, expected for completion by 2015, is an example. When these power plants are completed, Ghana will be expected to have an installed power generation capacity of 3,500 MW by 2013. The current electricity consumption of the country is estimated at 7,095 billion kilowatt hours (kWh); however, production capacity is at 6,489 billion kWh. Thus, increasing the demand for power to support the economy over the next five years is necessary. Several policy programs have been implemented to increase and ensure a secure supply of electricity, all while reducing negative environmental effects and creating easy, affordable access to energy.

2.12.4 *Renewable Source of Energy*

Ghana has the potential to generate electric power from renewable sources including solar, wind, biomass, and hydro. The government has been maximizing this potential by addressing all the necessary legalities involved in the rapid development of alternative renewable sources of energy to integrate them into the national grid through the enactment of a renewable energy law.

Such laws will compel utility service companies to procure an already determined percentage of electricity that can be provided through renewable sources of power. The government has assisted in the preparation of a training manual for solar PV testing, installation, and maintenance. This move is to strengthen strategy and attempt to address the energy problems in Ghana. Tamale Polytechnic University and Kwame Nkrumah University of Science and Technology have been given facilities by the government to take up the responsibility for the development of training, testing materials, and human resource capacity building for solar PV.

Additionally, the government has played a major role for designing protocol for off-grid solar electrification for schools, health centers, and security outposts. An operational manual provided by the private sector for managing grants that support renewable services, in addition to the installation of solar

PV systems in 75 rural health centers, has been published as a means toward this development. The government's projections are geared toward promoting renewable energy technologies (wind, solar, and small hydro), as well as the provision of solar electric power projects for schools, security, and health services. Another government initiative is the decision to build capacity for training on solar PV systems, operationalizing grid-connected solar PV and wind systems, rehabilitating grid-connected systems, and preparing a licensing and supervisory plan for the electricity companies.

2.13 Thermal Energy Sector

The addition of thermal energy has added a further boost to Ghana's energy capacity, with the establishment of two new plants in Tema. After its commissioning in 2009, the 126 MW Tema Thermal 1 Power Project (TT1PP) is now operational. Additional thermal projects still in progress include the installation of the 49 MW Tema 2 Power Project (TT2PP). This is about 95% completed, adding to the TAPCO-Takoradi I (330 MW) and Takoradi International Company (TICO)-Takoradi II (220 MW). There was expansion work in 2010 on the Takoradi Thermal Power Plant at Aboadze, in the Shema District of the Western region, and a 132-MW capacity combined cycle plant is also being developed. The plant is expected to have state-of-the-art specifications, such as four gas turbine components, four heat recovery generators, and two steam turbines. The gas turbines run on light crude oil, diesel oil, and natural gas. The signing of MoU has charged TAQA with the responsibility to expand the TICO power generation plant capacity from a 220 MW simple-cycle plant to a combined cycle plant of 330 MW. The 80-MW Mines Reserve Power Plant at VRA is also available to fill in the gap for any energy supply shortage in the country. This project was constructed at the cost of US$45 million in 2007. Previously, some mining companies, such as Newmont Ghana Limited, Goldfields Ghana, Anglogold Ashanti, and Golden Star Resources, used this plant during electric load sharing conditions. As a result of its high operational costs, the 126 MW emergency diesel power units purchased by the government had remained dormant.

2.13.1 Osagyefo Power Barge

The refurbished Osagyefo Power Barge is an added support to Ghana's energy generational capacity. A US-based energy company, Balkam Energy Company LLC, was responsible for its rehabilitation. It was done in partnership with the government of Ghana to set the Osagyefo Power Barge into full operation. Balkam Energy has agreed with the government of Ghana to manage the barge and convert it into a combined cycle power plant to increase energy capacity to 60 MW at an estimated cost of about $100 million. The government of Ghana is expected to receive an annual lease of $10 million from the company starting from its 6th year through its 12th year. This agreement is reviewable every five years. The sole objective is to assist Akosombo and Kpong hydroelectric power, as well as a few others, to tackle the energy challenges bedeviling the country. As a dual-fired unit that can operate on diesel and natural gas, the barge is expected to generate 185 MW capacity of power.

2.13.2 Private Sector Initiatives in the Energy Sector

The government of Ghana has created opportunities for Independent Power Producers (IPPs) to invest in energy production and power generation. The Asogli Power Plant, a full-fledged private sector financed plant with 200 MW capacity, has been completed, but yet to start its operations, instead waiting for when natural gas is available in adequate quantities. VRA and TemaOsonor Power Company, an IPP to undertake an expansion exercise of Tema Thermal Plant, has been reached to expand the plant by 126 MW and be converted into a combined cycle facility with a total capacity of about 330 MW. These measures are taken by the government to increase the power generation capacity in the country.

2.14 Mining

Ghana's mining subsector has continuously experienced a gradual growth over the years. The industry significantly adds to national revenues through its exports. In 2012, mining and quarrying contributed an estimate of 8.8% to GDP, which is equivalent to Ghc 956 million in Ghana. Minerals contribute about 37% to Ghana's total exports, with gold as over 90% of that proportion. Ghana is after South Africa, the first largest producer of gold. In the West African subregion, Ghana is the third largest producer of manganese, as well as aluminum, while bauxite and diamonds are also produced significantly. Ghana produces a significant amount of iron, limestone, kaolin, salt, as well as many other mineral resources; however, these minerals are generally of small scale. The mining industry provides more than

20,000 employment opportunities for people in large-scale mining, whereas there are over 500,000 opportunities for small-scale miners. The industry has undertaken a massive expansion project in order to improve the energy sector's revenue. In 2007, the government to develop a nuclear energy sector, which included the installation of a 400 MW nuclear power plant by 2018, approved the industry. If and when this plant becomes active, it will be the source of energy for the mining industry.

2.14.1 Mining Tax Regime

There is 35% rate of corporate income tax for businesses in mining. There is a strong restriction on mining taxation, which assesses mining companies for tax on the basis of the mining area, but not at the level of the whole entity. The mining area of a mining company is the area designated by a mining company and approved by the Minerals Commission (MC) of Ghana. There are also local content regulations restricting the procurement of locally available mining supplies and limiting the employment of expatriates to given quotas.

2.14.2 Mineral Rights

Mineral rights licenses are available in areas such as reconnaissance, prospecting, and mining leases, as well as restricted reconnaissance, restricted prospecting, and restricted mining.

2.14.3 Ghana Chamber of Mines

The Ghana Chamber of Mines (The Chamber) is the main association of the mineral industry in Ghana. The Chamber represents the shared interests of companies involved in mineral exploration, production, and processing in the country. The Chamber was established in 1928 and its members provide over 90% of all of the country's mineral production. The Chamber's main functions consist of the promotion and protection of the interests of the mining industry, the establishment and maintenance of effective membership governance, and the provision of good management for solving of national mining issues.

2.14.4 Benefits

Ghana has received massive FDI inflows into the country to boost the economy. The economy was ranked as the fifth largest recipient of capital inflows compared to others subregions in 2012. Capital inflows into the country rose to US$3.3 billion in 2012, up 2.2% from the US $3.2 billion received in 2011, according to the 2013 World Investment Report, as cited by UNCTAD and KPMG. The industry, in addition to reducing unemployment, generates revenue for the development of the economy.

2.14.5 Challenges in the Mining Sector

- The mining industry has major challenges, including illegal mining (popularly known as "galamsey" or artisan mining) on company concessions. Illegal mining poses health and environmental dangers for the operators and workers.
- Again, persistent power fluctuations have had negative effects on the mining industry. Notwithstanding with the development of a new hydropower plant at Bui and a nuclear power plant in progress, this problem should be minimized if not completely eradicated.
- Furthermore, the industry has had problems acquiring land. The land tenure system in Ghana makes negotiating with landowners for concessions difficult.
- Other obstacles include lower mineral prices in the international market, higher taxes, high interest rates, high inflation, and irregular electricity supply.

Notwithstanding the above concerns, Ghana still remains a great destination for investment. While there is high political risk, there are also high returns. Oil and gas discovery and exploration, available minerals, and other favorable sociopolitical and economic conditions put Ghana in a superior position for capital inflows than other economies.

2.15 Regulatory Framework

The Ministry of Lands and Natural Resources is responsible for regulating the activities of the MC (www.mincomgh.org), the sole government agency implementing mineral laws. The MC is the main promotional agency for the minerals sector in Ghana, and is mandatorily solely responsible for the regulation and management of the use of the mineral endowments of Ghana and the coordination of related policies. The industry is run by the Minerals and Mining Act, 2006 (Act 703), which considers different mineral rights, incentives issues, guarantees, and land ownership issues. Ghana has also developed a stability agreement, defined clearly in the 2006 Minerals Act, to protect the holder of a mining lease for a period of 15 years from any future legal amendments that are likely to impose financial difficulty on the license holder. With any investment over $500 million, the leaseholders have the right to engage in negotiations, which include a stability agreement and better fiscal terms and conditions. Small-scale (artisanal) mining is a reserve for local investors.

2.15.1 Registration Requirements

Investment in the mining sector in Ghana must meet the following requirements:

- An investor must register a company in Ghana – the company should be completely foreign-owned except, by law, a compulsory noncontributory equity shareholding of 10% is kept for the government;
- An investor must apply for operation rights and get legal approval from the Ministry of Lands and Natural Resources (Ministry); and
- Register with the Minerals Commission of Ghana.

There is no immediate minimum capital requirement to establish a mining operation in Ghana; however, before a license is released, the Ministry thoroughly reviews the level of equity and debt financing that the applicant intends to pump into the mining operation, based on the type of license.

2.16 How Globalization Is Affecting Market Structure and Business Opportunities

2.16.1 Definition of Globalization

Globalization determines the process of increasing social and cultural interconnectedness, political interdependence, and economic, financial, and market integrations (Eden and Lenway 2001; Orozco 2002). As such, trade blocs for sociocultural, economic, and political purposes can be the engines for globalization. Several forces act as determinants for globalization. One important effect of this phenomenon is the increased interdependence among nations. Technological, economic, political, and cultural exchanges between nations have increased exponentially (Curry 2000; Peter and Pierre 2006). With increased interdependence among countries, globalization has required further market liberalization and the removal of almost all trade bottlenecks (Lee 2005; Czinkota and Ronkainen 2007). As evidence, almost all countries, firms, and private individuals are affected by the forces of globalization, with trade liberalization and technology advancement as the necessary conditions for the realization of the full effect of globalization (Martin and Warr 1993; World Development Report 1990; Human Development Report 2004).

2.16.2 Globalization, Market Structure, and Business Opportunities

Globalization is the creation of interdependence and interconnectedness between countries and the people of the world unified into a single society that function together as such, in a global village. This global village phenomenon shows an integration of the economic, technological, sociocultural, and political forces across countries in the world. These are determined by grafting national economies into the international economy by means of trade, FDI, capital flows, migration, and widespread use of technology. Lee (2000) and Peng et al. (2008) claim that the speed of globalization is rapid and will continue to increasingly demonstrate its impact on business entities and practices. These impacts (both positive and negative) cannot be overemphasized.

2.16.3 Economic and Educational Benefits of Globalization

Domestic policies have enjoyed international advantages resulting from globalization and trade liberalization. Joyce (2003) identifies this as part of the precious opportunities globalization offers. Companies have been turning to developing economies in search of labor forces. This can be a solution to unemployment, generating income for the people in the country concerned. Additionally, trade liberalization allows for greater freedom of movement, leading to the creation of job opportunities as a result of migration. These migrants serve as a major source of income to help poor households, as well as to save and accumulate productive assets for their families and relatives back home. For instance, a recent study revealed that the global value of workers' remittances exceeded $100 billion by 2005. This was far more than the entire flow of financial aid from rich to poor countries. Trade liberalization involves the removal of all hurdles to trade, production, and investments. Liberalization stresses the freedom of business activities across regional or global borders, and also favors the dominance of private business entities (Agwu 2014). According to Agwu and Atuma (2015), globalization has created a platform for the spread of education worldwide. People can access numerous educational institutions anywhere on the globe and integrate with many varied cultures, rather than being limited to domestic institutions.

2.16.4 Business Expansion via Technological Advancement

The massive socioeconomic, political, and technological transformation associated with globalization can be attributed in a large part to information technology advancement (Dicken 2007). Technology and the emergence of a cheaper world communication system have given international business in the twenty-first century a new medium through which to grow. Currently, the use of computers is expanding as well as improving business operations and integration on a global scale. All businesses, including small and medium enterprises, have the ability to accumulate wealth through exports, especially with the Internet, which gives businesses the opportunities to access new ideas, products, and modern technologies. Baylis and Smith (2001) assert that globalization through the Internet can minimize the obstacles existing between specific businesses and the global market. Removing these blockades creates open doors for small and medium businesses, which would have otherwise been confined to domestic markets, to expand their market structure and growth to the global market, thus increasing their cash flows. Large-scale production companies also experience these opportunities. Through technology, many developing countries enrich their economic, cultural, and scientific base (Lall 2004).

2.16.5 Quality Products and Price Advantage

The global market creates easy access, as well as an immediate and available platform, to different quality goods and services provided to consumers. Multilateral trade regulations expect production companies to meet national requirements, taking into consideration certain safety and health-related standards. These trade regulations were devoid of discrimination between products of foreign and domestic companies; however, the rise of international trade has flooded the global market with variety of available products, creating strong competition. With this, consumers are offered the opportunity to choose based on products' price and quality. According to Hill (2009) poor quality is likely to negatively impact consumer satisfaction. Therefore, producers can stay continuously in business when their products have competitive advantage with regards to pricing and quality.

2.16.6 *Free Capital Transfer, FDI, and Communication*

For the economy of a country to become full-fledged and functional, capital flow into the country is paramount. Currently, the transfer of money through financial institutions has become and has reached light speed with the push of a button. Electronic transactions have simplified certain capital transfers, making life not only simpler but also more comfortable. ICT has been a powerful instrument in creating international networking among countries. Information dissemination has been fast and easy with the help of the Internet. Most large companies and strong economies are investing in less developed economies by establishing business branches outside their home countries through FDIs. This helps promote economic growth in the host countries (Dicken 2007). China has invested in Africa through free trade, the bedrock of globalization. Chinese investment in Africa rose from US$681 million in 2000 to US $9.3 billion in 2010. This has provided a boost to the African economies through infrastructural development, among other investments.

2.16.7 *Increase in GDP*

Currently, global trade has widened its scope through business outsourcing. In many occasions, concentration on a certain business is possible when there is an available business practice to outsource particular required services. Most countries that engage in open trade with few policy obstacles for export and import trading have become successful. With the marginal expansion of the domestic market to the international markets through import and export, countries and companies can increase their cash flows. These financial benefits improve the GDP of the developing economies involved.

2.16.8 Cultural Impacts

Free movement of people and firms often negatively interferes with the deeply held societal norms and cultural values of many countries. The culture of some foreign countries may be transferred to others through technology, causing the extinction of certain domestic cultural values and traditions that are held in high esteem by that home culture. When these cultural values, which form the moral fiber of a society, are destroyed, the cultural identity of a country may be lost. Therefore, countries such as France and Canada have put up specific policies to prevent foreign media, including Hollywood movies and American television programs, from dominating their cultural industries. Peru, India, and other developing nations have recently formulated regulatory frameworks to protect their plant resources, traditional folklore, and cultural traditions from unwanted use by international companies.

2.16.9 Easy Spread of Global Health-Related Problems

Free movement of goods, services, and people is one of the pillars of globalization. Despite the economic benefits, diseases can also spread rapidly across countries as people from different countries migrate into others and make closer contacts. Examples of new health threats posed to the world are the H1N1 "swine flu" virus and the Ebola virus.

2.17 Globalization and Its Disadvantages

2.17.1 Disparity and Unhealthy Competition

Globalization has created opportunities, such as employment and expansion of the market structure, but there is still a disparity in the development of several countries, including structural unemployment. Developed countries are moving their factories to foreign countries such as China, India, South Africa, and the Philippines, etc., in the form of FDI to obtain those countries' available cheap labor. The host country thus generates fewer revenues, since a greater percentage of profits are taken by the foreign firms. These foreign firms make huge profits, creating an even larger income loophole between the developed and the developing countries.

2.17.2 *Losses at the Domestic Firm*

Domestic businesses suffer losses when FDI takes advantage of local labor. Recently, the standard of living has been improving and consumers are prepared to spend more money on quality, but cheap, products. Modern marketing techniques such as advertising and branding have helped to create this impact. The result of such actions is the huge losses suffered by the domestic companies that lack the potential to advertise or export their products on a large scale.

2.17.3 *Trade and Technological Change*

International trade, especially with technological advancement, can cause uneven distribution of wealth across the people and countries of the world. Generally, free trade favors people, companies, and countries with the capacity to produce and export high-quality goods. As such, the plight of individuals, firms, and countries are, in terms of competition, at a disadvantage. Domestic companies cannot compete fairly with the imports and internal FDI in terms of quality production. In many countries, these effects cause uneven distribution of global wealth.

2.17.4 *Conflicts and Monopoly*

Developed countries in general strive to remain the supreme powers, which is in part responsible for the rise of terrorism and other forms of violence. When the more economically and socially disadvantaged state experiences dissatisfaction, it may choose to engage in violence, resulting not only in the loss of human life but also economic losses.

2.18 Trade Blocs: EU and AU

2.18.1 *Definition*

A trading bloc may be defined in four parameters. First, a trade bloc refers to a form of integration in which a special trade relationship is established by a formal agreement to promote and assist trade within that group of countries in preference to trade with outside nations by discriminating against nonmembers. Again, a trade bloc involves a union that has attained or intends to deepen trade liberalization or integration with the objective of ensuring a free trade area, customs union, or common market. Further, a trade bloc is an integration that endeavors to reach an agreement with developing countries, other trade blocs, or multilateral forums. Lastly, a trade bloc makes an effort to coordinate national economic policies and reduce obstacles to intra-bloc economic transactions. The trade blocs have stages of integration, which include the full political integration, economic and social integration, creating a common market, customs integration, and free trade among members.

2.18.2 Types of Regional Trade Blocs EU

The EU is an integration of 27 member countries working as a team toward a common economic, political, and cultural goal. Members delegate part of their competence or sovereignty to supra-national institutions. With over 500 million citizens, the EU can boast 24 official languages and a common currency, the Euro, used by 17 member states. As the world's biggest trader, the EU accounts for 20% of global imports and exports, and provides development assistance to many countries in the world. The Treaty of Lisbon, endorsed by all the member countries of the EU on December 13, 2007, provides the EU with the necessary legal instruments and tools to meet future challenges and respond to the needs of its citizens. The Treaty clearly states the most important values for the Union's external actions, which include democracy, rule of law, universality and indivisibility of human rights and fundamental freedoms, respect for human dignity, and principles of equality and solidarity, underlining all relations and cooperation activities with third-world countries. The Treaty also has implications for the roles of the EU delegations. By giving them stronger political references, they represent the new European External Action Service. Under the Lisbon Treaty, the EU has a single legal personality that enables the Union to conclude international agreements and join international organizations.

2.18.3 Main EU Blocs

The European Free Trade Association (EFTA) was founded in 1961 by Austria, Denmark, Norway, Portugal, Sweden, Switzerland, and the UK to promote free trade and economic integration. Currently, it consists of

Iceland, Norway, Switzerland, and Liechtenstein. The Agreement on the European Economic Area (EEA), which became fully operational on January 1, 1994, brought together the 27 EU members and 3 EFTA nations – Iceland, Liechtenstein, and Norway – in a single internal market, recognized as the "Internal Market." (Note: Switzerland is not part of the EEA Agreement, but has signed bilateral agreements with the EU.)

2.18.4 The North American Free Trade Area (NAFTA) Trade Bloc

The NAFTA was legalized on January 1, 1994. NAFTA's membership included the US, Canada, and Mexico. It abolished tariffs on 99% of the goods traded between the participant countries. Most obstacles on cross-border flow of services were removed and made sure that intellectual property rights were secured. Several restrictions on FDI between the three participating countries were cleared. NAFTA provided these standards in addition to the permit given to member countries in order to set its own environmental standards with a scientific base. Two commissions were established to impose fines and remove trade privileges when environmental standards or regulations relating to health and safety were violated. NAFTA ignores minimum wages as well as child labor, potentially to its detriment.

2.18.5 Other American Blocs

The Andean Community of Nations (formerly the Andean Pact), founded in 1969 based on the EU model, became unsuccessful by the mid-1980s. It was relaunched in 1990 and now functions as a customs union. MERCOSUR was formed in 1988 as a free trade pact between Brazil and Argentina. It was expanded in 1990 to include Paraguay, Uruguay, and the Central American Trade Market and was aimed at reducing trade barriers between the US and associated members. CARICOM was aimed at establishing a customs union.

In 2006, six CARICOM members formed the Caribbean Single Market and Economy – to reduce trade obstacles and harmonize macroeconomic and monetary policy between members. Talks began in April 1998 to establish a Free Trade Area of the Americas, which have not yet led to any tangible development.

2.18.6 Asia-Pacific Trade Bloc

The Association of Southeast Asian Nations (ASEAN) was formed in 1967 to ensure freer trade between member countries and to achieve some cooperation in their industrial policies. Current members include Brunei, Indonesia, Malaysia, the Philippines, Singapore, Thailand, Vietnam, Myanmar, Laos, and Cambodia. An ASEAN Free Trade Area between the six original members of ASEAN came into effect in 2003.

The Asia-Pacific Economic Cooperation was established in 1989 to increase multilateral cooperation in view of the economic rise of the Pacific nations and the growing interdependence within the region, and 21 members, including the US, Japan, and China, form the bloc.

2.18.7 African Union

The AU was established in 2002 as a result of the effort of Organization of the African Unity (OAU). Since the formation of OAU, regional integration has been the top most priority for the African continent. The Abuja Treaty (1994), to ensure the creation of an African Economic Community (AEC), is the regulatory framework for African integration. The Abuja Treaty clearly stated in Article 6 (2) the six stages that led to the formation of the AEC. Again, the Sirte Declaration of 1999 entreated African countries to speed up the implementation of the Abuja Treaty, while the Accra Declaration of July 2007 emphasized the necessity to quicken the economic and political integration of the African continent. Considering the above stated issues, the AU Commission was legally mandated to oversee the integration process at the continental and regional levels.

The AU Commission took advantage of the Conference of African Ministers, responsible to monitor integration, as a platform to deliver an update of integration in Africa. As of now, there have been five meetings. The first was on March 30–31, 2006, in Ouagadougou, Burkina Faso; the second on July 26–27, 2007, in Kigali, Rwanda and the third held on May 22–23, 2008, in Abidjan, Cote d'Ivoire. The fourth meeting was observed on May 7–8, 2009, in Yaoundé, Cameroon, and the fifth was held in Nairobi, Kenya on September 8–9, 2012.

AU Objectives

The main objectives of the commission include the creation of incentives for political unity while minimizing the tendency for conflict among member states. Again, integration focuses on giving individual countries greater political influence when dealing with other nations. Moreover, the AU Commission is the exemplar of an economic priority that removes tariffs and promotes healthy competition among member countries, leading to lower prices, and thus and better products. Fostering intra-regional trade/specialization, making economies of scale to possibly generate from various countries' endowments was a key issue. It finally protects the regional economy from competition from other national economies or regional blocs.

Monitoring the Integration Process of AU

The AU Commission undertook three assessments in 2008, 2009, and 2011, respectively, concerning the pace of the implementation of AU (Integration) program in connection with the Treaty establishing the AEC. The report on the assessments was delivered and thoroughly deliberated upon in the third, fourth, and fifth conferences of African ministers responsible for the integration. The reports were adopted and endorsed by the successive AU assemblies. The overall objective of the report is to inform the 16 political decisions-makers of the level of integration in Africa, and to provide some recommendations on how to speed up the process of economic and political integration of the continent of Africa.

Other trade blocs in Africa include:

- Southern African Development Community,
- Southern African Customs Union and Common Monetary Area,
- Preferential Trade Area for Eastern and Southern African States and Common Market for Eastern and Southern Africa,
- ECOWAS,
- Union Douanière et Economique de l'Afrique Centrale (Customs and Economic Union of Central Africa),
- East African Community.

Achievements of AU

The achievements of the AU are based on the capacity to respond to the implementation of more or less of the objectives it has clearly specified.

The AU created other relevant institutions with some delegated powers in order to fulfill its obligations to members. These political structures and institutions include the Peace and Security Council, the African Parliament, the Court of Justice, the Economic Council, the Social and Cultural Council, and the Financial Institutions were created as platforms. The operations of these structures and institutions will create a platform to address the relevant issues in specific quarters. Again, the provision of certain financial institutions, such as the African Central Bank, the African Monetary Fund, and the African Investment Bank, is similar to that of the EU, in that the EU assists the Union with financial issues.

Second, the building of an AU bloc has helped in the sensitive areas of conflict management, conflict prevention, and ensuring peace among members. One of the main reasons for the formation of the AU is linked to the successful management of continental violent conflicts. The Union has established the most comprehensive, complex and elaborates peace and security structures. At the heart of this structure is the Peace and Security Council, mandated to prevent violent conflict and ensure peace and security among members, akin to the UN Security Council.

The AU, as an African integration, has contributed to ensuring an improvement in the standard of living for the African people through economic development and solid governance.

Additionally, trade liberalization and the free movement of people, goods, and services among members have been ensured through the African trade bloc. Now, there is an African free trade market, allowing the free movement of African people as well as goods and services between and across borders.

The AU has been successful in the area of disaster risk reduction and management. At the African Ministerial Conference in Nairobi in 2009, African countries were entreated to speed up strategies for the implementation of disaster risk reduction policies to address issues regarding climate changes and other problems.

In addition, the AU does not only expect member states to ensure strong commitment to good governance and democracy, as well as preserving respect for human rights, but the integration also has helped with the energy initiatives which are aimed at transforming African energy endowments into sustainable opportunities in order to increase productivity and wealth creation, as well as improving the standard of living for all Africans. This initiative was mentioned in the New Partnership for Africa's Development (NEPAD), a complete and detailed strategic framework for

Africa's social and economic advancement. AU and NEPAD collaboration depends on self-assistance and self-reliance harnessing a collective approach to exploiting African opportunities. This involves the need for facilitating and establishing strong African partnerships between member countries and the advanced world on the premise of mutual agreement and shared commitment.

Moreover, AU has provided a common front in the eyes of the world to address all issues affecting African countries. This is the reason for AU to have some representatives even at the meetings and conferences of the UN.

2.19 Challenges

Irrespective of the massive advancements made regarding all sectors, Africa is still bedeviled with several challenges. These challenges include the following:

First, there are challenges emanating from harmonization of policies. A majority of AU members belong to more than one Regional Economic Commission (REC). This results in difficulties and confusion in managing the implementation of the multiplicity of programs in the same area of integration. The impact on the implementation of these adopted programs at the national level, as well as in the monitoring and evaluation process, constitutes one of the more massive failures of the Commissions.

A second challenge relates to the political reluctance to implement integration decisions. This is virtually the perceived result in the slow pace of members endorsing and ratifying the integration process. The mechanisms for implementing programs and decisions as well as inability to apply sanctions against States that fail to honor their obligations were absent.

A third challenge relates to a compensation package for temporary losers in the process of regional integration also is lacking. It should be noted that greater percentage of the revenue of most states was obtained from custom duties.

In addition, the Commissions lack adequate physical infrastructure for the integration. Insufficient infrastructure, especially in transportation and communication in the continent, negatively impacts the integration process, particularly intra-African trade. There are also many roadblocks erected by security forces as well as illegal barriers and insecurity on the roads. These barriers hinder free movement of persons, to and from regions.

Further, there is an absence of ownership of regional projects at the bottom level. This could be connected with the top-bottom system of administration employed for the development of the various regions, as well as continental policies and programs that have witnessed poor participation of the private sector and civil society organizations.

Another bottleneck is the absence of ownership of regional programs at the national level. African countries are faced with the problem of choices between the commitment to regional unions and concentrating on domestic challenges. The benefits obtained from integration could be long term, however, the cost of the process has to be met in the short term by members who are already saddled with much social, political, and economic problems at home.

Moreover, an area of difficulty is that of inadequate financial resources. This is the main hindrance to the implementation of the integration programs of all the RECs in addition to those who have employed a self-financing approach (e.g., ECOWAS). The RECs depend on developing partners to support their most prioritized programs and activities. Adding to this is the challenge in getting an African common currency for easy business transactions in Africa. This decision has been difficult for member countries since members are reluctant to relinquish national legal tender for regional currency.

Last but not least, there is lack or insufficient human resources to run the offices of the Committee. The RECs are strongly understaffed and this has a negative effect on the performance to coordinate the implementation of the regional programs.

2.20 Conclusion

Ghana's peaceful political environment has remained uninterrupted for over a decade. The economy is presently not only robust but also has a promising future in terms of development, resulting from its continuous economic stability. Comparatively, Ghana is considered one of the best destinations for investment in Africa. The private sector, the informal sector, takes dominance in economic activities, with agriculture providing employment at an estimate of 56% of the population of Ghana, despite its drastic decline in supporting the GDP. The service sector is the largest contributor to Ghana's economy. Despite challenges such as infrastructure, inadequacy of skilled labor, poor land tenure system, corruption, and difficulties with business registration, etc., Ghana has still been blessed with uninterrupted political and economic peace and stability, democratic governance, rich mineral endowments, and quality hospitality. Since Ghana is not isolated from the rest of the world, globalization and trade blocs such as the EU and AU have both positively and negatively impacted several aspects of its economy through integration. Ghana continues to be a promising destination for investment, especially since the government has implemented several measures to attract investment in order to meet the employment needs of its citizens and to improve its economy.

References

The Abuja Treaty. 1994. "Regional Integration in Africa: what has been done and what needs to be done, Faustin Mukela Lunga". Workshop on Transforming Political Structures: Security, Institutions, and Regional Integration Mechanisms, Florence, Italy, 2009.

Adams, A.N., and Lamptey, A.O. 2009. *Customer Perceived Value in Internet Banking in Ghana*. Winneba, Ghana: Lulea University of Technology, Sweden and University of Education.

"The Africa Competitiveness Report" 2013. At the World's Economic Forum, the World Bank.

African Development Bank & African Development Fund. 2012. Republic of Ghana Country Strategy Paper 2012–2016.

Agwu, M. E. 2014. "Strategic Impact of Inward Foreign Direct Investments on the Labor Markets of Developing Economies." Journal of Management, Marketing and Logistics 1(4): 297–310. Available at: http://www.pressacademia.org/journals/jmml.

Agwu & Atuma. 2015. "Strategic Review of the Impact of Globalization on the Sustainability of Communities and Business Organizations." International Journal of Business and Management Invention 4(4): April. 2015 55–62. www.mofep.gov.gh.

Amega-Selorm, Charles Internet Research. 2016. "Telecommunications Infrastructure and Its Impact on ICTs in Ghana."

Bank Group Doing Business. 2015. Going Beyond Efficiency. Regional Profile 2015. Sub-Saharan Africa. 12th edition.

Baylis, J. and Smith, S 2001. *The Globalization of World Politics*. (2nd Edition), Oxford, New York: Oxford University Press.

Bordo, Michael D., Alan M. Taylor and Jeffrey G. Williamson, editors, 2003. Globalization in Historical Perspective. Chicago: University of Chicago Press.

Curry, J.E. 2000. Internationales Marketing: Neue MarkteerschleieBen, Deutscher Wirtschaftsdienst GmbH, Koln

Czinkota, M.R., and Ronkainen, I.A. 2007. *Internatiaonal Marketing* (8 ed.), United States of America: Thomson SouthWestern.

The European Union and Republic of Ghana, cooperation that counts 2nd edition. "EU-Ghana: Four Decades of Development Cooperation."

Domfeh, Kofi Adu. 2013. Political Stability in Ghana to define Economic Outlook for 2013, http://www.modernghana.com/news/437856/50/political-stability-in-ghana-to-defi.html

Dicken, P. 2007. *Global Shift: Mapping the Changing Contours of the Global Economy.* 5th edn. London: Sage.

Eden, Lorraine and Stefanie Lenway. 2001. "Introduction to the Symposium Multinational: The Janus Face of Globalization." *Journal of International business Studies* 32(3): 383–400.

Ernst & Young's attractiveness Survey Africa 2013 Getting Down to Business http://www.ey.com/Publication/vwLUAssets/The_Africa_Attractiveness_Survey_2013/$FILE/Africa_Attractiveness_Survey_2013_AU1582.pdf, accessed February 2016.

George, Kusi. 2013. Kumasi Investment Road Show. Regulatory Framework for Investing in Ghana.

globaledge.com http://globaledge.msu.edu/countries/ghana/government.

globaledge.com https://globaledge.msu.edu/countries/ghana/statistics.

GSS. 2016. Ghana Statistical Services, statsghana.gov.gh

Hill, C. 2009. *International Business: Competing in the Global Market Place.* New York: McGraw-Hill/Irwin.

Human Development Report. 2004. http://hdr.undp.org/en/content/human developmentreport-2004

Kastning Thomas, na, Basic Overview of Ghana's Emerging Oil Industry, Friedrich Ebert Stiftung http://library.fes.de/pdf-files/bueros/ghana/10490.pdf

Keller, Wolfgang. 2004. "International Technology Diffusion." *Journal of Economic Literature* 42: 752–782.

KPMG. 2013. *Doing Business in Ghana.*

Lall S. 2004. "The employment impact of globalization in developing countries." In *Understanding Globalization, Employment and Poverty Reduction*, edited by E. Lee and M. Vivarelli, 73–101. New York: Palgrave Macmillan.

Lee, E. 2000. "Globalization and Employment: The New Policy Agenda." *Development.*43: 18–20.

Lee, K. 2005. *Global Marketing Management: Changes, Challenges, and New Strategies.* England: Oxford University Press.

Martin, W. and Warr, P.G. 1993. "Explaining the relative decline of agriculture: a supply-side analysis for Indonesia." *World Bank Economic Review* 7(3): 381–401.

Mikva, Keren, (2015), 10 Most Mineral-Rich Countries In Africa, AFK Insider http://afkinsider.com/67750/africas-mineral-rich-countries/11/

Ofori-Dwumfuo and Betty A. Dankwab. 2013. "Adopting Internet Banking in Ghana." *Journal of Social Sciences* 5(4): 143–151.

Osland, Joyce S. 2003. "Broadening the Debate: Pros and Cons of Globalization." *Journal of Management Inquiry* 12(2): 137.

Orozco, Manuel. 2002. "Globalization and Migration: The Impact of family Remittances in Latin America." *Latin American Politics and Society* 44(2): 41–66.

Peng, Mike W., and Hyung-Deok Shin. 2008. "How Do Future Business Leaders View Globalization?" *Thunderbird International Business Review* 50(3): 175–82.

Peters, G.G., and Pierre, J. 2006. *Handbook of Public Policy*. London: Sage.

Power Africa, Ghana Investment Brief. 2015.

PWC. 2014. Growth Accelerated. Doing Business and Investing in Ghana.

Terkper, Seth E. 2016. The 2016 Budget Statement and Economic Policy of the Government of Ghana. Also available at: www.mofep.gov.gh.

VENTURES,(2012) West African Economy Records 6.9% Growth in 2012-ECOWAS http://venturesafrica.com/west-africa-grows-economy-6-9-in-2012/

Willis, Amy. 2014. Global Corruption Index 2014: The World's Most Corrupt Countries in One Amazing Interactive Map, Metro.co.uk. http://www.transparency.org/cpi2014/results.

World Development Report. 1990. http://documents.worldbank.org/curated/en/671081468139770890/Worlddevelopment-report-1990-povertypublication-summary.

Zachary, G.P. 2003. Black Star, Center for Science, Policy and Outcomes. www.cspo.org/products/articles/Blackstar.pdf.

https://www.usaid.gov/sites/default/files/documents/1860/Ghana%20_IG_2015_05_03.pdf.

http://www.ginks.org/Telecommunications%20infrastructure%20and%20its%20impact%20on%20ICTs%20in%20Ghana.pdf.

http://www.MOFEP.GOV.GH OR http://www.HTTP://EEAS.EUROPA.EU/DELIGATIONS/GHANA http://www.africa-union.org

CHAPTER 3

Historical Perspective on Doing Business in Ghana

3.1 Introduction

Ghana has a population estimated to be 27.7 million people (Population Reference Bureau 2015) and growing, which makes it the second most populous country in sub-Saharan West Africa, behind Nigeria. It is also the 12th largest economy in Africa. For the last 15 years, Ghanaians have witnessed significant spells of steady economic growth, declining poverty, and increasing prosperity and peace and democracy (World Bank Study 89064 2014). This is impressive, given Ghana's somewhat turbulent political history prior to 1990s.

Ghana experienced a series of coups beginning in 1966, with additional coups occurring in 1972, 1978, 1979, and 1981. The rationale for these coups related to economic injustices, and the governments created by them created different economies and different perspectives on economic development, but with varying degrees of success. Some coups, though, have had negative consequences and degraded the Ghanaian economy (Kwaku Gyening 2008).

For the last 30 years, Ghana has been largely a stable democracy with multiparty system as the foundation of its political and governmental structure. This political stability has meant peaceful elections and successful changes of governments, with significant progress made in establishing democratic structures. There is now open and vigorous debate in the

J.E. Spillan, D.O. King, *Doing Business In Ghana*,
DOI 10.1007/978-3-319-54771-8_3

Ghanaian legislature, and the legislation that is constructed and passed provides opportunities for the macroeconomy and for the citizens of Ghana (African Development Forum 2015).

While Ghana possesses all the necessary prerequisites for continued political and economic stability, it is still a developing country in the developmental phase of its growth. Historically, the economy was focused on the agricultural industry, concentrating on the export of cocoa and other agricultural produce, along with timber(Travel to Ghana 2015). Now, though, the majority of Ghanaian business people are involved in small-scale businesses. Such businesses involve large personal investment and are therefore not big job creators. Most of the big business establishments in Ghana are foreign-owned or are joint ventures between Ghanaians and foreign investors.

The last two years, 2014–2015, has seen a slowdown in expansion after a period of high growth rates, which caused some macroeconomic imbalances. The 2014 current account deficit increased 10.4%, with inflation increasing to almost 17%. Additionally, the Cedi depreciated 30% in nominal terms and the national public debt increased from 55.8 to 67.1% of GDP. This increase in debt is alarming and, as a result, Ghana opened official negotiations with the International Monetary Fund (IMF) for relief and assistance (Okudresto et al. 2016).Over the last several years, the private sector has been promoted as the engine of growth. Over the last three decades, the Ghanaian economy has been on an upward and positive trajectory. Even so, there are a variety of other challenges that confront Ghana, especially in the area of growth, redistribution, and sustainability.

3.2 Background

Ghana over the last few decades has become better positioned to leverage its competiveness and attract foreign investment and can be said to be one of the most promising nations in West Africa. Its economic performance record over the last 10 years has been generally positive, with especially good increases in economic growth from 2009 to 2014. Economic challenges have emerged recently, however. Currency depreciation, energy production slowdown, and an imbalance in macroeconomic policy have occurred causing credibility issues and questions about economic stability.

Business in Ghana functions in a free market environment because the government has implemented market-friendly policies.

Ghana is second to Nigeria in the ECOWAS, with 10.3% of the total GDP for the region. Between 1984 and 2010 Ghana had a 5.2% annual growth rate in GDP. After a rebasing or setting a new level or rate for the period, Ghana's growth rate was 8.3% per year from 2007 to 2012, aided by the first year of commercial oil production, which has a major revenue impact on the economy, occurring in 2011. Unfortunately, economic growth has not universally affected the economy (Alagidede et al. 2013).

Traditionally, foreign firms locate in developing countries to seek markets or resources. Most of the foreign investment to Ghana is concentrated in the mining sectors, indicating that foreign firms that invest in Ghana are seeking resources (Chen et al. 2015).

3.3 Import Substitution Versus Domestic Economic Liberalization Versus Export-Led Growth

Economic development comes in many forms. While direct exporting is a valid and important mechanism to increase business in a country, import substitution can also provide a positive mechanism for initiating, promoting, and developing industrialization and economic development (World Trade Report 2014). In essence, import substitution is a popular tool that developing countries have used to increase self-sufficiency and decrease dependency on developed countries. One of the major features of this economic tool is the protection of infant industries so that they can grow, be come strong, and compete with imported (Cavusgil et.al. 2014).

Many sub-Saharan economies have demonstrated low growth, especially in manufactured exports. Many African economies have seen a major change in economic policy, with Ghana being one of the more successful. Export promotion has been seen as an important tool to achieve sustainable growth, and the adoption of export-oriented industrialization has created some issues about import substitution strategies. Over a lengthy period of time, success in manufactured exports has had a major positive impact on economic development. Export processing zones (EPZs), which are part of the import substitution strategy, have been a major factor or mechanism in developing economies in their quest to attract foreign investment and promote nontraditional exports. One of the benefits of an EPZ is that firms that are part of the EPZ receive benefits in terms of intermediate goods, taxation, and infrastructure. Their creation has generated economic benefit.

Ghana has private sector zones, which are comprised of private businesses that the people own. The businesses earn money by offering goods that customers like. This is an approach that has required limited government involvement. This approach was considered important for Ghana to take advantage of the global economy and for them to become a catalyst for employment development across the country. Private sector zones have become an important growth development mechanism in developing economies (Angko 2014).

Ghana initiated the free zones concept in the mid-1990s. It pursued this path so that firms could be competitive and produce exports that would assist in Ghana's economic development. EPZs and free zones are synonymous in Ghana. The rationale for free zones relates to the public policy notion that free zones are an important approach that developing countries can use for economic development (Angko 2014). Since Ghana is in constant need of economic development, it was believed that one approach to operationalize this idea was through the implementation of free trade zones.

To increase export-led growth, Ghana agreed to the free zone concept more than a decade ago by implementing the Free Zone Act of 1995 (Act 504). The free zones board named four areas – Tema, Ashanti, Sekondi, and Shama – as EPZs. These free zones provide a more favorable investment environment for a developing country. They can mitigate the infrastructural gaps and other bureaucratic routines that exist in developing countries.

In reality, though, businesses cannot affect exports unless they appeal to parties interested in pursuing FDI. Foreign exchange earnings is a major advantage of the free zones (Angko 2014). Profits from the export of goods and services a country increase, and the returns from its foreign investments have an impact on job creation, economic growth, and the overall sustainability of business and the country.

Producing jobs is a major emphasis of free zones activity. In Ghana, the free zones policy under the Gateway project concentrated on attracting exports-oriented investment (Angko 2014). EZP is a private concept that creates an attractive, inviting business environment. It is a "one stop shop" (Angko 2014, p.25) to promote and enhance domestic and foreign investment. All the incentives of EPZs are to decrease costs of doing business in Ghana and production.

With the import substitution rule in place, Ghana could now focus on developing its own businesses and manufacturing infrastructure that would provide economic opportunities and jobs. These strategies would create a multiplier effect of economic positives that would benefit Ghana in the long term.

Investment in the education sector, however, has not been matched to the demands of the economy and labor markets. In Ghana, education is thought to be the dominant channel by which a good life and improved prospects can be attained; yet Ghana needs to develop skills to sustain its competitive position. The right skills matter at many levels. Greater access to education has seen more women migrate to other countries to find jobs. The labor market is comprised of high levels of informal and vulnerable employment and high incidents of poverty, especially in rural areas.

3.4 Debt Issues

Ghana's economy has enjoyed high rates of economic growth over the past 25 years. The year 2006 posted a growth rate that exceeded 6%, which appears to be above previous years rates of growth. Because Ghana has relied on borrowing to fund its development, its indebtedness got to the point where, in 1999, the World Bank and IMF indicated that Ghana had an unsustainable debt level. Debt levels exceeded 100% of GDP in year 2000. Under the Highly Indebted Poor Countries (HIPC) program, however, Ghana received assistance in 2004. Additionally, Ghana benefitted from the 2006 Multilateral Debt Relief Initiative (MDRI), which provided it total relief from debt owed to the IMF, the International Developmental Association (IDA), and the African Developmental Bank (Kwakye 2012).

The assistance from these agencies reduced Ghana's debt to about 26% of GDP, a level that was, according to experts, sustainable. After achieving a reduced level of debt, Ghana again began borrowing to finance infrastructure. The result of this borrowing caused Ghana to increase its debt to 48% of GDP in 2012 (Kwakye 2012).This again raised concern that Ghana's debt would increase to an unsustainable level and cause other financial problems as the debt rose. These reductions were due to assistance from the HIPC and the MDRI initiatives. Then there was the rise of debt from $4,920 million to a whopping $35,146 million in 2012 (Kwakye 2012).

External debt decreased in 2000 from US$6,021 million to US$2,177 million in 2006.

Much of the increase in debt levels was caused by the change in exchange rates on external debt (Kwakye 2012).Using a Debt Sustainability Analysis tool, which reviews and analyzes future streams of debt service and studies future resources, it was found that Ghana's debt was unsustainable if Ghana policy makers continued on the same path of borrowing. Ghana's debt sustainability depends on several important elements, starting with exchange rates. As Ghana borrows from foreign sources, it, of course, must understand the level of exchange it is dealing with and also must be aware of the interest rates on that debt. Because interest rates are dynamic, they need to be monitored and managed intelligently. Finally, other macroeconomic factors also can have an impact on the debt situation. Policy makers must study and monitor these factors in order to make debt sustainability realistic (Kwakye 2012).The IMF has classified Ghana as in high-risk debt distress – raising money is more difficult because current debt levels according to the Bank of Ghana are US$94.5, or 70.9% of GDP. Ghana has issued a $1 billion dollar Eurobond – 15 years @ 10.75% interest (Dogbevi 2015).

A key factor in this debt sustainability situation relates to Ghana's economic growth, a variable not easy to control. Additionally, other items such as the amount borrowing needed to meet the needs of society must be taken into consideration. This means that domestic budgeting must be managed and monitored carefully, as controlling is a key and prime factor affecting long-term debt sustainability. Borrowing funds needs to be done cautiously, efficiently, and effectively. Adequate economic growth is imperative to decrease debt service and the debt burden that eventually will promote sustainability (Kwakye 2012).

3.5 Infrastructure

Improving infrastructure is a constant challenge for Ghana's government, as its ability to build and maintain infrastructure will affect its growth and development. Ghana's infrastructure situation, however, is quite hopeful when comparing it with its neighbors, even though it does have some deficiencies and resolvable issue in various infrastructure areas. It has an ongoing energy crisis because of its inability to complete arrangements with the West Africa Pipeline, which supplies gas from Nigeria's Escravos region of Niger Delta area to Benin, Togo, and Ghana. It provides gas to power plants in these geographic areas. Other areas that need improvement or reconstruction include:

- Water and sanitation, where water and sanitation needs $435 million annually and
- Housing, where housing is deficient and requires at least 170,000 new units every year for a decade to meet housing needs.

Ghana needs investment of significant expenditures for construction and operation of infrastructures. Such projects as regional integration, good road corridors, and internationally transportation links are essential.

Some of the major infrastructure projects that need to be addressed are listed below:

Electric: Ghana needs $1.2 billion over next 10 years to address energy needs.

3.5.1 Ghana's Ports

The Ports of Tema and Takoradi are increasingly becoming the main route to landlocked countries. Ghana's Gateway Program offers a major business development opportunity in the supply chain area for movement of goods in and out of Ghana and neighboring countries. One major obstacle is the capacity of the ports to handle the volume of ship and cargo traffic that is moving in and out of the region. With smart decision-making and attention to detail, Ghana has a strong platform from which to build a relatively solid economic base to fund infrastructure projects (Infrastructureafrica.org 2011).

Ultimately, the government of Ghana has the primary responsibility to provide infrastructure such as roads, power, water, sanitation, ports, airports, etc. Without proper functional infrastructure, it is not possible for Ghana to grow and develop. One method of resolving the infrastructure problems is to use the PPP arrangement that it has developed and uses in other sectors of its economy. This is one of the most efficient and cost-effective approaches to resolving the infrastructure problems. It becomes a win–win result for both private and public sectors (Magdalene 2013).

3.5.2 Ghana's Transport

Transport: The minister of transportation indicated that for the next 10 years Ghana must invest at least $307 million annually to provide infrastructure for transportation. Some of the projects include the following:

Roads

Road transport carries 96% of passengers and freight in Ghana. The main roads are generally good and can accommodate most of the traffic, but they do need upgrading and that costs money.

Roads: The Accra–Tema motorway and the Accra-Takoradi road project, totaling 185 km. These projects seem to be a priority because it can be a) an economic link, b) increase movement of goods, c) connect neighboring countries, and d) link the capital city with other destinations in the country (Magdalene 2013).

Railways

The railways are constructed in a triangular network that connects three cities – Takoradi in the west, Accra–Tema in the east, and Kumasi in the central part. Large passenger traffic is part of this type of transport. The Ghanaian government has recognized that the volume has significantly increased and therefore have initiated. Plans to expand and enhance rail transport (Magdalene 2013).

Air Travel

Ghana has the Kotoka International Airport in Accra. Presently it has an open sky policy that has led to Ghana becoming the main air route to West Africa.

Airport development (Magdalene 2013). This development will open up PPP in an attempt to strengthen the country's infrastructure. This is one more example of Ghana's government recognizing that its infrastructure needs major changes in order for Ghana to be competitive in world trade and its globalization effort.

Water Transport

Ports: Takoradi Port – rehab and expansion. This includes dredging of the channel to provide more access, construction of bulk and oil terminals, and construction of dual access roads to the port. All of this renovation activity will upgrade the port tremendously and allow for much more import and export activity.

Waterway: The Volta Lake is an important means of providing important and low cost alternatives to north-south road and rail transport. Ghana is in a unique position with its seaports and waterways to help service the neighboring landlocked countries. All kinds of cargo such as oil, cement, fertilizer, store products, etc., are carried on barges north and south. These water transport capabilities provide the ability of vendors, suppliers, and other supply chain members to transport their goods to a variety of destinations for a reasonable price. This is both advantages for the customers, the consumers, and the vendors. It promotes economic development along the water routes and also among the inland towns and cities (Ghana Investment and Promotion Center 2015).

The Africa Infrastructure Country Diagnostic Organization was developed to expand the world's knowledge of physical infrastructure in Africa. Ghana has made great progress in infrastructure, and has been successful in developing a broad infrastructural backbone. Ghana's road sector is generally well developed with 95% of the paved roads and 81% of the unpaved network in good condition. The power sector is the most challenging with respect to infrastructure. Because there is no ability to reconcile per kilowatt-hours and increasing demand that has to be met with increasing oil usage, large losses, which are about 3% of GDP, are generated. To meet its infrastructure needs, Ghana set up the Ghana Infrastructure Investment Group in 2014 to help alleviate the various infrastructure deficiencies that exist around the country (Dogbevi 2015).

3.6 Power Crisis

Ghana has a deficiency with power and ICT connectivity with neighbors. Overall, more than 50% of the expenditures relate to power sector. In1995, Nigeria, Ghana, Togo, and Benin agreed to the development of the West African Gas Pipeline, a project that originally was proposed by ECOWAS in 1982. Unfortunately, the agreement for the pipeline was not signed until 2003. Another crisis between 1998 and 2000 was provoked by climate. Again the demand and grow of demand for power created the shortage. Delayed investment in thermal power also caused much turbulence.

The power crisis has been a very challenging issue for Ghana's people and businesses. Ghana has had a major issue with energy and the supply of power from 1982 to the present. The issue relates to an environmental challenge, poor rainfall in the Volta River region in 1982–1984. This drought caused a shortage of power from the hydroelectric plants on the Volta River. To resolve the problem, the government reduced power to business and residents. Ghana did not have its first 220 MW plant till 1998, 12 years after it was recommended that this size of plant was needed.

3.6.1 *The 2006–2007 Crisis*

Again, reduced rainfall decreased the flow into the Volta Lake and, coupled with an insufficient supply of thermal power generation, caused a power shortage. Various short-term remedies were proposed but none were installed for the long term. Each crisis caused frustration about the energy shortages and the inconveniences that existed because of the scarcity of energy. To resolve the problem, Ghana needed long-term measures, including private sector investment in power generation from indigenous gas sources and liquefied natural gas projects.

While investments in appropriate energy sources are important and are necessary, it is not predictable that sufficient resources will be allocated to resolve the energy problem. The government must develop standards that define the type and quality of power generation that is needed. It also needs to determine the levels of fuel efficiency and availability and generation costs that would be necessary to resolve the energy problems throughout the country. The government also need to set realistic timelines for bringing the power on line. This should also take into consideration the time to rehabilitate and expand the transmission and distribution networks. Increasing generation capacity creates other challenges on how to distribute it (Amin Adam 2015).

The solution is to diversify the type of energy, i.e., gas-fired plants which would be cheaper and more efficient. Even while Ghana has had success with some of its energy infrastructure, service quality deficiencies have created some major problems.

3.7 Specific Businesses That Have Thrived or Failed

Many of the indigenous businesses fail because of poor succession plans. Other businesses fail due to the following reasons:

- Some businesses do not survive because they do not have sufficient family support or because the business is poorly administered;
- Owners fail to seriously plan for own success by developing effective business plans;
- Employers failure to train employees;
- Ghanaians businesses are not very interesting in sharing ownership of businesses;

- Ghanaian businesses are not successful because of politics. Politicians often may manipulate the system to frustrate businesses for their own political expediency;
- Businesses fail due to the inability to invest in technology. They fail to keep up with technology;
- Many indigenous Ghanaian businesses are unable to meet the various requirements of financial institutions. High cost of financing results in failure of businesses (ghanatrade.gov.gh 2015);
- Many business owners lack interest in networking or using interrelated contacts to achieve goals in their business. Ghana indigenous businesses do not use their personal contacts to promote business.
- They lack discipline in spending revenues and profits on unnecessary things like lifestyles, fancy cars, vacations, etc.
- Inability to make tough decisions regarding hiring or changing suppliers.
- Failure to set up R&D activities in business that lead to new product or procedures or improvement of existing products and procedures. R&D investments are critical if owner wants to prevent failure of company. If not products and procedures, then a company becomes obsolete (ghanatrade.gov.gh 2015).

These deficiencies in business operation and development have had in some ways a negative impact on Ghana's overall development. Knowing that these failures exist gives developers an opportunity to reform the business behavior and reinvest the capabilities into productive business development that helps the business owners and the economy as a whole.

3.8 Discussion

Ghana has had many challenges both positive and negative during the last decade and one half. It has been able to avoid some very catastrophic political upheavals while promoting economic growth. Since politics always plays a role in emerging market development, we can say that Ghana has positively evolved and successfully matured into an economically and socially growing country. Because of Ghana's incredible growth, it has been labeled as the gateway to sub-Saharan Africa or a positive economic face among many uncertain and unstable countries. It has been a showcase for economic development and has tried to demonstrate that economic opportunities and business development potential exists in sub-Saharan

Africa. With its free trade zone initiatives and its free market environment, it has been able to attract FDI from Europe and North America. The ability of a manufacturer to establish business in various parts of Ghana can be considered an opportunity. Using the readily available labor and other natural resources has given Ghana the upper hand in the economic development sector.

While there has been historic growth and positive change in Ghana, there have also been some major challenges that have created some difficulties and concerns for business and policy makers. Some of these issues are as follows:

- The existence of some narcotics trafficking. While it has not grown or manifested itself as a major problem, its existence is of concern;
- Slow transport infrastructure both on land and sea. The roads have improved, but not to the level that can support the ambitious supply chain needs of many new businesses. Additionally, the need for upgrading the seaports is critical. Because of the large volume of traffic, better-equipped and deeper ports are needed;
- The national debt issue is raising its head. While the economy has been doing well, the issue of borrowing has emerged as a possible threat to the economy. The level borrowing and accumulated debt are not sustainable and hence needs to be addressed;
- Electric power generation. This problem has emerged to become a major weakness in the Ghanaian economy. Without sufficient and consistent electric power, the ability to successfully promote economic development or business development is very difficult. Solutions need to be developed quickly.

There is great potential in Ghana, but attention needs to be invested in both the positive and negative aspects of economic development. The signs of hope are still present, and the desire, initiative, and perseverance of the Ghanaian people is the key to future economic success.

3.9 Conclusion

We can say that Ghana has a free market business environment that offers an environment that Africans from all parts of the continent can take advantage of. Yet Ghanaians recognize that it takes more than one successful venture to keep it going. Policy and business development structures need to be solidly established and constantly reformed or updated to keep pace with rapid globalization. Ghana, as a country and culture, has the will and the factors of endowment to achieve its goals. The question is which direction they want to take to sustain the free market economy they have so ambitiously worked for over the last few decades.

References

Alagidede, Paul, William Baah-Boateng, and Edward Nketiah-Anponsah. 2013. "The Ghanaian Economy: An Overview." *Ghanaian Journal of Economics* 1: 4–34.

Alexandres, Marc, Neelam Veriee, and Stephen Mogaka. 2015. "African Development Forum: The Challenge of Stability and Security in West Africa." World Bank Group International Bank for Reconstruction and Development.

Amin Adam, Mohamed. 2015. "Chronology of Power Crisis and Lessons from Enduring the Current Crisis." February 17, 2015.

Angko, William. 2014. "Analysis of Performance of Export Processing Zones in Ghana." *Journal of Business Administration and Education* 5(1): 1–43.

Cavusgil, S. Tamer, Gary Knight, and John R. Riesenberger. 2014. *International Business: The New Realities*. Third Edition. Boston; New York: Pearson.

Chen, Guangzhe, Michael Geiger, and Minghui Fu, 2015. "Manufacturing FDI in Sub-Saharan Africa: Trends, Determinants, and Impact." World Bank Group.

Dogbevi, Emmanuel K. 2015. "Quartey, Mona Helen (Deputy Finance Minister)-Ghana Requires $1.2b Investment Yearly to Meet Power Needs Minister." Ghana Business News.

Ghana Investment and Promotion Center. 2015. http://www.gipcghana.com/invest-in-ghana/whyGhana/infrastructure/transportation-infrastructure.html accessed on February 24, 2016.

Kwaku Gyening, Owusu. 2008. "Military Coups in Ghana, 1969–1985; A By-Product of Global Economic Injustices?" MSc International and European Relations School of Management and Economics LinköPings Universitet-Sweden. Date 03 June 2008, Liu-Iei-Fil-A–08/00332—SE.

Kwakye, J.K. 2012. *Ghana's Debt Profile and Sustainability*. Ghana: The Institute of Economic Affairs (IEA).

Infrastructure.org. 2011. http://infrastructureafrica.org/library/doc/824/Ghana-country-presentaiton.

Magdalene, Apenteng. 2013. "Voice of the Market." *World Finance*. http://www.Worldfinance.com/inward-investment/middle-east-and-africa/ghana.steps-up-infrastructure-investment-programme, accessed on February 24, 2016.

Okudresto, Eline, Wilberforce Aminiel Mariki, Sylvia Sefakor Senu, Radhika Lai. 2016. "African Economic Outlook." www.africaneconomicoutlook.org/en/country-notes/west-africa/ghana, accessed on February 24, 2016.

Population Reference Bureau. 2015. http://www.prb.org/DataFinder.aspx, accessed on February 18, 2016.

Travel to Ghana. 2015. http://www.travel-to-discover-ghana.com/business-in-ghana.html accessed on February 24, 2016.

World Trade Report. 2014. "Trade and Development: Recent Trends and the Role of the WTO." World Trade Organization.

World Bank Study 89064. 2014. "Demand and Supply of Skills in Ghana: How Can Training Programs Improve Employment and Productivity." Peter Darvas and Robert Palmer, pp. 10185.

http://www.ghananewsagency.org/economics/Ghana-s-manufacturing-sector-growth-declining-agr-96349 accessed on October 2015.

http://www.myjoyonline.com/opinion/2015/february-17th/chronology-of-government-responses-and-lessons-for-ending-the-current-crisis.phpNABILITY.

http://www.ghanatrade.gov.gh/trading-tips/why-most-indigenous-businesses-areunable-to-survive-beyond-the-second-generation/print.html 2015.

CHAPTER 4

Cultural Issues Affecting Business Activities in Ghana

4.1 Introduction

This chapter takes a critical look at the way national culture and subcultures, social structures, religion, values and attitudes, education, manners, and customs impact business activities in Ghana. The chapter then ends with a summary of the various discussions related to the issues listed above.

4.2 National Culture and Subcultures

Culture refers to a lifestyle as shown by a particular people or society. Culture can be shown in both tangible and intangible forms. Tangible forms of culture can be seen in, for example, the kinds "of food procurement and preparation, diverse technology and crafts, clothing, body decoration, visual art and symbols, secular and religious architecture, monetary medium of exchange, transport, systems etc." (Anquandah 2006). Intangible forms, on the other hand, can be expressed in the manner of "languages, dialects, philosophical thought, cosmology, morals and ethics, religious beliefs and rituals oral traditions, folklore, festivals, political ideas, music and dance, social customs related to birth, puberty, marriage, family life, work, death etc." Tangible and intangible forms of culture permeate the lifestyle of people who share common values and goals. Culture and business activities are inseparable; culture influences

J.E. Spillan, D.O. King, *Doing Business In Ghana*,
DOI 10.1007/978-3-319-54771-8_4

business activities, and the nature of business activities is an aspect of culture. Ghanaian culture, therefore, will affect how business in Ghana is carried out.

4.2.1 Ghana's Cultural Policy

Ghana contains several ethnic groups with similar cultural values and institutions integrated to represent a collective national heritage. These ethnic groups are united by history but have special cultural features and traditions that reveal identity, self-respect, and pride of the indigenes. Since gaining independence in 1957, the people of Ghana have seen the importance of promoting national unity in the midst of cultural diversity.

In Ghana, the "Provisional National Council Law 238" gave birth to the National Commission on Culture in 1990, with the sole responsibility of managing the country's cultural traditions, practices, and values. The National Commission on Culture task includes ensuring the promotion of the changes in an integrated National Culture, playing a supervisory role in implementing programs to preserve, promote, and represent Ghanaian tradition and values, and undertaking other responsibilities as may be prescribed by government.

The 1992 Constitution of Ghana recognized culture as a vital instrument for national integration and development, using the Directive Principles of State Policy (Article 39). This state policy holds that: 1) "The State shall take steps to encourage integration of appropriate customary values into the fabric of national life formal and informal education and the conscious introduction of cultural dimensions to relevant aspect of national planning. 2) The state shall ensure that appropriate customary and cultural values are adapted and developed as an integral part of the growing needs of the society as a whole; and in particular, that traditional practices which are injurious to the health and wellbeing of the person are abolished. 3) The state shall foster the development of Ghanaian languages and pride in Ghanaian culture. 4) The state shall endeavor to preserve and protect place of historical interest and artifacts" (Directive Principles of State Policy, Article 39).

The purpose of the policy is to help the citizens of Ghana to "respect, preserve, harness and use cultural heritage and resources to advance the development of a united vibrant and prosperous national community with distinctive African identity and personality and collective confidence and pride" (Directive Principles of State Policy, Article 39).

Admittedly, though, Ghana has experienced several forms of ethnic and tribal rivalry, particularly among small communities in the north, mostly over land boundaries. However, the peace and stability of the country have not been tampered with. The northern and the southern parts of Ghana have sharp cultural contrasts; the north has more poverty, less education, and low infrastructural investment than the south. Figure 4.1 shows the recognized ethnic groups as well as their percentage distribution in Ghana.

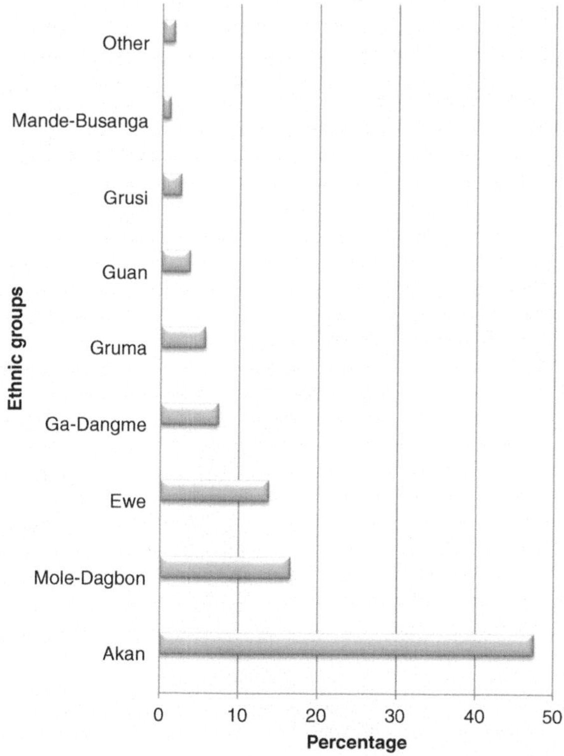

Fig. 4.1 Major Languages

Source: The World Factbook, 2015

4.2.2 Ghanaian Cultural Components

Language

Ghana is a country with multiple languages, thanks to the over 70 different tribal groups who live there. Approximately, 80 different languages are spoken, with Akan the one that is spoken most widely. The official language, as well as the *lingua franca*, is English. Eleven of the Ghanaian languages have received government sponsorship, however, including the "four Akan ethnic languages (Akuapem Twi, Asante Twi, Mfantse, and Nzema), two Mole-Dagbani ethnic languages (Dagaare and Dagbanli), and Ewe, Dangme, Ga Gonja, and Kasem" (www.ghanaculture.gov.gh. As can be seen in Fig. 4.2, the major languages spoken in Ghana and their tribal percentage distributions include Asante, 14.8%; Ewe, 12.7%; Fante, 9.9%; Boron, (Brong) 4.6%; Dagomba, 4.3%; Dangme, 4.3%; Dagarte, (Dagaba) 3.7%; Akyem, 3.4%; Ga, 3.4%; Akuapem, 2.9%; and the official language,

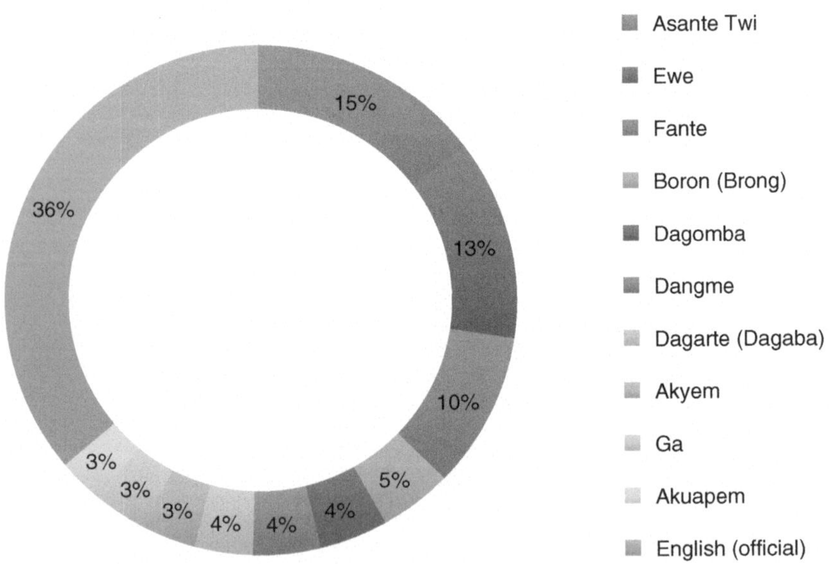

Fig. 4.2 Major Religions

Source: The World Factbook, 2015

English, 36.1% (2000 census). The English also is the official language of the educational system from kindergarten to the tertiary level, and it is the language used internationally for business and services (National Commission on Culture, 2004).

Ghanaian Cuisine

A variety of traditional dishes originates from the various ethnic groups, tribes, and clans across the country. Generally, a large percentage of Ghanaian dishes are prepared from starchy foods such as rice, banku, tuo, gigi, akplidzii, yekeyeke, etew, ato, etc. and a sauce or soup mixed with fish, snails, meat, or mushrooms. The main starchy Ghanaian recipes include cooked rice, waakye (rice and beans), fufu (pounded cassava and plantain or yam and plantain or cocoyam), banku/akple (cooked fermented corn dough and cassava dough), kenkey/dokono (fermented corn dough and cassava dough wrapped in corn or banana leaves and cooked into a solid paste), kokonte (prepared from dried cassava chips), and gari (prepared from cassava). Most Ghanaian recipes are often served with a stew (prepared with tomato and a protein) or soup. The most popular soups include groundnut soup, light soup, and palm nut soup, followed by okra soup and stew.

Main Staple Foods

For people in the southern part of Ghana, the typical staple foods are cassava and plantain. Among the north, the major staple foods are millet and sorghum. Foods such as yam, maize, beans sweet potatoes, and cocoyam are eaten across Ghana.

National Holidays

Holidays are observed thoroughly by Ghanaians as part of their culture, with 13 public or statutory holidays celebrated annually. Government workers and many private sector employees do not go to work on statutory holidays, and schools are closed nationwide. Some business, however, such as food vendors and restaurants, provision shops, shopping malls, fuel stations, hotels, transport operators, tourist centers, etc., are open. Statutory holidays in Ghana are connected with historical as well as religious events, and include major religious holidays for Christians and Muslims, New Year's Day, Independence Day (March 6), Worker's Day (May 1), and Republic Day (July 1).

Fig. 4.3 Ghana national flag
Source: The World Factbook, 2015

4.2.3 Ghana National Flag, Colors, and the Black Star

Ghana's national flag (see Fig. 4.3) is made up of three colors – red, green, and gold, with a Black Star in the middle, which represent the nation and its history. Red, the top color, remembers and celebrates the heroes who sacrificed their blood for the independence of the country. Gold, the middle color, stands for the country's rich minerals, and green, the bottom color, represents vegetation since the country lies in the tropics. The five-pointed single black star in the middle symbolizes African emancipation and unity in the struggle against colonialism. Incidentally, the national coat of arms and the national anthem capture the Black Star as part of their features, Ghana's soccer team proudly is called the Black Stars, and a central ceremonial ground in Accra for ceremonial activities is named the Black Star Square (welcome to Ghana, accraexpat.com).

Just as every Ghanaian citizen is expected to treat the flag dignity and respect, so too are foreigners in Ghana.

4.2.4 Ghana's Coat of Arms

The coat of arms of Ghana (see Fig. 4.4) was created in 1957 during independence. It shows a blue shield divided into four segments by a St. George's Cross with a golden edge. In the middle of the cross lies the golden lion of the UK of Great Britain and Northern Ireland, which represents Ghana's relationship to the Commonwealth and the UK. The sword on the upper left is called "okyeame," which is used at ceremonies. It symbolizes the regional governments of Ghana. The area on the upper right shows a castle on the sea, representing the presidential palace in Accra on the Gulf of Guinea and symbolizing the

Fig. 4.4 Ghana's coat of arms

Source: The World Factbook, 2016

national government. A cacao tree, which embodies the wealth of Ghana, is on the lower left. The fourth and last field – on the lower right – reveals a gold mine, which stands for the richness of natural resources in Ghana. Above the shield are beads with the national colors red, green, and gold. Above that is a black five-pointed star with a golden border, symbol for the freedom of Africa. Holding the coat of arms are two golden eagles, which have black stars on a band of the national colors hanging around the neck. They are perched on a motto ribbon, which bears the national motto of Ghana: FREEDOM AND JUSTICE. All government offices and official documents must bear the coat of arms to demonstrate its authenticity and validity.

4.2.5 Ghana National Anthem

Ghanaians have a patriotic song that is sung on special occasions such as Independence Day and special international sporting events which involve Ghana. This song, which every Ghanaian is required to learn, is sung to demonstrate the high sense of good spirit and patriotism required of every Ghanaian in all endeavors. Lyrics to the national anthem are presented below. (welcome to Ghana, accraexpat.com)

> National Anthem
> God bless our homeland Ghana,
> And make our nation great and strong,
> Bold to defend forever
> The cause of Freedom and of Right;
> Fill our hearts with true humility,
> Make us cherish fearless honesty,
> And help us to resist oppressors' rule
> With all our will and might evermore
> *Source:* Goversnment of Ghana website, Ghana.gov.gh
> Ghana Currency

The Ghanaian currency is the cedi. The cedi has both notes and coins, pesewas, which were introduced in 1965 to replace the pounds, shillings, and pence of the British. The name "cedi" was derived from the word "sedie" meaning cowrie, a kind of shell money which gained popularity and wider circulation in the later part of the nineteenth century. The "pesewa" represents the smallest denomination (quantity) of the gold-dust currency regime. The cedi currency has undergone several changes, resulting from change in government and fiscal policies over the years.

4.2.6 *Other National Symbols of Identity*

Other essential national emblems originate from Akan traditions incorporated into the national culture. These are the ceremonial sword, the linguist's staff, the chief's stool, and the talking drum. The Ghanaian national dress, kente cloth, is another identifiable common identity and source of pride.

4.2.7 *Independence Day Celebration*

Independence Day, a statutory holiday, falls on March 6th in remembrance of the freedom Ghanaians gained from their colonial masters, the British, in 1957. Celebrations are held nationwide, and all public institutions and schools are closed. During this occasion, a statutory holiday, special celebrations are observed nationwide, and the President addresses the entire nation on certain important and sensitive economic, political, and social issues. The state organizes this program with parades and political speeches where similar of this program is also observed across all the administrative regions and districts in the country. The national anthem is sung on this day to remind Ghanaians of the need for selflessness and patriotism for the development of Ghana. Independence Day is also a good day for commerce, especially for Ghanaian-oriented paraphernalia, food restaurants, and recreation-oriented destinations.

4.3 Social Structures in Ghana

Social structures in Ghana can be discussed in connection with social classes, marriage and family systems, and even healthcare delivery. The Ghanaian society has been stratified according to pre-colonial and modern ways. There are social classes in Ghana based on historical tradition dating from the pre-colonial period. Before colonialism, the traditional kingdoms were segmented into hereditary classes including the royals and commoners. The royals had the exclusive rights to occupy the political offices as kings and queen mothers. The royals always had the right to marry the commoners. This is the result of a rule of lineage out-marriage. Traditional royalties are still in the custody of the royals. In Ghana, a king and a queen mother distinguish themselves significantly by the use of certain traditional regalia such as special umbrellas, staves, and expensive kente cloth. Nowadays, people of hereditary offices spend and use much of Western consumer goods such as luxury cars, clothing, and food.

Currently, Ghana's social structure is experiencing a paradigm shift to education and wealth. Wealth differences in Ghanaian society have been noted as another good determinant of social class. The rich and the highly educated exhibit their elevated social class by using both Western and traditional consumables such as luxury automobiles. The concept of shared responsibility among extended family members, however, has reduced the magnitude of the effect of marked wealth differences. Social status is demonstrated by the rich in open display of wealth through expensive funerals, weddings, and other celebrations. Both the royals and the rich demonstrate their status through dozens of women they are able to marry.

Family support obligations and the communal rights that most Ghanaians hold in land are major aspects of this tradition. Majority of the people in the north are poor, hence form a noticeable underclass. They also occupy low status jobs in Ghana.

4.3.1 Marriage and Family

Ghanaian traditions and customs determine how a native should get married. According to the traditional customs of Ghanaian societies, family elders are responsible for the arrangement of marriages of their members. Marriages cannot be contracted between people of the same lineage; however, cross-cousins can be allowed to marry. In Ghana, the groom and his family are solely responsible for the payment of a bride-price. People are permitted to marry more than one wife depending on their wealth and the ability to care for them. Child bearing is considered an important focus of traditional marriages, and fresh marriages can be broken due to childlessness. Western civilization, education, and modernity, though, have modified the traditional approach to marriages in Ghana. Christian values and virtues endorse single-wife marriages, and prospective young men and women are permitted to make their own choices in terms of their marriage partner and greater tolerance to cross-ethnic marriages.

4.3.2 *Family Unit*

The family is the basic household unit formed on a complex set of traditional and modern systems in Ghana. There are two family systems in Ghana, the nuclear and the extended family systems. The nuclear family consists of the father, mother, and siblings, whereas the extended family structure involves all of the members of the nuclear family together with other members such as uncles, aunts, grandfathers, grandmothers, and other relatives. The nuclear family system is now widespread in Ghana due to modernity, education, economic conditions, and geographical mobility. In the nuclear family, the father takes the responsibility in providing for the basic needs of the family, but other extended family members can also provide assistance. There are much stronger bonds between siblings. The shared responsibility concept continues to provide a strong economic bond, cementing the unity of extended family members who stay in their separate physical homes and still assist one another. The Ghanaian family system also has two forms of inheritance – matrilineal (inheritance from the mother's lineage) and patrilineal (inheritance through the father). People in the north of Ghana practice patrilineal, while the south is into matrilineal.

4.3.3 *Medicine and Health Care*

Ghana practices both the modern and traditional systems of healthcare. The government of Ghana, through the Ministry of Health, finances and supervises the medical system in Ghana. Religious groups (churches and Muslim groups), international agencies, and NGOs also assist in the administration of the health system. Health facilities are inadequate and are mostly sited in the cities and the district capitals. Indigenous Ghanaians believe in using both traditional and orthodox medicines for the treatment of diseases. As a result, practitioners of the two forms of medical treatment are considered very useful. Several scientific investigations into Ghanaian herbal medicine have started to ascertain the degree of curative potency of the herbs that suggest new ways of developing new local drugs.

4.4 Religions in Ghana

Religion according to Rudolf Otto (religion.oxfordre.com) refers to "the experience of the holy." He refers to this experience as "mysterium, tremendum, fascinum" – an awe-inspiring mystery, a fascinating mystery.

It is a means by which man expresses himself to his object of worship, being it God or a deity. In Ghana, religion is woven into the fabrics of the society. Put differently, as part of its traditions, the Ghanaian society is religiously inclined; religion permeates social, economic, and political life, and embodies all spheres of Ghanaian life from cradle to the grave (Sarpong 1974; Tweneboah 2012). The bedrock of the existence of the society is religious. Therefore, religion becomes an indispensable part of the traditional Ghanaian's daily routine (Tweneboah 2012). This can be likened to the assertion of Mbiti (1969, also cited by Tweneboah 2012) that "the African is notoriously religious."

Religion has contributed massively to Ghana's development. Religion, especially Christianity, has become a strong social force in every aspect of the Ghanaian life, from family life, economic activities, occupation, and health to education (Fredua-Kwarteng 2007). In Ghana people are judged on the basis of church attendance and their religion. The dominant religion in Ghana is Christianity, which is practiced by approximately 71.2% (Pentecostal/Charismatic 28.3%, Protestant 18.4%, Catholic 13.1%, other 11.4%), of the total population. Next is Islam, estimated at 17.5% of the population, followed by traditional religion with 5.2%, none with 5.2% and "others" at 0.8% (2010 census) (see Fig. 4.5.)

There is no significant correlation between ethnicity and religion, but geographical influence plays a major role. A greater percentage of Muslims stay mainly in the north and in the urban centers of Accra, Kumasi, Sekondi-Takoradi, Tamale, and Wa. As Christians are spread across the country, the majority of the traditional worshipers can be found in the rural areas. Muslims and Christians have always lived peacefully in Ghana, unlike other countries in the same subregion.

4.4.1 Days of Worship

Like all religious peoples, Ghanaians have specific days of worship. Muslims in Ghana worship on Fridays in addition to the intermittent daily prayers. This means that the Ghanaian Muslim either uses the whole or part of the Fridays for worship. Christians in Ghana worship largely on Sundays, although the Seventh Day Adventists use Saturdays as Sabbath days. The Christian believers in Ghana do not work on Sundays and Saturdays. Some Christians, in addition, observe morning devotional prayer meetings and evening services. Presently, most Ghanaian Christians use Fridays and other

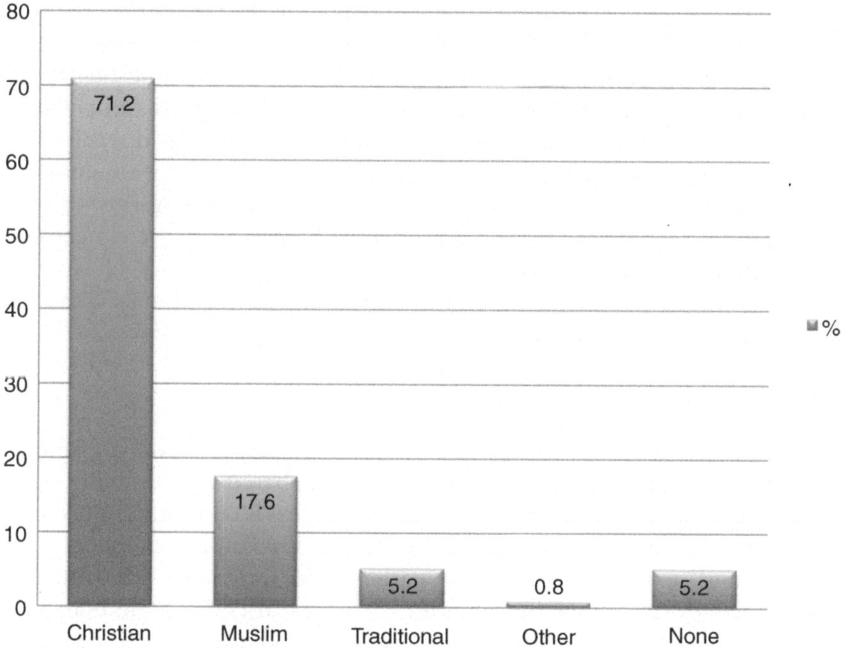

Fig. 4.5 Major Ethics Groups
Source: CIA Factbook, 2014

days for prayer meetings and night vigils. As for believers in traditional religions, the days of worship vary from tribe to tribe or ethnicity in Ghana.

Ghanaian religious believers absent themselves from work or take some time out to perform religious rituals on all the days of worship. As a result, it has become the practice of Ghanaian businessmen to start their business of the day with worship and prayers.

4.5 Values and Attitudes in the Ghanaian Society

A value is a measure of the worth or importance a person attaches to something, and our values are often reflected in the way we live our lives. An attitude refers to a learned and existing tendency to act toward a person or a situation in a certain way (Akuoko 2008). It can also be seen as the way a person expresses what he believes or values in life through words and action. In Ghana, there are several common sociocultural values and attitudes which are inseparable from daily life. Despite numerous rapid transformations that have evolved over time due to religion and civilization, Ghanaian society still demonstrates many of its old-aged traditional values, norms, and attitudes transmitted from generation to another through word of mouth (Sarpong 1974). These traditional norms, values, and attitudes include the respect accorded to funeral rites, the concept of "Dwanetoa" (the perception of time and lateness), the act of sharing responsibilities among family members, discrimination, and male chauvinism. All these have some degree of impact on Ghanaian businesses.

4.5.1 Funerals

Ghanaians are generally recognized for the high respect given to funeral rites. The Ghanaian indigenous people have a shared responsibility with family members such that one's problem or success is considered a responsibility for all. Therefore, when there is funeral the family members (both nuclear and extended) have to gather and celebrate the funeral. Sometimes, during funeral celebrations workers, friends of the bereaved as well as relative's acquaintances have to attend the funeral and give donations in the form of cash or drinks.

4.5.2 Lateness and Absenteeism

Generally, Ghanaians are noted for their persistent lateness and absenteeism at work. It is only in Ghana where lateness is referred to as "Ghanaian time" and in most cases left unpunished. Occasionally, most Ghanaians are late or absent from work and blame it on either lack of transportation or fatigue resulting from attending a relative's funeral at their hometown. Mostly, workers exhibit lateness or absenteeism on Mondays and Fridays. These days are considered special since on Fridays Ghanaians prepare for funerals, church, or weddings. On Mondays, these people are unable to return to work from their weekend trip and funerals, as expected.

4.5.3 Discrimination

Discrimination, demonstrated in social stratification, has a negative impact on the worker and work performance in Ghana. Tribalism and ethnicity bias are prevalent in the society, and in many businesses, appointments to certain sensitive positions are not done based on competence, merits, and efficiency. The heads of many institutions prefer giving appointments to their tribes, ethnic, or family men regardless of qualifications and experience. The worst scenario is where business opportunities and/or financial credit facilities are given mostly to political party faithful and cronies. There seems to be a high level of what Ghanaians term as a "whom you know attitude," meaning that the success of one's business or job appointment is relatively and largely dependent on a person's connectedness to many "big" people in the society.

4.5.4 *The Concept of "Dwanetoa"*

This is a tradition of dispute settlement where a third party of high reputation is made to intercede on behalf of an offender. This concept is an arrangement in the traditional setting for making peace in the midst of a misunderstanding between two parties. Mostly, the third party, who is probably a traditional leader, a reputable person in the society, or a kinsman of the complainant, is sought by the offender to intercede on his or her behalf when he admits his or her offense and knows the gravity of the punishment awaiting the offense. This known intercessor, "dwanetoa," then goes to the complainant and pleads with him for the offender. The use of a "dwanetoa" often is found in business situations in which a worker has violated the code of conduct but ends up being pardoned following the "dwanetoa's" intervention. In situations like this, heads of business institutions are left in a dilemma whether to apply the organizational codes of conduct or to accept the plea of the reputable person and absolve the offender at work.

4.5.5 *Male Chauvinism*

Male chauvinism has been persistent in Ghana's social system. Many jobs, such as the driving of public buses and long vehicles, are reserved for the male gender. In many Ghana societies, men occupy the headship positions at homes and families, clans and tribes, and this practice is transferred to the formal work setup such that male dominance is widespread, clearly posing a threat to the growth of women in business in Ghana (Ackuaku 2014). Presently, though, modernity, education, and much awareness-creation are relatively and gradually improving the situation for women in Ghana.

4.6 Ghana's Educational System

4.6.1 Educational Structure

Ghana is endowed with a good educational system as compared to her neighboring countries (Education USA Advisory Center). Before the advent of the colonial masters, the system of education was purely informal where information was passed on to the younger generation through the word of mouth. Education in Ghana has seen many major reforms since independence. Presently, Ghana operates a 12-year educational system at the pre-tertiary level and a four-year university. The educational structure of Ghana operates on a 6:3:3:4 system which consists of a six-year primary school education operating on a Free Compulsory Universal Basic Education (FCUBE) program to give opportunity to every Ghanaian child of school going age the right to enjoy a quality education. The educational curriculum is free and compulsory for those aged 4–14, and is defined as the minimum period of education required to ensure that children get basic literacy, numeracy, and problem-solving skills, and skills to ensure creativity and a healthy lifestyle. The 1992 Constitution of Ghana stresses in Article 38 the need for the government to provide opportunity for FCUBE and, based on available resources, extend it to the senior secondary, technical, and tertiary education as well as for life-long learning (Education USA Advisory Center).

Kindergarten education lasts for two years (age 4–6) and forms part of basic primary schooling. Then basic education comes next. Then there is an additional three-year junior high education, which ends with the Basic Education Certificate Examination, followed by another three-year senior high, and a four-year university education. The Senior High School also ends on a final exam known as the West African Senior Secondary Certificate Examination (WASSCE), previously known (before 2007) as the Senior Secondary School Certificate. After a Senior High School education, graduates have the privilege to further their education in any vocational institution, teacher education institution, polytechnic, or any tertiary educational institution.

In Ghana, enrollment into tertiary education depends on one's qualifications. The performance requirement for entry into any tertiary institution for a bachelor degree program is pegged at a maximum of 24 points in the WASSCE. A Bachelor degree is awarded after completion of a four-year program, majoring in a specific field of study. The universities offer academic programs ranging from Bachelors to a PhD. While the Master's degree program is offered for two years after the Bachelor degree, the PhD is done over three years after the Master's degree. Polytechnic institutions, which offer a vocational education, are also an option. Polytechnic institutions offer a three-year curricula, leading to a Higher National Diploma. Again, Ghana has many colleges of education. Usually, these colleges specialize their programs in specific areas of study (colleges of agriculture, for example) or in work-training (nursing training colleges, teacher training colleges). Fresh graduates from tertiary education, it should be noted, are required to serve the state for a year under the National Service Scheme. These graduates are usually posted by the National Service Secretariats to serve in any of the following sectors: agriculture, health, education, local government, rural development, military and youth programs, and other private organizations (Ameyaw, 2003).

4.6.2 Medium of Instruction of Ghanaian Education

The sole official language used as a medium of instruction throughout the Ghanaian educational system is English. The language policy allows students to study in any of eleven local languages in the period between the first three years, after which English becomes the primary medium.

4.6.3 Educational Institutions in Ghana

The available 2010 record on education performance in Ghana indicates the wide range and numbers of educational institutions spread across the country. Currently, Ghana has 17,471 KG schools, 18,579 primary schools, 10,768 junior high schools, 697 senior high schools, 280 technical and vocational education training centers, 7 public universities including GIMPA and 55 accredited private tertiary educational institution, 10 polytechnics, and 38 colleges of education. Table 4.1 presents the statistical data of educational institutions in Ghana (MoE Ghana, Education sector performance report 2010).

4.6.4 The Education Sector and Agencies of Ghana

Education in Ghana falls under the auspices of the Ministry of Education (MoE). The Ministry is responsible for overall education sector policy, planning, and monitoring. The delivery and implementation of education is given to institutions, districts, and regions using various agencies of the Ministry.

4.6.5 *Ghana Education Service*

The Ghana Education service (GES) is the recognized body charged with the implementation of the basic and senior high education segment as well as technical and vocational institutions. GES is given the responsibility to oversee schools.

4.6.6 *Other Agencies in the Education Sector*

Other educational agencies, such as the National Council for Tertiary Education and the Non-Formal Education Division, have vital subsectoral roles in connection with education delivery and policy implementation.

4.7 Manners and Customs in Ghana

Ghanaian society puts a premium on certain customs and social manners. The people of Ghana are noted to be polite, hospitable, and very formal. The practice of shaking hands and sharing pleasantries when acquaintances meet is prevalent in Ghanaian social life. Visitors to a house are expected to greet and shake hands with each family member. The guests are then offered seats and greeted in turn by the hosts. In Ghanaian custom, the host is required to serve the guests with welcome drink and food. Prayers

Table 4.1 Academic institutions in Ghana

Institutions	*Number*
Kindergarten (KG)	17,471
Primary schools	18,579
Junior high schools (JHS)	10,768
Senior high schools (SHS)	697
Technical and vocational training centers	280
Colleges of education	38
Polytechnics	10
Universities and GMPA	7
Other accredited private universities	55

Source: Ministry of Education, Ghana, Education sector performance report 2010

are often said to ancestors for persons making or returning from a long journey. If someone is eating, he or she must invite an unexpected visitor to join him or her. Normally, an invitation to eat should not be objected. Ghanaian society respects cordial human relationships such that friends of the same age and gender may hold hands when walking. Age and social status also are recognized; for example, elderly men and women are addressed as father or mother (Anquandah, 2006).

4.7.1 Abusive Gestures and Taboos in Ghana

In Ghana, the use of the right hand to shake hands, touch, eat food with, or handle money is compulsory. To use the left hand for these things is considered rude and dirty. It is rude to offer or take an object with the left hand. Gestures such as waving with the left hand and the thumbs up sign are seen as rude. It is equally rude or insulting among Ghanaians to stare or point at people in public. While people of the same age, gender, and social status generally accept direct eye contact, too much direct eye contact (too much stare) is probably interpreted as rude and a possible threat. Children are not expected to directly look the elderly in the eye during conversation. Very few people are allowed to look at a village chief or highly respected elderly men in the eye when speaking to them, as it is customarily accepted as a sign of respect to avoid direct eye contact when speaking with an elder or superior.

4.7.2 Law and Order

Ghanaians do not generally endorse the behavior of drunkenness and smoking in public. The legally accepted age for drinking and smoking is 18. Sanctions are meted out for the illegal possession of firearms and the use, or trade in illegal drugs. Offenders can be given long jail sentences and heavy fines.

4.7.3 Dress

Ghanaians, in general, take pride in dressing well and having a positive appearance. With Ghanaian men, the most widely accepted clothing choices include nice pants, a collared shirt, and a tie, although in several situations a tie is not desirable. Some foreigners may be seen in shorts, but many Ghanaian indigenes hardly wear them. Shorts are generally meant for school children or sport. For women, simple dresses, skirts or pants, and blouses are accepted. The majority of Ghanaians dislike dressing provocatively (clothes that are too transparent or tight fitting). Shorts or miniskirts and skimpy clothing are also considered provocative. During funerals, Ghanaians put on funeral or mourning clothes fashioned in many designs. The color of the funeral cloth could be black, red, or any acceptable color that demonstrates mourning. Additionally, Ghanaians have accepted the wearing of locally made clothing to be worn on Fridays. This is made a national agenda to promote locally made-in-Ghana goods and stimulate the growth of local industries. On Fridays, both workers in the public and private sectors wear their locally made Ghanaian prints to their offices.

4.7.4 Titles and Business Cards

Ghanaians commonly address strangers by "Sir" or "Madam." Known persons are also addressed as "Mister or Mr." in addition to the first or last name. Madam is used for females together with the first or last name. Age plays a vital role in how Ghanaians address their fellow humans. Peers, however, usually call themselves by their first names. Ghanaian society also accepts addressing people by their profession. For example, the driver of a bus can be called "driver" and a teacher can be called "teacher." While it is normally advisable to exchange cards (using the right hand, of course), there are no set procedures on how to exchange business cards in Ghana.

4.7.5 Conclusion

For businesses to triumph in Ghana, foreign entrepreneurs and investors are advised to know and understand its cultural climate and operate businesses accordingly. Knowing the Ghanaian people means knowing their way of life – what they eat, what they wear, where they sleep, their language, religious beliefs and practices, traditions and customs, manners and attitudes, education, etc. Culturally, Ghanaians are noted worldwide for their hospitability, peace loving attitude, and interest in promoting and maintaining national unity in the midst of diversities. Ghana's national culture has been formed out of a collection of varied traditions, customs, values, and practices from many ethnic groups. The Ghanaian and his religion are highly inseparable and that religion permeates all spheres of his endeavors. The society of Ghana is woven under class systems in which royalty is highly esteemed. In Ghana, one's social status is determined by his education, wealth, position, and, to a lesser extent, family. The level of poverty in most cases is not massively felt because of the belief in the concept of shared responsibility among family members (nuclear and extended family units). Marriage and childbearing are considered paramount. In understanding the cultural climate of Ghana and deciding to set up businesses there, companies, firms, and other small businesses need to tailor their operations in accordance with the cultural knowledge in order to have the best chances for success.

References

Ackuaku, Charity. 2014. "The Determinants of Gender Asset Gap in Ghana." Master's Thesis, University of Ghana, July 2014.

Akuoko, K.O. 2008. Traditional Values, Socio-Cultural Factors and Human Resource Management Practices in Public Sector Organizations in Ghana.

Ameyaw, Akomfi. 2003. "Ministry of Education, Government of Ghana Education Strategic Plan 2003 to 2015." Volume 1: Policies, Targets and Strategies.

Anquandah, James. 2006. "Culture, National Identity and Developments."

CIA Factbook. 2014. The World Factbook – Africa: Ghana http://www.rodaknet.com/cia_factbook_2014/geos/print/country/countrypdf_gh.pdf accessed on July 27, 2016.

Fredua-Kwarteng. 2007. "Religiosity vs Spirituality." Ghana Web, http://www.ghanaweb.com/GhanaHomepage/features/artlikel.php?ID=123593.

Ghana, International Religious Freedom Report for 2013 United States Department of State • Bureau of Democracy, Human Rights and Labor CIA World Factbook.

Ghanaian Culture, National Identity and Development 18/12/2006

Mbiti, John S. 1969. *African Religions and Philosophy*. 2nd ed. Oxford: Heinemann.

Ministry of Education. 2010. Education Sector Performance Reforms.

National Commission on Culture. 2004. Cultural Policy of Ghana.

Tweneboah, Seth. 2012. The Sacred Nature of the Akan Chief and its Implications for Tradition, Modernity and Religious Human Rights in Ghana.

The World Factbook (2015). https://www.cia.gov/library/publications/the-world-factbook/docs/whatsnew.html.

The World Factbook, (2016). https://www.google.es/?gfe_rd=cr&ei=CdMRWd21OOGs8weqnbm4Cw&gws_rd=ssl#q=The+World+Factbook+2016&spf=554

Sarpong, Peter. 1974. *Ghana in Retrospect: Some Aspects of Ghanaian Culture.* Tema: Ghana Publishing Corporation.

http://www.ghananation.com/recipes/.

http://globaledge.msu.edu/countries/ghana/cultures.

http://www.everyculture.com/Ge-It/Ghana.html#ixzz4D68NipPH.

http://www.officeholidays.com/countries/ghana/index.php.

http://www.businessdictionary.com/definition/national-culture.html#ixzz3z5oUYRYz.

https://en.wikipedia.org/wiki/Ghanaian_cuisine.

http://www.accraexpat.com/pdfs/Ghana%20-%20A%20country%20profile.pdf, accessed July 27, 2016.

https://www.google.com.gh/search?q=Ghana%27s+coat+of+arms+image+pdf&rlz=1C2EJFA, accessed July 27, 2016.

CHAPTER 5

The Political Climate and Entrepreneurship in Ghana

5.1 Overview Of Chapter

This chapter provides a descriptive picture of political climate in Ghana, with reference to how it affects doing business in the country. In addition to looking at the overall political climate, issues such as regional politics transparency, and political risk will be discussed. Political risk, legal systems, contracts and agreements, and obstacles to entrepreneurship will also be addressed.

5.2 Introduction to Ghana's Political Climate

As mentioned earlier, Ghana gained its independence from the British in 1957 through the relentless efforts of Dr. Kwame Nkrumah, the first President of the Republic of Ghana and his CPP. Since then, the country has witnessed many political regimes through military interventions, a second and third republic, another military intervention, and the back to Fourth Republic.

For over a decade, though, Ghana has enjoyed uninterrupted political peace and stability. This success has come through smooth democratic transitions and transfers of power since the Fourth Republic began in 1993. Transitions include moving from the eight-year regime of Jerry John Rawlings and the NDC to John Agyekum Kuffour and the NPP in

J.E. Spillan, D.O. King, *Doing Business In Ghana*,
DOI 10.1007/978-3-319-54771-8_5

2000, and then from that to John Evans Atta Mills and the NDC again in 2009. Due to President Mills' illness and untimely death, his Vice President, John Dramani Mahama, became interim president and was then elected president in 2012.

It must be emphasized that all these presidents have contributed in deepening the young democracy by ensuring good governance, boosting the economy, reducing poverty, and fighting corruption. Though Ghana's democracy is still young with its multiparty status, the country has done well compared to other African countries in the region. The political parties are properly institutionalized. Traditional leaders and the military restrain themselves from interfering in the functions of the executive office and politics. According to World Bank document (2009, No. 47432-Gh), there is a quite more delicate governance picture behind the scenes, showing that political incentives in Ghana are set to only favor the country as the grabber but not as a producer, meaning that "with grabber friendly institutions more natural resources push aggregate income down, while with producer friendly institutions more natural resources increase income" (Mehlum et al. 2005: 1).

The political system mimics a clientele situation in which government responds to a few interest groups – those who relate well with the government in power or government cronies. According to FAFT (2015), Transparency International's Global Corruption barometer 2010/2011 showed that Ghana was ranked high in ensuring good governance and the fight against corruption compared to the countries in the subregion. In a political terrain like this where there are some powerful interest groups, big business investments are likely to flourish with strong influence from either personal relationships or political campaign financial support.

As specified by the 1992 Constitution, Ghana's political framework has checks and balances between the three arms of government – the executive, the judiciary, and the legislature. Each of these branches is supposed to provide a certain amount of check on the others. However, these checks and balances are generally known to be fragile. One example of a check is that, through the mandate given by the Standing Orders of Parliament, the minority party effects the appointment of the chair of the Public Account Committee. This constitutional entrenchment has been respected since the Fourth Republic. An example of where a check on power can be weakened, however, is that the president, in his capacity provided by Article 28(1) to appoint a majority of cabinet ministers from parliament. This can reduce the independence of the legislature and its efficiency in ensuring accountability through checks (2009, No. 47321-Gh).

Despite the relatively peaceful political climate that has been in place since 1993, according to globaledge.com (2015), the current political and economic climate of Ghana has been ranked "C," indicating a highly volatile environment interspersed with numerous disturbing weaknesses and risks. The recent survey of Afro barometer (2014, round 6) indicates as well that democracy and governance in Ghana are becoming weaker and deteriorating, and a greater percent of Ghanaians are becoming fed up with the regime of the incumbent NDC. The reasons advanced could be traced to the perceived increase in the level of corruption among incumbent government and public officials, the recent decline or extinction of the effectiveness of social intervention programs such as the National Health Insurance Scheme, National Youth Employment Program, the School Feeding Program, etc.

Currently, there is greater public dissatisfaction with the governments' repetition of unfulfilled political promises, rising inflation, currency depreciation, frequent energy crises, a high cost of living, and delays in the disbursement of district assembly common funds. The level of political risk now is perceived to be at 60% (Afro barometer survey report 2015). It must be stressed, though, that democracy in Ghana remains unperturbed and the dissatisfied public have the political right and responsibility to wait until the 2016 election to voice its opinion about the incumbent government through the electoral process.

5.3 Regional Political Issues That Affect Business in Ghana

Ghana engages in regional politics to advance the course of its massive economic, social, political, and cultural developments. The first president of the Republic of Ghana, Osagyefo Dr. Kwame Nkrumah, performed credibly as part of Ghana's foreign policy in the area of regional integration. He was the leader of the CPP and believed in advocating for anticolonialism and independence for Africa.

Ghana's decisions on regional integration as a branch of foreign policy are taken not only by the executive arm of government but by the constitutionally elected representatives that play a vital role in the signing and ratification of international treaties and demonstrating the regulatory framework in which foreign policies must operate in the democratic system of governments. International agreements, treaties, and conventions are incorporated into domestic laws through parliamentary act or resolution (under Article 75(2), 1992 Constitution). This means that international agreements and other specific treaties are dependent on parliamentary ratification prior to their effectual operations in the country.

5.3.1 *The Executive, Constitution, and Foreign Policy of Ghana*

The 1992 Constitution of Ghana gives the Executive branch the legal right to formulate and implement foreign policies on matters relating to regional integration. There is a provision in Article 40 in addition to other matters that "in its dealings with other nations, the Government shall... adhere to the principles enshrined in... the aims and ideals of – (i) the Charter of the United Nations; (ii) the charter of the Organization of African Unity; (iii) the Commonwealth; (iv) the Treaty of the Economic Community of West African States; and (v) any other international organization of which Ghana is a member." More importantly, Article 75(1) states that "The President may execute or cause to be executed treaties, agreements, or conventions in the name of Ghana." Ghana's foreign policies on regional integration in West Africa are specific, and focused on the promotion of peaceful mutual relations with neighboring countries. As of 2005, Ghana had engaged in the ratification of 45 out of 46 ECOWAS protocols, except the ECOWAS protocol on education and training.

Ghana's foreign policies help in ensuring bilateral agreements to enhance good security and the integrity of its territorial borders in addition to the general cooperation with countries in the West African subregion through the application of ECOWAS protocols such as the free movement of goods and services, intra-community trade, common infrastructural development, regional peace, and security, as well as addressing cross-border criminal issues (Friederich-Ebert-Stifung 2009).

5.3.2 *The Ministry of Foreign Affairs, Regional Integration*

Ghana's regional and international relationships fall under the auspices of the Ministry of Foreign Affairs. The Ministry is responsible for promoting mutual economic relationships between Ghana and other countries, as Ghana performs a positive and creative function as an

ECOWAS member in ensuring peace, stability, economic development, and provision of support for member states.

5.3.3 *The Ministry of Trade and Industry*

The Ministry of Trade and Industry is another regulatory body responsible for implementing and monitoring the internal and external trade and other related policies of the industries. Besides ensuring the promotion of trade with other neighboring and developing economies in the African subregion, the Ministry of Trade and Industry sees to it that import and export laws are well administered. The major agencies that collaborate with the Ministry of Trade and Industry include the Ministry of Foreign Affairs, Lands and Forestry, CEPS, GIS, Ghana Civil Aviation Authority, the Ghana Ports and Harbor Authority, COCOBOD, and other players in import/export, manufacturing and trading segments. With regard to trade, Ghana's policies for sub-Saharan Africa should include the formulation and harmonization of frameworks that will ensure free trade and industrial collaboration at national and regional levels. Ghana is poised to formulate and implement trade policies using statistical systems that meet the standards of both the domestic as well as international market in order to assist in the development as well as the promotion of nontraditional export products, and advancing production capacity on the basis of free trade across borders.

5.3.4 *Private Sector Development (PSD)*

This is a unit of the Ministry of Trade responsible for providing a good atmosphere, permitting private firms to function efficiently. The unit also provides the needed support for certain agencies and policies that ensure the promotion of the private sector domestically and regionally.

The country is well connected both at the African trade bloc level, such as the OAU, the AU, the Nonaligned Movement, the ECOWAS, etc., and the international integrations which include the EU, the WTO, the UN, etc. Generally, the integrations aim at considering the sociopolitical, economic, and cultural benefits that member countries can exploit to their advantage [Friederich-Ebert-Stifung (2009)].

5.3.5 *Ghana's Bilateral Investment Agreements*

There have been bilateral trade and economic agreements and permanent joint commissions involving Ghana and its immediate neighbors, sometimes in the face of latent ideological and political differences and mutual respect, as well as numerous reciprocal state visits by high-ranking officials. These measures have contributed significantly to subregional cooperation, development, and the reduction of tension.

The following countries have had their Bilateral Investment Treaties (BIT or agreements) signed and ratified with Ghana. They include China, the Netherlands, Denmark, Germany, Malaysia, Switzerland, and the UK. Ghana has concluded BIT negotiations with 26 countries, 19 of which are still pending ratification by parliament. The countries that have BIT awaiting ratification include Zimbabwe, Barbados, Zambia, Benin, Yugoslavia, Botswana, Spain, Bulgaria, Romania, Burkina Faso, Cote d'Ivoire, Cuba, Egypt, Mauritius, Mauritania, France, Italy, and Guinea. Discussions are in progress for treaties between Ghana and the US, Pakistan, South Korea, North Korea, and Belgium. The US has signed a BIT with a Trade Investment Framework Agreement and the Open Skies Agreement, which have expanded international passenger and cargo flights in and out of the US (State Department, USA) (www.state.gov, 2016). Exploratory BIT discussions were initiated between US and Ghana in 2012. Eligibility requirements have been met by Ghana in order to enjoy the benefits afforded by the African Growth and Opportunity Act (AGOA), and Ghana is eligible for the opportunities under AGOA. On the issue of taxation treaties, double taxation treaties have been signed and ratified between Ghana and countries such as France, Germany, Italy, Belgium, South Africa, Denmark, Switzerland, the Netherlands, and the UK (US Dept. of State 2015 Investment Climate).

Politically, Ghana has been fantastic in its contribution to peacekeeping activities both at the international level and the African subregion. The country has given wonderful assistance to international peacekeeping under the auspices of the UN in countries such as Lebanon, Afghanistan, Rwanda, the Balkans, and Liberia. As a member of the International Criminal Court, Ghana's foreign policies, since the time of independence, have been demonstrated through adherence to the principles and ideals of Pan-Africanism and Nonalignment. Ghana's foreign policies aim at maintaining friendly relationships and cooperation based on mutual respect with all countries regardless of political differences.

These relationships have been devoid of internal interference from the parties involved.

Culturally, Ghana's foreign policies demonstrate the possibility of creating a platform of cultural exchange with neighboring countries such as Togo, Ivory Coast, Burkina Faso, Nigeria, etc. The free movement of people, and goods into the country from the developed economies also introduces foreign cultures and products to the Ghanaians.

Ghana's foreign and regional relationships with other countries have enormous investment impact. Economically, Ghana gains access to African and international markets to engage in more export and import trade. A bigger global market is created for the country to produce and export local goods such as cocoa, gold, coffee, bauxite, manganese, and oil.

Again, the free movement of people, goods, and services resulting from trade liberalization in the African subregion and the world is another major economic impact. Ghana enjoys free cross-border trade among Africa and the world, and there is transfer of skilled labor as well as FDI into Ghana to make room for healthy competition in the local market to ensure the production of quality goods and services. This kind of trade is fast-tracked by the advancement of technology and the internet. Ghana's technology and internet development is fast-paced compared to the other countries in the subregion.

5.3.6 Challenges to Ghana's Regional Issues

Ghana has performed credibly in the regional and subregional integration of Africa. However, Ghana's foreign policies and their implementation have witnessed uncountable challenges and bottlenecks; the following are few of them.

Most economic analysts are of the view that the idea of regional integration still remains a political dream, and the political will to ensure full implementation of regional policies backing the integration is a mirage. Many companies complain that the framework required to ensure free trade regionally and subregionally is unavailable. More to the point, the private sector, which plays an important role in most economies, has received no consultation for its input prior to regional integration. The existing trade blocks do not facilitate Ghana's ambition of being the gateway to West Africa, since large-scale exports to the African subregion are hindered. Such countries like Burkina Faso, which is landlocked, require over land transport of goods (Sundaram et al. 2011).

Inadequate or poor infrastructure has been noted as a major obstacle to integration. Promoting the free movement of goods and services as well as people across the subregion requires certain modern infrastructure such as good roads, ports, and other physical structures linking countries that form the integration. Even though roads connecting Ghana to countries in the subregion are properly constructed to ensure the smooth transport of goods and services as well as people, the numerous security checkpoints and the difficult procedural process used by the security agencies render road transport highly uncomfortable and expensive (Friedrich-Ebert-Stiftung 2009).

In general, road networks connecting ECOWAS countries are poor. Transportation on the sea has challenges relating to the absence of direct shipping links within the subregion. The port facilities are in bad condition, if not unavailable, whereas some port officials show less or no commitment in ensuring the quick clearance of goods at the ports. Although roads in the subregion have seen improvement recently, there are still problems with transportation. First, there is no railway line to link countries in the subregion. Second, air transport among subregional countries is underdeveloped, poorly patronized, and very expensive. Last but not least, there is a poor telecommunication network in the subregion to inject some fast pace into the integration process (Friedrich–Eberto-Stiftung 2009).

5.3.7 *Transparency and Regulatory Issues*

Ghana's trade liberalization and investment promotion policies are directed and implemented by the government's preparedness to ensure a clear and transparent legal framework. According to the 2015 rankings of the World Bank's Ease of Doing Business, Ghana stepped backward to 70th position. The Ghana Investment Promotion Center (GIPC) law enshrined the preparedness of the government to provide foreign investors with a liberal and transparent foreign investment regulatory regime. The GIPC has created a fast-track outlet for investment registration. This outlet facilitates the investment registration process. Regulatory agencies have been established to perform some supervisory roles. Such regulatory agencies include the NCA, the National Petroleum Authority, the PC, the Energy Commission, and the Public Utilities Regulatory Commissions

(PURC), all charged with, for example, the responsibility of overseeing the operations in telecommunications, downstream and upstream petroleum flows, along with electricity, natural gas, and water resources. Though the creation of these regulatory agencies was a positive initiative by the government, they are relatively not well resourced and are plagued with political interference. Therefore, they remain inefficient in the discharge of their duties (US Dept. of State 2015. Investment Climate).

5.4 Political System

Ghana's political system demonstrates three branches of government: the executive, the judiciary, and the parliamentary branches, with each ensuring some level of checks and balances on the other. Other important political institutions in Ghana's democratic system include political parties, local and regional authorities, and civil society, including chieftaincies. The institutions in Ghana's political system are as follows.

5.4.1 The Executive and the Cabinet

The Constitution of Ghana gives the executive power to the President, who is also the Head of State, Head of Government, and the Commander-in-Chief of the Armed Forces. The President and his Vice President are directly elected through democratic means for a four-year term and are eligible for a second tenure of four years. The President is empowered by the 1992 Constitution with the executive powers to make vast political appointments. According to Ninsin (2008), the 1992 Constitution vests in the Executive Branch of Government, specifically the President, exclusive power and control in making appointments. The Cabinet and Ministers are appointed by the President to determine general government policies (OSIWA and IDEG 2007: 23; Abdulai 2009; FES 2011).

The President is responsible for the appointment of between 10 and 19 cabinet members. The Cabinet comprises the President, the Vice-President, and other Ministers of State not exceeding 19. The ministers are appointed through parliamentary approval to assist the President in the administration of the various ministries. The greater percentage of the ministers must be appointed from members of parliament with the ruling party having the largest share. The specialized government ministries to which ministers are appointed to run on behalf of the President include the Ministry of Defense, the Ministry of Health, and the Ministry of

Education and Sport. Deputy ministers are appointed to help the various ministers appointed by the President to form his cabinet. The appointment of other ministers to oversee the day to day administration of the ten regions of Ghana rests with the President. Each regional minister is the chairman of the regional Coordination Council, which comprises the minister and his deputies, the presiding member including the District Chief Executive representing each district in the region, as well as two chiefs chosen from the Regional House of Chiefs.

Other constitutionally mandated agencies which receive varied forms of appointment from the President to help in ensuring good governance and deepen democracy include the National Security Council, the National Development Planning Commission, the Council of State, the Commission on Human Rights and Administrative Justice, the National Commission for Civic Education, and the Electoral Commission. These bodies do not only serve as advisory bodies, but also render some level of check and accountability on the executive branch.

5.4.2 *The Legislature*

According to the 1992 Constitution, Parliament is the lawmaking body of Ghana. The Legislature is the organ of government responsible for making legislation as its primary function. Ghana's constitution requires the President to appoint a greater percentage of his cabinet from Parliament (Abdulai 2009). The Parliament of Ghana has witnessed numerous significant changes over the years (Abdulai 2009). The proportion of parliamentary members by party affiliation after the return to 1992 constitutional rule has undergone a tremendous metamorphosis, starting from the NDC getting 198 (95%) out of 200 seats in the third (2001–2004) and fourth (2005–2008) parliaments of the Fourth Republic. The number of parliament seats shot up to 230 in 2012, and the split between the NPP and the NDC (the ruling party) shifted from 94 to 128, respectively (with the remaining eight representing minority parties). Currently, the legislature of Ghana is unicameral in nature, with 275 members democratically elected as representatives of their constituencies, and a Speaker. Parliamentarians are elected for four-year terms. After the 2012 election, the ruling NDC had 147 seats (53.5%), with the NPP getting 123 (44.7%), and the People's National Convention getting one seat in addition to four independent Members of Parliament (MPs).

Parliament debates and passes bills, which receive presidential assent to become laws. The Speaker, who is in charge of all parliamentary proceedings, makes sure activities are done through the established procedure and protocol of the house. The Speaker, in addition, functions as a spokesperson for the House in matters involving other state institutions and the President. The Constitution specifically states the numerical capacity of the elected MPs as not less than 230. Besides making laws and supporting party allegiance, the MPs are the representatives of the various constituencies in parliament. Several committees are formed in parliament to enable members to scrutinize and deliberate in detail many various bills, policy matters, and public issues in the House. The main committees in parliament are three in number: "Standing Committees," "Select Committees," and "Ad Hoc Committees." Each committee has a special role assigned by its mandate. Select Committees have the responsibility of supervising specific ministries, departments, and agencies (Friedrich-Ebert-Stiftung 2011; Abdulai 2009).

5.4.3 Customary Law

The political, social, and economic terrain of Ghana is interspersed with customs and traditions. In Ghana, customary laws play a vital role in conflict resolutions as well as protecting human rights. The 1992 Constitution of Ghana sets prohibitions on any customary practice that abuses human rights in terms of causing body or mind injuries of any person, men and women alike. Such customary practices prohibited under the 1992 Constitution include the widowhood rite, subjecting women to pain and mental torture, female genital mutilation, the banishment of women from communities due to witchcraft and other forms of inhumane practices.

Again, the traditional chiefs (chieftaincy institutions) are charged with the powers to interpret customary laws, with backing from the African Peer Review Mechanism Report (2005: 18) recognizing a "strong consensus on the relevance of the chieftaincy institution and chiefs in state and society...." To acknowledge the importance of traditional institutions, the 1992 Constitution does not only support the chieftaincy institutions as well as the traditional councils that are established by customary laws and usage, but in addition ensures that the National and Regional House of Chiefs are established and charged with the interpretation and codification of all customary laws among others. Traditional authorities have the mandate to regulate matters in their own jurisdictions, including their influence over lands even though they are prevented from meddling in politics. In Ghana, many land holders, especially in the rural areas, own their land in the form of "customary tenure," and getting the opportunity to hold land is heavily managed in reality by chiefs and or family heads (Crook 2005: 2).

5.4.4 Local and Regional Government

Ghana's constitution endorses the decentralization of the executive powers to involve local participation at the regional and the district levels to deepen and consolidate democracy. By this, the central government transfers some of its powers to the regions and the districts in order to bring the administrative and financial machinery of government close to the people to ensure local participation in decision-making. According to Article 240(1) of the Constitution "Local Government and administration [should]...as far as practical be decentralized", and Article 240(2) specifies the functions, powers, responsibilities, and resources transferred from the central government to local government entities. The current local government system in Ghana depends on the decentralization program that started in 1988 during the regime of the Provisional National Defense Council. In achieving this objective, 10 Regional Coordinating Councils (RCCs), 110 District Assemblies, and other district administrative structures were created to undertake various functions at the regional district and subdistrict levels. It must be noted that the RCCs are not the regional government; however, they are responsible to the central government, which appoints its members (Friedrich-Ebert-Stiftung 2011; Abdulai 2009).

5.5 Political Risk

Political risk has been the subject of many scholars and has received many different interpretations. Even though risk assessment is part of any business venture, the issue of political risk analysis caught the attention of many scholars and firms only after the Second World War, and particularly after FDI started flowing from the US to Europe (Moffett et al. 2006). Political risk is an essential component of the business environment for numerous firms, particularly those in the field of global business operations, and the fact that contracts are almost not possible to effect at an international level (Thomas and Worrall 1994; Restrepo 2012).

The World Bank (2012) opined that political risk is "the probability of disruptions of the operations of companies by political forces and events, whether they occur in host countries or result from changes in the international environment." It is caused by uncertainties that can be blamed on the actions of both governments and political institutions on one side and the minority groups and separatist movements on the other (Marchetti and Vitale 2013).

Wagner (2000) believes that political risk can be explained in terms of its types in order to determine whether a particular government action poses a threat to an investment (at the firm-specific and country-specific levels). Firm-specific political risks are directed at a particular company and are discriminatory in nature. In contrast, country-specific political risks are directed at a country and result from a systemic problem. Examples include a government's decision to forbid currency transfers out of the country or the outbreak of a civil war within the host country.

Expropriation and nationalization of assets have been noted as posing the greatest threats to foreign firms in the country. The effects of politics on business operations have often been considered as a negative. Unexpected political activity by despotic governments or other political groups has been another means of political risk. In the 1990s and beyond, terrorism has been a source of worry to international investors with specific reference to the attacks to the World Trade Center in the New York City. This has been noted as a form of political risk (Berry and Dalton 2010).

Nationalization, restrictions on earning repatriation, unexpected changes in government policies, corruption, civil and social wars have been additional negative effects on international business in foreign countries (Mawanza 2015).

Korbin (1982) demonstrates the two categories of political risk as (1) country-specific (or macro) and (2) firm-specific (or micro). Expropriation (nationalization) is the most extreme form of political risk. On the contrary, other forms of political risks result from currency and trade controls, changes in tax or labor laws, regulatory restrictions, and requirements for additional local production.

Moffett et al. (2006) determined political risks in three ways – firm-specific risks, country-specific risks, and global-specific risks. Firm-specific risks affect the investment at the firm level but originate from goal conflict between the firm and its host government (e.g., breach of contract, sabotage, kidnappings, discriminatory regulations, "creeping" expropriation, firm-specific boycotts, etc.). Country-specific risks affect investments at the firm level but emanate from activities at the country level (e.g., transfer risk, war risk, nepotism, and corruption). Other risks include mass nationalizations, regulatory changes, currency inconvertibility, mass labor strikes, and urban rioting). Global-specific risks are those that affect the investment at the firm level but erupt from the activities at the global level (e.g., terrorism, antiglobalization, poverty).

5.5.1 Political Risks and Ghana

Ghana provides a relatively stable and predictable political climate for investors. There is a strong democratic tradition that is wrapping up its sixth peaceful democratic election in December 2012. The election in 2012 saw the losing party challenge the Presidential election results through a petition at the Supreme Court. The petition and the Supreme Court ruling in favor of the winning party gave Ghana a narrow escape from political instability in 2013, but it created a season of uncertainty for investors, causing them to be reserved with a "wait and see attitude" (US Dept of State 2015). Presently, the rivalry between the two dominant political parties (the ruling NDC and the opposition NPP) has deepened, polarizing the country politically along party lines and threatening the country's hybrid democracy. Surprisingly, the two major political parties have policy programs that are relatively similar – targeting Ghana's economic transformation and liberalization (David W. Throup 2011).

Ghana has for some time now witnessed an eruption of intense economic constraints, resulting from higher inflationary pressures due to a continuous rise in seemingly unsustainable public fiscal debt financing and large currency depreciation. Unemployment, energy challenges, poverty, and a high cost of living have minimized the purchasing power of most households, breeding much discontent toward the ruling government (AMB 2015; IMF Report 2015). GDP is at a slower growth rate due to lower oil prices, electricity crises, water shortages, and the effect of higher inflation on consumer and business confidence. GDP is predicted at 3.5% and 6.4% for 2015 and 2016, respectively, rating Ghana as a high risk country for business at CRT-5 (AMB Company Inc. 2015).

According to an IMF report (2015), the short and medium-term economic policies to improve the economy are faced with substantial risks. The IMF team believes that though Ghana has received a three-year financial assistance package from the IMF, if the current energy challenge is not dealt with and the energy sector restructuring is delayed, there is a probability of lower economic growth than the 2015 projections. Without prudent measures to address economic difficulties, the IMF team predicts social tensions before and during the 2016 election, making the government withdraw some policies.

According to the IMF report (2015), volatility in oil prices and changes in the global financial situation are likely to put the medium-term economic policies of Ghana at risk.

As a result of increasing public fiscal debt and slower future growth predictions, the country entered into a new three-year loan arrangement with the IMF, increasing the country's national debt at an "unsustainable pace" (IMF Report 2015). Increased terrorists operations from Islamic organizations such as Al-Qaeda and Boko Haram have reduced investor confidence, negatively impacting capital inflows or FDI inflows to sub-Saharan Africa, including Ghana. These situations have led to growing social dissatisfaction coupled with related recurrent labor and social unrests emanating from wage policies in the midst of abundant resources. In addition, widespread corruption among public officials has increased public distrust of government agencies (AMB Company Inc. 2015; US Dept. of State 2015; Friedrich E. Stiftung 2011).

Notwithstanding the aforementioned hostile political and business environment, Ghana is still considered stable as well as the best investment destination (Taylor 2012). Comparatively, Ghana is well rated among countries in sub-Saharan Africa, ranking 70th out of 189 countries in the World Bank's 2015 Ease of Doing Business survey (Bratton and Gyimah-Boadi 2015). The government of Ghana does not only make FDI a priority but also understands that heavy capital inflows requires an enabling regulatory environment, and allows a discussion of issues that impede FDI (AMB Company Inc. 2015).

The Constitution of Ghana states some exemptions and includes a clear procedure toward the payment of compensation in exceptional cases of expropriation or nationalization, meaning that investors are provided some security against expropriation and nationalization. The government of Ghana also supports due legal process so that investors are generally not subject to differential or discriminatory treatment in Ghana, and official government expropriations have been absent presently (US Dept. of State 2015).

Ghana is comparatively less corruption-prevalent than other subregional economies. However, a few investors have identified corruption as the main constraint to foreign direct capital inflows. Ghana tied with Croatia at 61 out of 175 in 2014 on the Transparency International Global Corruption Perceptions Index. This recorded a little improvement from 2013. A number of corruption allegations involving government officials were made in 2014. The government of Ghana has taken measures to amend, if not enact, laws on public financial administration and public procurement. The Public Procurement Law, passed in January 2004, aims at harmonizing the public procurement framework used in the country and to make procurement conform to WTO standards. The law seeks to improve accountability, value for money, transparency, and efficiency in the use of public resources (US Dept. of State 2015).

Political stability and peace puts the country at a better position against any threat of political ramblings than any other country in the subregion such as Cape Verde, Benin, etc. Therefore, the free and fair elections of 2016 coupled with the smooth and peaceful transfer of political power is probably a sign of hope for consolidating democracy. Based on the smooth and transparent 2015 elections and transition of power in Nigeria, there is likely lower political risk to democracy in Ghana should the country glide over the 2016 election hurdles peacefully (Braton and Gyimah-Boadi 2015).

5.6 Judiciary and the Judicial System

The Judiciary is another arm of government whose primary function is to interpret the law. The 1992 Constitution provides judicial independence and makes the judiciary impartial and subject only to the Constitution. Article 127(2) clearly demonstrates that "neither the President nor Parliament nor any person whatsoever shall interfere with judges… or other persons exercising judicial power… " The Chief Justice is the head of the judiciary. He or she and other judges of the superior courts are appointed by the President upon parliamentary approval and in consultation with the council of state or judicial council. The Chief Justice performs administrative and supervisory role over all judicial matters. The judicial council is responsible for administering justice as provided in the Constitution. According to the Constitution, the council helps in "proposing for the consideration of Government judicial reforms to improve the level of administration of justice and efficiency in the Judiciary."

Ghana's judicial system is made up of the superior courts and lower courts, with a hierarchical arrangement of the court system starting from the high-ranking courts such as the Supreme Court, through the Court of Appeal, the High Court, and the Regional Tribunals. Next are lower courts such as the Circuit Courts and Tribunals, the District Courts, as well as additional lower courts established by parliament (OSIWA and IDEG 2007: 34; Transparency International 2007; Abdulai 2009; Friedrich-Ebert-Stiftung 2011).

5.6.1 *Judiciary and the Legal System*

Ghana's legal system mirrors British common law and customary law. Investors should understand that statutory and customary laws control the acquisition of real property in Ghana. The judiciary of Ghana is another arm of government responsible for interpreting the law. This regulatory body consists of the superior and the lower courts. The superior courts include, in a descending order of supremacy, the Supreme Court, the Court of Appeal, the High Courts, and the Regional Tribunals. Lawsuits usually begin in the High Court. The High Court has jurisdiction over all cases – civil and criminal and others except matters of treason. The lower courts comprise the circuit courts and tribunals, the district courts and other lower courts that parliament probably establishes (Abdulai 2009; US Dept. of State 2015; Friedrich E. Stiftung 2011).

The independence of the judiciary is clearly spelt out in the 1992 Constitution. Article 127(2) states: "neither the President nor Parliament nor any person whatsoever shall interfere with judges . . . or other persons exercising judicial power. . . . " However, government interference with the activities of the judiciary in addition to widespread corruption in the judicial system undermines judicial independence (CDD-Ghana 2003; APRM 2005; Abdulai 2009; Friedrich E. Stiftung 2011).

5.6.2 *Dispute Settlement*

There are situations where the courts have issued a judgment with which the government is not in favor. With commercial cases, there is much interest in alternative disputes settlement. Most lawyers render services relating to arbitration and/or conciliation. Arbitration decisions can be enforced on condition that they are registered in the courts. Fast-track courts have been established to quickly abdicate certain cases. The fast-track courts are High Court branches charged with the responsibility of resolving disputes meant to be concluded within six months. Many times, however, the courts have not been swift in abdicating cases. This is because the courts are faced with resource constraints and institutional inefficiencies in enforcing decisions.

However, they have been unsuccessful in dispute resolutions consistently within six month (US Dept. of State 2015).

The government of Ghana established commercial courts in 2005 to exclusively sit over all commercial cases. The courts in addition settle cases in connection with commercial arbitration as well as awards enforcement, intellectual property rights such as patents, copyrights and trademarks, commercial fraud, applications under the companies code, tax issues, and insurance and reinsurance matters. The commercial court uses mediation or other alternative dispute settlement approaches, which are mandatory in the pretrial settlement conference stage. (US Dept. of State 2015).

There is also a Financial and Economic Crimes Court in Ghana, which is a specialized branch of the High Court with the jurisdiction of abdicating high profile corruption and economic crime cases (US Dept. of State 2015).

Enforcing foreign judgments in Ghana depends on the doctrine of reciprocity. By virtue of this, court decisions from Brazil, France, Israel, Italy, Japan, Lebanon, Senegal, Spain, the UAE, and the UK are considered enforceable. Judgments from American courts are currently not enforceable in Ghana (US Dept. of State 2015).

The GIPC, free zones, labor, and minerals and mining laws stipulate clearly dispute resolution procedures and make provisions for arbitration when cases cannot be resolved alternatively. They also make room for the referral of cases to arbitration in conformity with the rules of procedure of the United Nations Commission on International Trade Law, or within the framework of a bilateral agreement between Ghana and the investor's country. The 2010 Alternative Dispute Resolution Act (Act 798 of 2010) allows the settlement of cases, using mediation and customary arbitration as well as regular arbitration processes (US Dept. of State 2015).

5.6.3 *Traditional Laws*

Ghanaian political, economic, and social life is greatly interspersed with customs and traditional values. Therefore, customary laws still play a pivotal role in the settlement of disputes as well as redressing human rights violations relating to customary practices. The 1992 Constitution clearly prohibits any customary practice, which is an infringement of human rights. Any customary act that dehumanizes or is injurious to the body and mind of all persons, women and men alike, is prohibited. The 1992 Constitution frowns on 31 customary practices, including widowhood rite (subjecting women to pain and mental torture; female genital mutilation, the banning of women from communities for witchcraft, and all other forms of customary slavery or servitude). The institution of chieftaincy is the sole traditional administrative body responsible for interpreting the customary laws (Abdulai 2009).

5.7 Contracts and Agreements

Numerous scholars use the term "contract and agreement" interchangeably; however, they are semantically different. According to Duhaime's Law Dictionary, a contract refers to "an agreement between persons which obliges each party to do or not to do a certain thing." It is also considered as an agreement which is legally binding on two or more parties involved, creating room for obligations that are probably enforceable in the courts of law. The core element of a contract is agreement. Duhaime defines "contract" as a specific form of agreement that satisfies certain requirements crafted to ensure constitutionally binding obligations between parties and that are enforceable by a recognized court of law (Pester 2003). Black's Law Dictionary sees the term "contract" as: "An agreement between... parties creating obligations that are enforceable." A contract requires a more critical and stricter, as well as precise, agreement.

On the contrary, an "agreement" refers to any understanding or arrangement made between parties toward effecting a specific engagement (Duhaime's Law Dictionary). Black's Law Dictionary also defines an agreement as a mutual understanding between parties about their relative rights and responsibilities. In reaching an agreement, the parties involved require just a simple understanding of their rights and responsibilities (Pester 2003). This is referred to as a "meeting of the minds."

5.7.1 Contract Requirements

The essential elements required for the formation of a contract include the following:

a. Offer and acceptance;
b. Every contract must contain a definite offer and the acceptance of the definite offer. Mutual consent;
c. The offer and acceptance must be willingly consented to by the parties involved and devoid of compulsion.

A party's genuine consent is an important requirement for a legally binding contract. The same terms and conditions intended for the contract must be set and agreed upon by all the parties involved.

5.7.2 *Consideration*

This involves an exchange of a phenomenon or something of high value between the players or parties involved. Consideration may be in the form of cash or money, or the provision of goods or services. However, the parties involved should give something of value for the formation of the contract. A contract is considered a gift should a single part provides something for the contract.

5.7.3 *Competence*

It is expected of both parties involved to fully understand every situation and other details of the contract. The parties should be of "sound mind" to comprehend the implications of the situation and all other requirements. This requires that neither of the parties be a minor nor mentally handicapped, but should be sober.

5.7.4 *Legal Purpose*

The purpose of the contract should be within the parameters of lawful conduct. Put differently, a court would never enforce a contract relating to a phenomenon that has illegality. A contract may be regarded as illegal if its subject matter is prohibited by a statutory act or if it is an infringement on a public policy rule. A contract that has illegal conduct, promises, or objects infringes upon this condition.

In the Constitution of Ghana, Section 11 of the Contracts Act, 1960 (Act 25) says that a contract does not need to be in writing in all case before it can be considered enforceable by the court of law.

The court has the ability to enforce an oral agreement between parties just like any written agreement.

5.8 Entrepreneurship

The term "Entrepreneurship" has several scholarly definitions. One definition refers to the term as the establishment of any fresh business entity for income generation. Others opine that entrepreneurship involves the creation of wealth for oneself through the process of starting a business venture, making the required resources mobilization and considering the risks and rewards involved.

Entrepreneurship involves the process of risking available resources (time, money, and materials) to pursue opportunities and create value and growth through innovation irrespective of available resources controlled by an individual or group. The three key factors in this definition include: (1) the pursuit of opportunities, (2) innovation, and (3) growth. Business entrepreneurs pursue opportunities and ensure the growth of a business by effecting transformation through innovative means as well as the introduction of new goods or services. Entrepreneurs are seen as being bold, innovative, initiative-taking, venture-some, and risk-taking, with their prime objective maximizing growth and profit (Robins and De Cenzo 2007). According to the European Commission's Green Paper (Brussels 21.1.2003), "Entrepreneurship is the mindset and process to create and develop economic activity by blending risk-taking, creativity and/or innovation with sound management, within a new or an existing organization."

5.8.1 Entrepreneurial Process

There are four major processes of entrepreneurial activities. Entrepreneurs must consider these main factors before staring and managing their businesses. The primary step is to explore the entrepreneurial context. Exploring the entrepreneurial context involves the analysis of the realities of the new economy, society's laws and regulations that constitute the legal environment, as well as the dynamisms in the world of work. It is advisable to consider each of these items of the entrepreneurial context since they form the key determinant "rules" of the game and inform the decisions and actions likely to ensure success. The identification of opportunities and possible competitive advantages in a venture are equally important in the entrepreneurial process. After exploring the entrepreneurial context, identifying opportunities and other possible competitive advantages, entrepreneurs should factor in the issues of starting and sustaining the ventures. As part of starting up a business includes feasibility research on the business venture, planning, organizing, and launching the business. The final process is managing the business. Here, the entrepreneur manages the process, people, and growth of the venture (Stephen and De Cenzo 2007; Boateng et al. 2014).

5.8.2 *Benefits and Obstacles to Entrepreneurship*

Much as there are numerous benefits to entrepreneurship, hurdles to the phenomenon cannot be overemphasized. The following are the discussions on both benefits and obstacles to entrepreneurship:

- Benefits of entrepreneurship;
- Job creation.

It is worth noting that entrepreneurship:

a. provides opportunities for job creation, and
b. ensures the reduction of unemployment, poverty, and crime in a country.

> This brings improvement in the economic conditions of a country and ensures political stability. Based on a Global Entrepreneurship Mentor survey conducted in 29 countries in 2001, almost 150 million people engage in some form of entrepreneurial activity (Bridges.org 2002). This suggests that more people are employed through entrepreneurship as a method of economic development among Ghanaian citizens. The driving force of global economic development, then, depends essentially on the increase in small-scale businesses. (Forbes Insights 2015)

In Ghana entrepreneurial activity provides numerous benefits for the country, both at a micro level by creating stable and sustainable employment for individuals and at a macro level by significantly increasing the GDP (Prince E.W. Attipoe 2013).

5.8.3 *Wealth Creation*

Entrepreneurship creates an opportunity for poverty reduction and ensures wealth creation for both individuals and the economy of a country. Ghana has the ability to minimize poverty, reduce joblessness and underdevelopment, and ensure growth through entrepreneurship. To sum up, the significance of entrepreneurship includes the creation of opportunities for the reduction of unemployment, the sustainable production of much local goods and services, the creation of healthy competition in the market to ensure good consumer choices, the promotion of innovation and resilience through experience-based learning, the promotion of a strong social and cultural identity, and the reduction of crime rate due to unemployment (Gilbert O. Boateng and Commission of European Communities Brussel 2003: 21.1).

5.8.4 *Obstacles to Entrepreneurship*

Despite the many benefits of entrepreneurship, some obstacles exist.

Infrastructure
As discussed earlier, infrastructural deficiencies with respect to roads and electricity is a barrier to entrepreneurs. In Ghana, electricity and transport pose a major threat to businesses. Most businesses complain of the current energy problem, which has resulted in frequent irregularity in electricity supply over the past four years. To keep businesses running, generators have to be used, with their associated high cost of fueling. These high costs discourage business sustenance and growth. In Ghana, most of the private businesses have collapsed as a result of power rationing and to a larger extent lack of electricity supply (Laary 2015). Additionally, in Ghana, there is a problem with the transportation of merchandise. The distance to cover before transporting products from the production site to the market is relatively long. The roads are also bad, leading to unnecessary delays. This not only increases the cost of transportation but also, in the case of produce, causes spoilage (Prince E.W. Attipoe 2013).

Transparency, Regulation, and Standards
The absence of transparency is another blockage to innovation and entrepreneurship in Ghana (Agyeman-Duah 2008; Johnson and Lund vall 2003). This arises from land ownership in Ghana. According to a World

Bank Survey (2010), the economy of Ghana faced massive threats to development and growth due to difficulties in getting access to land, a lack of security of land tenure, and improper management of the country's land resources. Traditionally, chiefs in Ghana possess the ownership rights of public lands and therefore play a pivotal role in managing them (Berry 2009). "Legal and judicial recognition of customary claims to land and community membership tend to reproduce layered claims to land and recurring disputes over custom and historical precedent" (Berry 2009: 1351). Most landowners often require advance rent payment of two years or more, which could be a difficult expense for young entrepreneurs to pay. Another land problem is that a landed property may be sold to more than one individual simultaneously. The government of Ghana therefore needs to improve how to accommodate domestic businesses in its formal sector (Imani News 2015). In 2015, Ghana dropped one place, to 70th, in the World Bank's Ease of Doing Business rankings (US Dept. of State 2015).

Access to Finance and the Banks

The greatest difficulty confronting numerous potential entrepreneurs worldwide, including Ghana, is lack of smooth access to financial support and banks. Apart from their inability to mobilize funds from family and friends, entrepreneurs' access to credit from banks to startup businesses is always an obstacle. In most cases, it is not that the banks are reluctant to issue loans, but the risks involved are very high. Most banks in Ghana require collateral security, which may be difficult, if not possible to provide by entrepreneurs. Also, a greater percentage of the government and commercial banks which could provide financial support to the entrepreneurs are only centered in the cities and big towns, places which are far removed from most of the village entrepreneurs. On the other hand, interest rates could be extremely high due to high borrowings by the central government and therefore young entrepreneurs do not have the urge to access the loan facilities from the banks (Prince E.W. Attipoe 2013).

Corruption

Even when parameters for standards have been set properly, the enforcement of regulations in Ghana is often a challenge. Corruption is one of the reasons impeding the funding of private enterprises. There is a belief that credit decisions are politicized, leaving room for government officials to offer cheap loans to party supporters. In Ghana, well-shielded cronies have greater access to public resources than talented and risk-taking entrepreneurs. According to a US Department of States investment climate report (2015), "Corruption in Ghana is comparatively less prevalent than in other countries in the region, but remains a problem. A few American firms have identified corruption as the main obstacle to foreign direct investment. Ghana's 2014 score and ranking on the Transparency International Global Corruption Perceptions Index improved slightly from 2013, tying with Croatia for 61st place out of 175. In 2014, there were a number of corruption allegations involving government officials" (US Dept. of State 2015 Investment Climate Statement, Ghana).

Human Capital, Education

Another challenge to entrepreneurship has to do with human development and education. Ensuring sustainable economic growth through poverty reduction depends on education as the bedrock. Unfortunately, it is estimated that 48% of women, versus 37% of men, are illiterate. With this high rate of illiteracy, it becomes very difficult for them to come up with innovative and creative ideas in order to establish and expand their entrepreneurial activities (World Bank, 2010).

Unnecessary Competition

Entrepreneurs are faced with the challenge of coming up with an innovative ways of overcoming the difficulties involved in creating a competitive advantage for themselves with their goods or services as they compete with both foreign and local firms for the larger market. Entrepreneurs thus need to get easy access to available information and knowledge, relevant contacts, and training and highly recognized entrepreneurial support services. As a result, the Ghana Export Promotion Council, Office of the PSD, National Board for Small Scale Industries (NBSSI), Business Advisory Centres, Ministry of Trade and Industry, and other relevant bodies become indispensable. Ironically, getting connected with these bodies for assistance is very cumbersome (Prince E.W. Attipoe 2013).

Fear of Uncertainty

It is worth noting that to set up a business entity requires a certain drive, innovation, creativity, and persistence, but sustaining the business depends on good managerial skills, efficiency, and reliability. There is the fear of the unknown future on the part of the entrepreneurs as to whether their businesses will be able to survive the environmental challenges at the initial stages and succeed. This fear should be overcome even before the business commences. The skills needed to help make entrepreneurs confident enough for the running of their businesses should be made available and taught in the educational institutions in order to ensure a good and well-equipped labor force (Prince E.W. Attipoe 2013).

Tax System
When entrepreneurs are hit with higher taxes, businesses are likely to suffer. Several Ghanaian budgets have made giant attempts to provide some tax incentives to attract entrepreneurs to the Northern Regions of Ghana, but the expected results have not yet been realized. The nature of the Ghanaian tax system, such as income and corporate tax, labor tax and VAT, have an impact on the ability of firms to grow. The difficulties of different tax systems create an administrative challenge for entrepreneurs. A marginal increase in income tax rates results in entrepreneurs ensuring slower business expansion, investing less and hiring fewer staff. The labor tax impacts firms' decisions on staff recruitment (Prince E.W. Attipoe 2013).

5.8.5 *Youth Entrepreneurship Support*

Entrepreneurship has been recognized as a great policy framework to ensure strong economic development (www.ndpc.gov.gh). Even though there exists in Ghana a kind of support structure to improve Ghana's entrepreneurship, it is better to evaluate the degree to which their effort contributes to entrepreneurial sustainability, which could create more employment for the growing population.

This is demonstrated by the creation of numerous support institutions such as rural enterprise programs established by the government to provide financial assistance and ensure improvement in operational efficiency in the micro and small enterprises sector (www.home.moti.gov.gh. The following are the current agencies responsible for ensuring efficiency and promotion in youth entrepreneurship in Ghana: the Ministry of Trade and Industry, the Ministry of Youth and Sports, the National Youth Authority, the Ghana Youth Employment and Entrepreneurial Development Agency, the NBSSI, vocational and technical training centers, and microfinance schemes such as the Micro and Small Loans Centre. These agencies have reported some recent developments in funding, training, and mentorship programs targeting youth in enterprises or those interested in starting their own enterprises. There are also other structures at regional, metropolitan, and Municipal and District Assembly levels (Prince E.W. Attipoe 2013).

5.9 Conclusion

It can be observed from the above discussion that Ghana's political climate is comparatively conducive to business, making the country a good destination for investment and entrepreneurial activities. The country has good political relationships with other neighboring economies in the African subregion. Ghana is noted for its effort and contribution to ensuring peace and security in Africa and the world as a whole through its membership with the AU and other trade blocs. Since Ghana is not in isolation, it is not excluded from the impact of global social, political, cultural, technological, and economic activities. Ghana has well-established political structures and clearly defined legal systems that regulate all political and business activities. This notwithstanding, the country seems to have high political risks and high returns for doing business. There is much assurance, and entrepreneurs should not be afraid doing businesses in Ghana since they will get the government support and returns from their investment if they work hard and manage their businesses successfully.

References

Abdulai, Abdul-Gafaru. 2009. "Political Context: Study-Ghana." pp. 1–42.

African Peer Review Mechanism (APRM). 2005. "Country Review Report of the Republic of Ghana." June 2005.

Agyeman-Duah, I. 2008. *An Economic History of Ghana: Reflections on a Half-Century of Challenges and Progress.* Banbury: Ayebia Clarke Publishing Limited.

A.M. Best Company, Inc. 2015. AMB Country Risk Report on Ghana.

Berry, S. 2009. "Building for the Future? Investment, Land Reform and the Contingencies of Ownership in Contemporary Ghana." *World Development* 37(8): 1370–1378.

Berry, Charles and Tony Dalton. 2010. "Trading on Housing Wealth: Political Risk in and Ageing Society." *The Blackwell Companion to Economic Housing: The Housing Wealth of Nations.* Published online, http://onlinelibrary.wiley.com/doi/10.1002/9781444317978.ch10/pdf.

Boateng, G. O. et al. 2014. "Barriers to Youthful Entrepreneurship in Rural Areas of Ghana." *Global Journal of Business Research* 8(3): 108–119.
Bratton, Michael and E. Gyimah Boadi. 2015. Political Risks Facing African Democracies: Evidence from Afrobarometer. Working paper No.157.
Bridges.org's publication titled "Entrepreneurship in Developing Countries" – Survey of the Field and Inventory of Initiatives (2002).
Centre for Democratic Development [CDD-Ghana]. 2003. "The Growth of Democracy in Ghana despite Economic Dissatisfaction: A Power Alternation Bonus?" Research Paper II, CDD-Ghana, Accra.
Commission of European Communities (Brussels 21.1.2003), Green Paper Entrepreneurship in Europe, 27 Final.
Crook, R. 2005. "The Role of Traditional Institutions in Political Change and Development." CDD/ODI, Policy Bried, No. 4, November.
Dasmani, Laary. 2015. "Electricity: Ghana's Power Crisis." African Report, February 4, 2015.
Dreyhaupt, Ivan Nimac and Kusi Hornberger, The World bank. 2012. Investment Climate In Practice-Political Risk: The Missing Link in Understanding Investment Climate Reform? Investment Policy, No. 20, https://openknowledge.wroldbank.org/bitstream/handle/10986/10416/682950NEWSoinv00Box367908B00PUBLICO.pdf?sequence=1
Document of the World Bank. 2009 (Report No. 47321)-GH Economy-Wide Impact of Oil Discovery in Ghana.
Financial Action Task Force (FAFT). 2015. Ghana: Risk & Compliance Report.
Forbes Insight. 2015. Job Creation in Sub-Saharan Africa, Enterprises, Governments and Innovations, in Conjunction with DJEMBE, Communications.
Friedrich-Ebert-Stiftung. 2009. Ghana in Search of Regional Integration Agenda.
Friedrich-Ebert-Stiftung. 2011. Structure of the Ghanaian State. www.fesghana.org.
Globaledge. 2015. Ghana: Introduction. www.globaledge.com.
Imani New Room. 2015. "Is Ghana Ready for Business?" July 10, 2015. IMANI News Room – IMANI Center for Policy & Education. http://imanighana.com.
IMF. 2015. Ghana Request for a Three-Year Arrangement under the Extended Credit Facility.
Johnson, B., Lundvall, B.-A. 2003. "National Systems of Innovation and Economic Development." In Putting Africa First: The Making of African Innovation Systems, edited by. M. Muchie, P.Gammeltoft, B.-A.Lundvall, 13–28 Denmark:Aalborg University Press.
Korbin, S. 1982. *Managing Political Risk Assessment: Strategic Responses to Environmental Changes.* Berkeley, CA: University of California Press.
Marchetti, R., and ENI, M. V. 2013. The Transnational Dimension in Political Risk Analysis.

Mawanza, Wilford. 2015 "An Assessment of the Political Risk Management Strategies by Multinational Corporations (MNCs) Operating in Zimbabwe International." *Journal of Business and Social Science* 6(3):.116–127.

Mehlum, Halvor, Karl Moene, and Ragnar Torvik. 2005.Cursed by Resources or Institutions, pp. 1–23. http://www.sv.ntnu.no/iso/Ragnar.Torvik/worldeconomy7.pdf.

Moffett, Michael, et al. 2006. *Political Risk Assessment and Management, Fundamentals of Multinational Finance.* 2nd edition www.aw-bc.com/scp/0321280318/assets/downloads/ch17.pdf.

Ninsin, K.A. 2008. *Executive-Parliament Interface in the Legislative Process (1993–2008): A Synergy of Powers?* Accra, Ghana: WOELI Publishing Services.

OSIWA [Open Society Initiative for West Africa] and IDEG [Institute for Democratic Governance]. 2007. Ghana: Justice Sector and the Rule of Law.

Pester, David. 2003. *Finding Legal Information: A Guide to Print and Electronic Sources.* Oxford, England, New Hampshire, U.S.A.: Chandos Publishing.

Prince E.W. Attipoe. 2013. "Challenges of the Entrepreneur." *Business & Financial Times.* May 31. https://www.newsghana.com.gh/challenges-of-the-entrepreneur/newGhana.

Report No. 47321-GH Economy-Wide Impact of Oil Discovery in Ghana November 30, 2009 Document of the World Bank.

Restrepo, Diana et al. 2012. "Political Risk and Corporate Investment Decisions." Working Paper # 4, Universidad Carlos III De Madrid, pp. 1–22.

Robins, Stephen P, and David A. DeCenzo. 2007. *Fundamentals of Management.* 5th edition. Pearson Education, pp.56–57.

Sundaram, Jomo Kwame, Oliver Schwank, and Rudiger von Arnmin. 2011. "Globalization and Development in Sub-Saharan Africa, Economics and Social Affairs, DESA." Working Paper, No. 102.

Taylor, Scott. 2012. *Globalization and the Cultures of Business: From Patrimonialism to Profit.* U.S.A: Indiana University Press.

Thomas, Jonathan and Tim Worrall. 1994. "Foreign Direct Investment and the Risk of Expropriation." *The Review of Economic Studies* 61(1): 81–108.

Throup, David, W., Jennifer G. Cooke and Richard Downie. 2011. "Ghana: Assessing Risk to Stability." Center for Strategic & International Studies. ISBN # 978-0-89206-644-5(pb).

Transparency International. 2007. https://www.infoplease.com/world/political-statistics/2007-transparencyinternational-corruption-perception-index.

U.S. Department of State Investment Climate Statement. June 2015.

Wagner, D. 2000. Defining "Political Risk." https://www.irmi.com/articles/expert-commentary/defining-political-risk.

World Bank. 2010. The World Bank Annual Report, http://siteresources.worldbank.org/EXTANNREP2010/Resources/WorldBank-AnnualReport2010.pdf.

World Bank Group, Enterprise Survey. 2010. www.enterprisesurveys.org.
http://www.irmi.com/expert/articles/2000/wagner10.aspx.
http://www.diffen.com/difference/Agreement_vs_Contract.
http://biztaxlaw.about.com/od/contractsandagreements/a/Principles-Of-Contracts-And-Agreements.htm.
http://biztaxlaw.about.com/od/contractsandagreements/a/Principles-Of-Contracts-And-Agreements.htm.
www.state.gov/e/eb/tra/ata/.

CHAPTER 6

The Economic Climate of Ghana

6.1 Introduction

The term "climate" generally refers to the atmospheric condition of a place over a long period of time. By extension, "economic climate" touches on the prevailing conditions of the economy and its predictable patterns of growth, decline, resuscitation, and movement. The term is normally employed to explain how a country's economic climate varies widely. This chapter throws more light on the economic climate of Ghana with special reference to certain economic variables such as the monetary, economic, and commercial systems. Specific subtopics under each of these variables will be discussed for better clarity and understanding.

6.2 Introduction to Ghana's Economic Climate

As a developing country with a low middle-income status, Ghana has experienced a slow structural transformation over the years. The country's informal sector is a major part of the economy with varied degrees of small- and medium-scale businesses highly clustered in the big cities and towns. The informal sector absorbs approximately 90% of the private business entities.

The economy of Ghana is strongly endowed with resources such as cocoa, gold, and oil, whose combined exports amount to 75% of Ghana's

J.E. Spillan, D.O. King, *Doing Business In Ghana*,
DOI 10.1007/978-3-319-54771-8_6

total exports. The country has the capacity to be a part of the regional value chain through export in ECOWAS communities. Since Ghana is well positioned in terms of geographical proximity to ECOWAS markets, the rise in consumption as well as minimal standard requirements create windows of opportunities for Ghanaian business entities to increase production levels (Okudzeto et al. 2014).

As a member of the league of oil producing countries, Ghana is expected to witness some economic relief from the benefits of oil reserves and production since 2012. Oil production was considered to become the new driving force of the economy; however, the impact of oil proceeds still has been less than expected.

According to the BoG 2015 monetary report, domestic prices of petroleum products have not responded to the downward international price trends of crude oil as expected, particularly due to an introduction of a 17.5% Special Petroleum Tax in November 2014. Consequently, Ghana has seen the price of petrol at the pump increase marginally by 0.9% during the last quarter at the end of December 2014. For the entire year, fuel prices increased by 54.3%. However, in January 2015, the domestic price of petroleum products was lowered by 10%, partially reflecting developments in international markets. Due to the sharp fall in international crude oil prices and challenges in the energy sector, the PURC maintained tariffs on electricity and water during the last quarter of 2014 and first quarter of 2015 (BoG 2015, vol. 4 No. 1/201).

The recent decline in the world market prices of these export commodities compared to 2013 price levels is linked with the occurrence of a trade imbalance for 2015. The government is likely to find it very difficult addressing an increasing current fiscal deficit as well as balance of payment constraints in the rest of 2015. The fall in export commodities from US $5.89 billion in November 2014 to 5.46 billion in December 2014 is the result of the heavy depletion of the country's foreign exchange reserves (Acheampong and Barker-Okwan 2015a).

Ghana's huge deficits emanating from the fiscal and current account witnessed over the years have been blamed on the massive public sector wage bill, energy subsidies, low domestic tax revenues, and low commodity prices. Total public debt as on December 2014 stood at GH¢ 76.1 billion (67.1% of GDP), up from 55.3% of GDP in 2013. This consists of GH¢34.6 billion (30.5% of GDP) domestic debt and US $13 billion (36.6% of GDP) of foreign debt (Acheampong and Barker-Okwan 2015a).

The economic climate of Ghana can be determined by its diverse economic activities. The economic operations that support and sustain the Ghanaian economy can be categorized under three sector variables – agriculture, industry, and service. These sectors do not only form the economic structure of Ghana but are also seen as the driving force that gives support, sustainability, and growth to the economy. Available records indicate that the service sector largely provides massive support and share of 54.1% of the growth of the economy, followed by industry with 26.9% and then agriculture with 19.0 in 2015. The agricultural sector absorbs a little over 56% of the Ghanaian labor force, yet its contribution to economic growth is minimal. The current economic structure of Ghana can be statistically presented below in Fig. 6.1.

Figure 6.2 shows real GDP growth in Ghana from 2007 to the first quarter of 2016. Available data show that the economy grew at 4.3% in 2007, followed by an increase in 2008 to 9.1%. The country in 2009 witnessed a sharp decline in terms of growth with 4.8% from 9.1% in 2008. The growth rate then rose to 7.9% in 2010 and continued to record an astronomical increase to 14.0% in 2011. This was as a result of the benefits obtained from oil exploration to boost the economy. Since 2012 to the first quarter of 2016, economic growth has

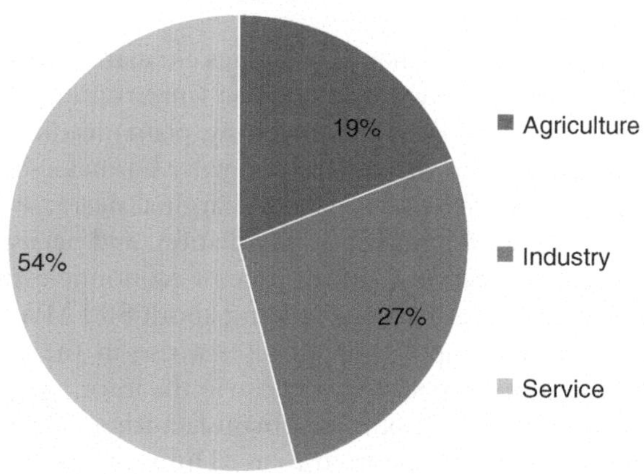

Fig. 6.1 Ghana's economic structure 2015

Source: 2016 budget statement and economic policy of Ghana

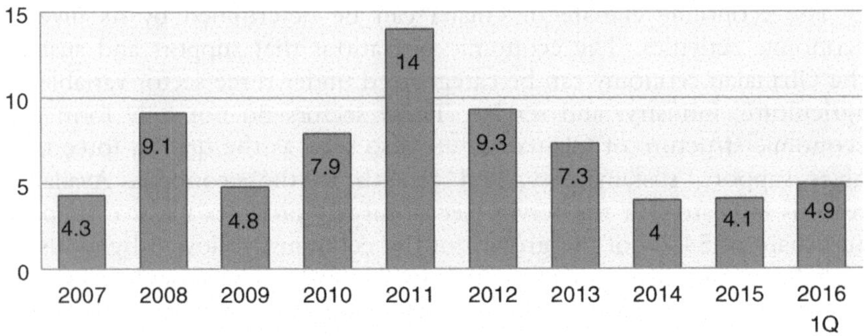

Fig. 6.2 The trend of Ghana's GDP growth 2007–2016 1Q in %

Source: The 2015 and 2016 budget statement and economic policy of Ghana

experienced a persistent decline from 9.3% in 2012, 7.3% in 2013, 4.0% in 2014, 3.9 % in 2015, and 4.9% in the first quarter of 2016. The persistent marginal decrease of the GDP between 2012 and 2016 can be blamed on the aftermath of 2012 elections, a protracted energy crisis, increased inflation, persistent increase in public debt, and financial constraints that Ghana is presently grappling with (Acheampong and Barker-Okwan 2015a).

Ghana has been faced with many challenges emanating from the energy sector in the form of load shedding exercise (interrupting the electricity supply to avoid excessive load at a generating plant) leading not only to low productivity but also to the collapse of many businesses in the private sector in 2014. The energy crisis and the marginal decrease in key commodities prices in the world market, high inflation, and persistent increase in public debt have resulted in a slower pace of economic expansion since 2012 and 2014. Ghana is currently shedding about 500 MW of electricity daily due to insufficient supply. This causes a rise in the cost of doing business in the economy, especially for those in the informal sector and for industries such as mining, telecoms, and manufacturing. The current load-shedding program, popularly referred to as "Dumsor," continues to have heavy impact on industry profitability, liquidity, efficiency, productivity, cost, and quarterly profit forecasts. (Acheampong and Barker-Okwan 2015a).

According to Acheampong and Barker-Okwan (2015a), "The Association of Ghana Industries (AGI), the umbrella body of industries, remarked in its Q1 2015 Business Barometer Report that several other companies and industries in the country may be forced to lay off thousands of workers if the current energy crisis continues. The Ghana Employers Association reported that as of the end of April 2015, about 13,000 workers have been laid off by several businesses due to the ongoing power crisis and the resultant increase in the cost of production."

Other foreseeable effects of the power challenges include high unemployment and rising social costs such as an increased crime rate, and the general despair of Ghanaian people, resulting in anti-government unrests. From an international perspective, this could lead to the loss of investor confidence in the Ghanaian business climate. The business environment can be considered as noncompetitive within the subregion and reduce the country's investment destination attractiveness (Acheampong and Barker-Okwan 2015a).

Recently, the present NDC government has been severely criticized by the opposition NPP, labor unions, and civil society groups bringing to the public domain their frustration and general hopelessness over the economic hardships (Acheampong and Barker-Okwan 2015a).

These challenges have informed the policy stance for 2015 to turn around macroeconomic imbalances and restore confidence in investors as macroeconomic stability is gradually regained. The policy stance is expected to be controlled by complete implementation of all the fiscal consolidation measures slated in the 2015 budget, maintaining a tight monetary policy stance as well as keeping the foreign exchange market stable (Okudzeto et al. 2014).

Again, the exchange rate of Ghana has been under continuous pressure from 1Q 2014 through 3Q 2014, until the Eurobond and the syndicated Cocobod loan brought some relief to the cedi and offered support to the foreign exchange market (GoG 2015 vol. 4 No. 1/2015) in the midst of declining international reserves. The cedi continued to depreciate, registering a further decline due to continuing weak economic fundamentals. The government has the hope that IMF credit facility will bring sanity in its fiscal policy consolidation by creating global credibility and confidence in its economic policies. The first tranche of the long-awaited credit facility aimed at improving BoG forex reserves is unlikely to do much to stabilize the cedi (Acheampong and Barker-Okwan 2015a).

Considering these developments, it becomes highly unlikely for the government to be able to demonstrate the required political will and fiscal discipline to fulfill the IMF conditionalities looking at the impending 2016 elections. Historically, governments have run huge budget deficits in election years. A key challenge faced by government is how it proposes to reduce the wage bill from its current expenditure, which is one of IMF loan conditionalities (Acheampong and Barker-Okwan 2015a).

On the part of governance, Ghana has shown its commitment to good governance and stable democracy. The country ranked seventh as the best performing economy in terms of governance after Mauritius, Cape-Verde, Botswana, Seychelles, South Africa, and Namibia. Ghana has maintained or improved its rating on most governance indicators, including participation and human rights, public management, and human development. Significant measures have also been taken to improve transparency and accountability, including the submission to parliament of the Freedom of Information Bill, the commitment of government to extend the Extractive Industries Transparency Initiative to the oil and gas sector (ADB and ADF 2012–2016).

6.3 Ghana's Monetary System

A monetary system of a country can be considered as the institutional arrangements formulated to transform savings into investments. These institutional arrangements are conducted using legal rules regarding the framework of monetary instruments and regulation of banks as well as banking practices (Amidu 2006).

The monopoly of government over the supply of money is the reason for the growth of monetary systems. For a monetary system to be able to function accurately, it is necessary that the supply of money is controlled in a suitable way. Gordon and Wang (2004) suggest that the danger associated with the monetary system could be avoided by moving to a "metallic currency" and by eliminating "any government control of the quantity of money," which would encourage a "balanced actual budget."

Monetary policy involves the use of different measures with the aim of regulating the value, supply, and cost of money in concert with the expected level of economic activity. Common with any monetary policy is the objective of dealing with price stability, maintenance of balance of payments equilibrium, creation of employment, output growth, and sustainable development. In order to be effective and globally acceptable, monetary policies have to be dynamic (Quatey and Mensah 2014).

In Ghana, the BoG, which is also the central bank, is the legal financial institution responsible for managing the monetary system. Ghana's monetary policies have undergone transformations over the years from the use of direct instruments to the market-oriented approach, where the main policy objective is the money supply. For example, prior to the start of financial sector reforms in 1992, the BoG operated a system that meant to manage the amount of money in the economy by using direct controls and a fixed exchange rate system. Ghana, together with other countries, regulated the monetary targeting framework and opted for inflation targeting tool for conducting monetary policy (Quatey and Mensah 2014).

The BoG as the central bank is charged with the responsibility by the Bank of Ghana Act 2002 to regulate inflation targeting as indicated by BoG Act 617, Section 33(2) that: "The Bank, in counteracting unusual movements in the money and prices in the country, shall use any of the instruments of control conferred upon it under this Act or under any other enactment to maintain and promote a balanced growth of the national economy." It appears that the core object of monetary policy in Ghana has been to stabilize prices and later provide an enabling climate for both foreign and domestic investors (Quatey and Mensah 2014).

The available data from the BoG indicate that the policy of Ghana as of February 2015 recorded 21% compared to 22% of the month of May, 24% of July, 25% of September, 26% of November, and 26.1% in the month of December of the same year. The current policy rate (PR) as of the month of January, 2016 is 26%. This PR can be attributed to the slower pace of growth in the Net Domestic Assets of the banking system as well as the moderated increase in the Net Foreign Assets of the banking system (BoG 2016, vol. 4, no. 1/2016). The trend of Ghana's monetary PR can be statistically represented in Fig. 6.3 as follows.

6.3.1 Interest Rate Developments in Ghana

In response to rising inflation and heightening inflation expectations, the Monetary Policy Committee (MPC) of the BoG increased the monetary PR by 500 basis points (bps) to 26% in 2015, from 21% in 2014. In reaction, trends in interest rates at which banks and other financial institutions borrowed on the money market showed mixed

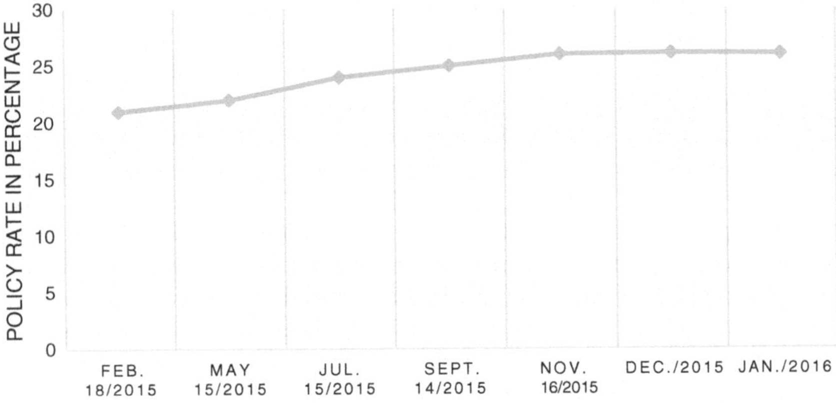

Fig. 6.3 The trend of Ghana's monetary PR February 2015–January 2016
Source: BoG's monetary policy and inflation report, Jan 2016 vol. 4 No. 1/2016

outcomes. The rates on Government Treasury Instruments such as the 91-day and 182-day bills decreased by 267 bps and 199 bps year-on-year to 23.12 and 24.40%, respectively, at the end of December 2015. However, the rates on the one-year note and two-year note increased by 25 bps and 30 bps year-on-year to 22.75 and 23.0%, respectively, while the rate on the three-year bond declined by 191 bps to 23.49% at the end of December 2015. Over the same period, the rate on the five-year bonds increased by 496 bps to 24.00%, while the rate on the seven-year bond remained unchanged at 18% (MoF 2016).

6.3.2 *Exchange Rate Developments in Ghana*

The foreign exchange market saw increased volatility in the first half of the year, resulting in a faster depreciation of the currency, 26.2% against the US dollar. The trend, however, moderated in the last quarter as foreign exchange inflows improved amid policy tightness. Foreign inflows from the Cocoa loan and Eurobond issue summing up to about US$2.8 billion provided a strong buffer to the foreign exchange market. Consequently, the cedi appreciated by 14.5% during the second half of 2015. Cumulatively, however, the cedi depreciated by 15.7% on a year-to date basis in 2015, a much slower pace than 31.3% depreciation in 2014 (Bank of Ghana Monetary Policy Report 2016, vol. 4, No. 1/2016).

6.3.3 *Inflation Targeting and Whipping Inflation in Ghana*

Amato and Gerlach (2002) define inflation targeting (IT) in terms of price stability and considered it as the most important goal of monetary policy. Taylor (2005) claims that achieving the IT is the primary goal of monetary policy. Hence, as a framework, IT in practice requires a quantitative statement as to what inflation rate is consistent with the pursuit of price stability in the long run. IT directly aims at inflation without using monetary aggregates as a route. The important instrument used in IT is the interest rate.

In Ghana, the Central Bank has used the PR, which denotes the base rate for lending to banks and thereby functions as the benchmark for other interest rates in the economy. Under the IT method, the Central Bank decides its forecast of inflation based on a larger set of indicators that determine the economic growth of a country, including real economic activity, business and end-user confidence, external factors, the fiscal stance, and even money supply.

The BoG employed a strict monetary policy to address the problems of rising inflation as well as cedi depreciation in Ghana in 2013. The PR was increased to 16% in an attempt to limit liquidity, as inflation outlook increased (Okudzeto et al. 2014).

In Ghana, recent available data from the Ministry of Finance (MoF 2016) showed that inflation pressures remained elevated over the first six months of 2016 due to the pass through effect of upward adjustments in prices of utilities and petroleum products and transport fares. Headline inflation rose from 17.7% in December 2015 to 19.2% in March 2016, before moderating to 18.7% in April 2016. Inflation rose slightly to 18.9% in May 2016 and reduced to 18.4% in June 2016. Over the review period, food inflation went up from 8.0% in December 2015 to 8.6% in June 2016, while nonfood inflation also increased from 23.3% in December 2015 to 24.1% in June 2016, as shown in Fig. 6.4.

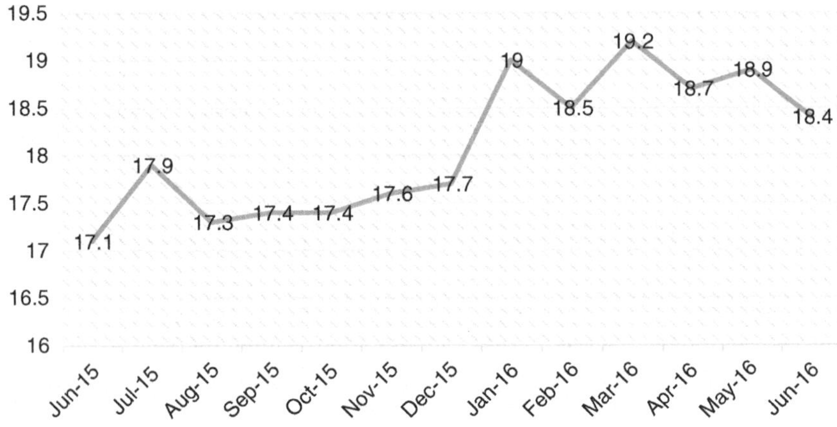

Fig. 6.4 Inflation trends, June 2015–June 2016

Source: Ministry of Finance 2016 review of the budget statement, economic policy, and supplementary estimates

6.3.4 *Financial Liberalization*

Financial liberalization may be considered as the provision of a greater role and freedom to markets. Ghana, as a low middle-income economy, has implemented a financial sector reform program since the 1980s, resulting from severe decline experienced by the banking system over the years. The financial sector reforms involved the liberalization of delegated controls on banks, restructuring of insolvent banks as well as reforms on prudent regulations and supervisions. The objective of the reforms was to promote quality competition that will create efficiency in the banking sector (Adams and Agbemade 2012).

Ahiawodzi (2007) examined the impact of the financial liberalization policy on financial savings in Ghana from 1988 to 2000. Using the elasticity's approach, he concluded that the financial liberalization policy modestly improved financial savings during the period. Specifically, financial savings went up by 14% to support private investment and other activities. These combine study report some significant association between financial liberalization, however, the varying degrees of influence are unequal.

An important feature of the financial liberalization process for developing economies is the influx of new banks, which are mostly foreign. In Ghana, for example, the Ghana Bank Survey (2008) shows that at the end of 2007 there were 12 Ghanaian and 12 non-Ghanaian banks (Adams and Agbemade 2012).

According to Adams and Agbemade (2012), for a country to enjoy the full benefits of competition, the government should deepen the liberalization process to enable more banks and nonbanks to be established in its economy. High competition leads to the marginal decline of returns, yet the industry remained attractive. The banking sector in Ghana is noted as one of the sectors with the brightest opportunities despite increasing competition. Net interest income has doubled between 2003 and 2007 and net profit also increased by 120% over the period. Despite keen competition, Barclay Bank of Ghana (BBG), Ghana Central Bank (GCB) and Standard Charter Bank (SCB) still reign as the dominant players in the market with respect to market share of deposit, assets, and profit.

6.3.5 FDI Flow Patterns

FDI is defined as long-term investment by foreign direct investors in an enterprise resident in an economy other than that in which the foreign direct investor is based. FDI should consist of a parent enterprise and at least on foreign affiliate which together form a Multinational Corporation (MNC). Developing countries like Ghana are confronted with the challenge of an annual resource gap, increase in government expenditure, high propensity to consume imported goods, and inadequate foreign exchange resources. So, the bulk of resources needed will have to come from abroad; from official sources (finance from multilateral organizations such as the World Bank), foreign indirect investment (which includes portfolio investments, bond finance, and bank lending), or FDI (IMF 2008).

In considering Ghana's data, it is obvious that most companies prefer to locate their businesses in either Accra or Tema for reasons that include the availability of social amenities such as good schools and hospitals, roads, and access to public services.

This observation dampens the impact of tax incentives as a major attraction for FDI in Ghana and elsewhere. In effect, the attraction of FDI has been a main feature of Ghana's Economic Recovery Program (ERP), which started in 1983 under the auspices of the World Bank and the IMF. Encouraging foreign investment in Ghana is therefore an integral part of Ghana's economic policy. This policy has also become a basis for Ghana's foreign policy direction. Ghana embarked on a privatization program, which has resulted in the sale of about two-thirds of approximately 300 state-owned enterprises. Foreign firms comprise most of the bidders for these businesses. Few local investors participate in this process except in partnership with foreign firms because of an inability to raise sufficient capital. From the foregoing discussion, it becomes clear that the relationship between FDI and economic growth has been and continues to be a subject of considerable academic and research interest. Much of the empirical research findings in this area have produced differing opinions and results. Some authors have found that increase in FDI to a country leads to increased economic growth, while others have found either the reverse or no relationship at all (IMF 2008).

In 2012, capital inflows marginally shot up over US$17 billion in key sub-Saharan African frontier markets and contributed 2.7% to the GDP of those markets. FDI inflows, though, have witnessed a fall since 2012 in Ghana, where statistics indicate that between 2012 and 2013 FDI decreased by 19.5% to $3.95bn. In early 2013, low bond yields, weak economic growth, as well as excess liquidity in advanced economies such as UK and US influenced capital inflows in Ghana. Again, pull factors such as robust macroeconomic management, low debt levels, and improved structural reforms by countries such as Nigeria and Ghana contributed to this effect. The Ghanaian government has plans to issue another $1bn dollar Eurobond in August 2015 to refinance its short to medium-term expenditure. In August 2013, Ghana sold a $1bn bond with a maturity of 10 years and a yield of 8%. The benefit was marginal compared to those attached to international debt issues of other sub-Saharan African economies, reflecting Ghana's deteriorating financial condition. A successful August issuance could ease pressure on the currency and provide government some room to invest in capital expenditure (Acheampong and Barker-Okwan 2015a).

6.4 Economic Systems in Ghana

The economic systems in Ghana touch on all aspects of business activities in the country. Further elaborations have been made below to demonstrate the type of economic systems commonly operational in Ghana.

6.4.1 *Typology of Economic Systems in the Region*

Economic systems exist in every country. This is because every economy is made up of a set of interrelated activities in which the production of goods and services is organized to satisfy the needs of people. Simply put, an economic system is seen as an organized way of providing for the needs/wants of people in a country. There are three main typologies of economic systems and every country in the world subscribes to one of these economic systems. They are the traditional economic system, the command economic system, and the market economic system. The traditional economic system considers the allocation of economic resources and activities which stem from habit, custom, or ritual. In this economic system, individuals cannot make their decisions as they want them; rather, their decisions are influenced by the customs and traditions of their elders and ancestors. Ghana used to embrace this economic system in colonial times. The command economic system is the one in which the central government makes most of the what, how, and from whom decisions for the people. The state makes the dominant decisions on economic issues; whilst the people have little, if any, influence over how basic economic questions are answered. The market economic system is the most common economic system of many countries. Here, instead of the government taking decisions on economic situations, the people themselves also have influential power in making economic decisions.

Currently, the economic system in Ghana is the mixed economic system. Unlike the case of Sweden, where its market economic system is dominated by the government which plays major economic roles, Ghana's mixed economic system is dominated by private individuals where economic decisions are taken in the market place but the government plays an important role in modifying the functioning market. In the Ghanaian setting, the roles of the government are to maintain full employment, ensure price stability, and promote economic growth and keep exports and imports in balance.

- Development of nations – The composition and distribution of national production and human development

The economic development of Ghana is mixed, consisting of a large traditional agriculture sector, including small-scale farmers, small capital-intensive mining concessions, a few manufacturing establishments, and growing informal small-scale businessmen, artisans, and technicians. The agricultural sector takes care of three-fifths of the country's labor force and accounts for 34% of the GDP (GSS 2013). The service sector, which is growing at a 10% rate (the fastest growing sector of the economy), also contributes one-third toward the country's GDP, while the industrial sector contributes a little over one-quarter (26%). However, this trend is changing as recent developments in the country show a declining trend in the agricultural sector, compensated by a booming service sector (GSS 2012)

- Demographic trends

According to National Population Council (NPC 2011), the population of Ghana compared to other developing countries has experienced marginal growth over the years, starting from 1960 with 6.7 million to 18.9 million in 2000. In 2010, the population recorded another rapid increase to 24.2 million, with an average growth rate of 2.4–2.7%. Based on the current growth rate of 2.4%, Ghana's population is expected to double in the next 29 years (NPC 2011).

The age structure of the population indicates that about 40% of the Ghanaian population is in the youthful bracket, under the age of 15. With its lower middle-income status, the country is witnessing demographic instability, especially with its decline in both fertility and mortality levels. However, with a youthful population there is an in-built momentum for further growth despite the decline in fertility. This is reflected in the preliminary results of the 2010 Population and Housing Census, which show that overall, the population of Ghana increased by 28% with all regions of the country experiencing growth. Ghana's population is rapidly urbanizing, with close to 50% of the population living in urban areas with urban primacy being a key feature. The determination of the government of Ghana to effectively manage the population for development is reflected in its commitment to global and regional agreements and conventions on population and development, including the International Conference on Population and Development, the Millennium Development Goals, Beijing Platform for Action, the World Summit on Sustainable Development and the NEPAD" (National Population Council 2011) Fig. 6.5 presents the demographic trend of Ghana's from 1960 to 2010.

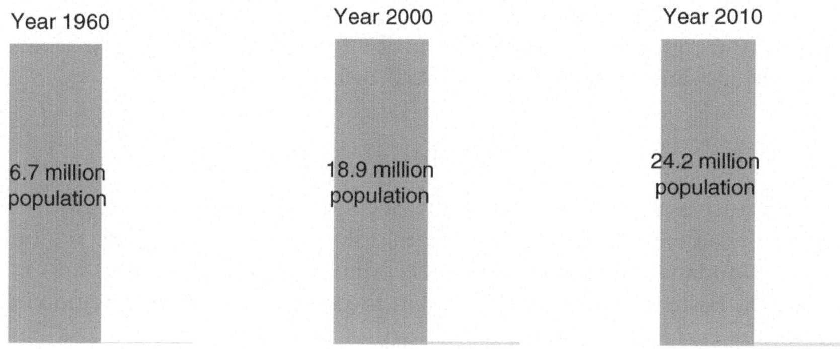

Fig. 6.5 The trend of Ghana's population 1960–2010. This graph shows the population growth over a 50 year period of time. Since demographics are important for business development, knowing the trends in population growth provides a good perspective for planning and growth projections

Source: Ghana National population Council (GNPC), 2011

6.4.2 *Evolving Comparative Advantage*

This looks at the various endowments and opportunities available in the ten regions in Ghana. It also considers the reasons some regions attract more investors than others.

6.4.3 *Geographic Influence on Business*

Location decisions significantly affect the profit margins and eventual success of a firm due to many variables, such as the availability and proximity of raw materials and labor, proximity to customers and competitors, infrastructure and transportation costs, etc. (Schiele 2008). When prices and profit margins are fixed, firms choose their locations in order to maximize their profits by increasing their demand (Stevenson 2007). In Ghana, most of the businesses are centralized in the big cities and towns. Factors, such as population, easy access to electricity, transportation, water, accommodation, Internet, etc., influence the decision to site businesses in the big cities and towns. The majority of the informal sector businesses such as bigger financial institutions, numerous small and medium-scale enterprises as well as other private companies are located in the cities and towns, while the rural areas can only boast agricultural farming, few rural banks, and other petty trading activities. Further geographic influence of doing business in

Ghana can be considered using the endowments of each of the ten regions found in the country. The regional contributions to the growth of Ghana's economy and businesses can be discussed below.

6.4.4 The Ashanti Region

The Ashanti region of Ghana is the second most populous region in Ghana. It is centrally located in the middle belt of Ghana. The region shares boundaries with four of the ten political regions: Brong-Ahafo in the north, Eastern in the east, Central in the south, and Western region in the southwest. Kumasi is the capital city of the Ashanti region, and has four municipalities, Obuasi, Bekwai, Offinso, and Mampong (Kpmg 2012 & 2013). The region has a total land area of 24,389 sq. km, or 10.2% of Ghana's total land area. The population of the region stands at 4,780,380, or 19% of the total. It has an urban population of 61%. In terms of geography, more than 50% of the region located in its western part lies in the semi-equatorial forest zone.

In terms of economic activity, agriculture – crop cultivation, hunting, and forestry – dominates. This constitutes about 30.5% of the economic activity in this geographic area. The region has a strong retail and wholesale trading activity (25.4%). Other contributions to the economic activity in the region are manufacturing, 10.5% and accommodation and food services, 6.1%. Workforce in the managerial category is reported to be 2.7%, professional 6.3% and technicians, and associate professional occupations 1.8%. Most managers (4.5%) are in the age group 55–59 years and the fewest are in the 20–24 age groups (1.3%). Cocoa growing in the region is very common among farmers, making cocoa an important crop cultivated in other parts of Ashanti region (Kpmg 2012 & 2013).

Other natural resources the region is endowed with are timber and livestock. The Ashanti region has air, road, and rail transportation available to its businesses and its citizens. The region has the second largest teaching hospital (Komfo Anokye Teaching Hospital) in the country. The inhabitants of the region own telecommunication facilities that are above the national levels (Ghana Statistical Service 2012).

With respect to the Ashanti region workforce defined as population aged 15 years and older, 69.4% were economically active though the situation indicates a comparable decline compared with 76.9% in 2000. This depict that many more residents in the region are economically not active in 2010 (30.6%). Other features that define the region are the fact that 92.5% of real estate activities, 90.2% of financial and insurance activities, 85.8% of electricity gas stream and air conditioning supply, and 85.7% of professional scientific and technical activities are concentrated in the urban areas in the region. The majority (58.7%) of the workforce is self-employed without employees (Kpmg, 2012 & 2013).

6.4.5 *The Eastern Region*

The capital of the Eastern region is Koforidua. The Eastern region comes as the region with the highest variety of culturally distinctive groups. It is home to some Asantes, Ewes, Krobos, Akuapems, and Dangbes. The region is dominantly an agricultural one. Chief among the agriculture activities are palm oil production, fishing, rubber production, and other crop-related farming (Ghana Tourism Board 2015; Ghana Statistical Service 2012). In the rural parts of the region, its indigenous population contributes to the food basket of Ghana by engaging in petty trading, animal raising, and cattle rearing, especially along the eastern borders of the region. Commercially, some parts of the region contribute to Ghana's production in the areas of pineapples, cocoa, coffee and oil palm on a large-scale, and cola nut. The exportation of these produce are minimal, as a chunk are sold to the local market within the region and to the nation's capital. The mining of diamonds at Akwatia is chiefly limited in the Eastern region. There are some factories that are sited in some of the regions. These include pharmaceutical, lumber processing poultry feed, alcoholic beverages, furniture, textiles. The region is home to one of the nation's scientific cocoa research centers, which is located at Koforidua Tafo (Kpmg 2012 & 2013).

6.4.6 *The Brong Ahafo Region*

The Brong Ahafo region is located in Ghana's midlands 400 km north of Accra. The region spans 320 km, when measured from the border between Ghana and Cote D'Ivoire in the west to Lake Volta in the east. In terms of landmass, the region comes as the nation's second largest, characterized by hills and mountain ranges. Land for cultivation in the region comes available since the region has about 30,400 sq. km of which only 3,706 sq. km has been used for cocoa planting. A few factories are located at Mim (the Mim Timber Company and Scanstyle Limited) and Wenchi (a tomato factory). The Brong Ahafo region is an ideal region for tourist-related investment because it comes with a greenery landscape that is free from industrial pollution, congestion, and noise pollution compared to other regions of the country. Economically, agriculture production is key in most communities in the region (Kpmg 2012 & 2013).

The region is known for its abundance of forest reserves, cocoa farms, plantain production, and large oil fields. The production of cashew and other related crops are done on plantations and on a traditional basis. The myriad production of agricultural produce from the region and its potential for investment in related areas has caused the region to earn the name the "breadbasket" of the nation. Market operations in the region are very busy with numerous market days. This serves as a good opportunity for investment platforms. Traditional skills and artisanal works are found in domains such as pottery, which are common in the region in addition to woven handicrafts. Included in the list of major towns in the Brong Ahafo regions are Sunyani (the capital), Techiman Kintampo, Yeji, Brekum, Dormaa Ahenkro Atebubu, Nkoranza, and Wenchi. Entertainment-related businesses consist of night clubs and drinking pubs which, though few, continue to boom each day. Hotels, restaurants, and guest houses in the region are descent but with moderate charges. The region is easily accessible by road from the north and south, by Lake Volta at Yeji and Buipe and by air. The region has a regional airport located in its capital Sunyani, which handles three domestic flights per week (Kpmg 2012 & 2013).

6.4.7 The Central Region

The Central region is one of the earliest historical regions in Ghana. It is characterized by beautiful beaches, fishing harbors, and ancient forts and castles which were built by European missionaries and traders. The capital of the Central region has two of its major towns being UNESCO World Heritage sites, that is, Cape Coast and Elmina Castles. Most of the economic activities in the Central region resolve around no commercial agriculture, and fishing on a small scale. Due to the historical nature of most towns in the region, tourism is a major area for investors. The Central region produces large quantities of fish and exotic fish products for export. Other economic activities that make the region business-friendly are tree crop farming (fruits for export and agroforestry) and smallholder salt production bodies. The region has an Intermediate Technology Transfer Unit that supports the expansion of the informal sectors in the region. Other enterprises in the region include small-scale salt and allied chemical production, kaolin, and allied products. Some members in the region engage in small-scale gold mining and palm oil/kernel enterprises (Kpmg 2012 & 2013).

6.4.8 The Greater Accra Region

The Greater Accra region comes as the smallest of all the regions in Ghana. Its capital, Accra, doubles as the national capital of Ghana. It serves as both the commercial and administrative hub of Ghana. Two major entries to Ghana, thus gateways, by both air and sea, are located in Accra. These are Kotoka International Airport and Tema Harbor. Geographically, the Greater Accra region has sandy beaches and lies very low. The region has luxury hotels, a variety of restaurants, golf courses, conferences and exhibition centers, colorful markets, museums, and historical monuments. The Ga-Adangbe are the indigenous occupants of the Greater Accra region. However, the cosmopolitan nature of the region with its dual function as the commercial and administrative region of Ghana has made it accommodate different people from different origins. The Greater Accra region is home to the Tema industrial and commercial towns, where Ghana's largest harbor is located. Other spectacular establishments found in the region are the Ghana's chocolate factory, Golden Tree, the National theatre. The business environment is very busy with relatively high cost of living than all the other parts of the country. During the evenings, other business including cinemas, bars, restaurants, and casinos flourish. There are over 200 manufacturing industries in the region (KPMG 2012 & 2013).

Key among these industries is the nation's oil refinery located in Accra and Tema. This makes the region to consume almost half of the total electricity generated nationwide. In terms of marketing and produce, the region serves as Ghana's largest market areas for manufactured products. The location of the region along the sea borders makes it good thriving grounds for fish farming. A ready and large market exists for the production of fish in large quantities. It is estimated that about 30,000 fishermen are located in the Greater Accra region. The region has a mixture of all business typologies, which makes it a hub for doing business.

6.4.9 *The Northern Region*

The Northern region is the largest region in Ghana in terms of landmass. It is estimated to have an area of 70,390 sq. km. Thus, it covers close to a third (31%) of the total landmass of the country. The Northern region borders the upper east and west on the north, and shares boundary to the south with the Brong-Ahafo and Volta regions. On its west and east coast are Cote d'Ivoire and Togo, respectively, which shares boundary with the northern region.

Most of the Northern region inhabitants are Muslims. A majority of the people in the northern region, more than 70%, are engaged in agriculture, and many are peasant farmers. The temperatures in the Northern are very high. Similar to other regions, the Northern region is connected to other regions through road transport, by air, and water (Lake Volta). The production of crops, such as maize, rice, sorghum, yams, tomatoes, and cotton shea nut, is common in the Northern region. In addition, rice and groundnut cultivation is common to the Northern region. Though iron ore deposits have been identified in some parts of the region, its production is on a small scale. This comes as an area where investment could suffice. Businesses that have the potential to be profitable are those that deal with craft shops, weaving, tanning, and pottery (Kpmg 2012 and 2013).

6.4.10 *The Upper East Region*

Bolgatanga is the Upper East region's capital. It occupies 842 sq. km of nearly flat land. There are four main ethnic groups who inhabit the region. These are the Gurenes of Bolgatanga, Builsas of Sandema, Kusassis of Bawku, and Kassena-Nankana of the Navrongo/Paga. Maize growing is common in the Upper East region. The buildings of the inhabitants are done mostly with mud and with thatched roofs. Agriculture is the most common economic activity in the region, engaging more than two-thirds of the region inhabitants. In terms of tourism, the region boast of the famous crocodile pond at Paga known for their friendliness. Two major irrigation projects to enhance crop production are located in the Upper East region; these are the 2,490 ha and 850 ha of irrigation located at Tono and Vea. This has enabled the cultivation of paddy rice, tomatoes, onions, millet, groundnuts, sorghum, and maize. There are an additional three major manufacturing establishments located in Pwalugu (a tomato canning factory), Zuarungu (a meat processing factory), and Bolgatanga (a rice mill). Notable areas of investment are smock weaving, leatherwork, pottery, and shea butter and groundnut oil extraction (Kpmg 2012 and 2013).

6.4.11 *The Upper West Region*

Ghana's smallest region is the Upper West region. The Upper West region is predominantly Muslim. Wa is its capital. With respect to its economic opportunities, the region produces large quantities of cotton, groundnuts, millet, and sorghum. The Upper West plays home to Wala, Dagarti, Sissala, and Lobe people. The Upper West region contributes uniquely to some tourist attraction destinations. These include, but are not limited to, Kaleo, with the nation's biggest crocodiles located here, two mushroom-shaped rock formations in the village of Wuling. It has been estimated that eight in every ten persons in the region is engaged in subsistent agriculture. Crops such as guinea-corn, millet, rice, yams, beans, groundnuts, and cowpea become the cultivating crops. Through the hard efforts of the farmers in the region, it produces cotton and shea nut in large quantities. The savannah vegetation in the region serves as an opportunity to produce cattle, goats, sheep, and poultry. The Upper West has several industries, ranging from pottery, shea butter processing, groundnut oil extraction, and soap-making (Kpmg 2012 and 2013).

6.4.12 *The Volta Region*

The Volta region is found in the eastern part of Ghana. It shares Ghana's eastern border with Togo, its western border is Lake Volta, the southern border the Atlantic Ocean, and the north boundary with the Northern region. The Volta region is a flat and undulating with coconut-clad sandy beaches and mangrove swamps. This makes tourism in the region a common occurrence. The Volta region has different sets of populations. Some are the Akan, Ewe, Guans, Ga-Dangme have settlements in the Volta. Six in every ten inhabitants depend on agriculture for subsistence (KPMG 2015). Among the crops produced on a large scale are cassava, maize, rice, and yam. With respect to Ghana's marine catch, 13% of it comes from the Volta region, and with Volta Lake running through the region, fish farming is a good prospect (Kpmg 2012 & 2013).

6.4.13 The Western Region

The Western region serves as a major tourist destination in Ghana. The region is found at the South-western coast of Ghana. It shares boundaries with Brong Ahafo to the north, and Ashanti and Cote d'Ivoire to the east and west, respectively. The region, with its tropical climate, has a moderate temperature and has the country's highest annual rainfall. Takoradi is its capital town. Some of the indigenous dwellers in the region are Ahanta, Aowin, Nzema, Sefwis, and Wassas. The economic opportunities of the Western lie in the availability of recreational facilities where internally generated funds could be realized. All parts of Ghana could be linked to the Western region through all the forms of transportation. More than half of the residents in the Western region are in agricultural sector-related businesses. Crops grown by those engaged in agriculture include cocoa, coffee, rubber, oil palm, citrus, coconut, rice, cocoyam, plantain, cassava, and vegetables. In terms of cocoa production, the Western region produces the most. The recent location of oil in the Western region makes it a destination point for oil-related businesses to thrive. The Western region additionally has a high concentration of forest that causes it to be the region with the highest production of timber. Mining in the Western region is found in towns such as Tarkwa, Prestea, and Hunni Valley. The Western region comes only after the Ashanti region and Greater Accra in terms of the most industrialized regions. In Ghana, the Western region appears to be the region that produces the most raw materials for further production; cases in point are cocoa and tobacco, edible and industrial palm oil, paper products, rubber tire and tubes, cement (Kpmg 2012 & 2013).

6.4.14 Comparative Cost of Doing Business Over Time in Ghana

Ghana is located in the sub-Saharan Africa and became a middle-income country in the year, 2010 (KPMG 2015). Ghana's foreign exchange is influenced by the exportation of oil, electricity, timber, diamond, bauxite, manganese, and individual remittances. In 2011, the real GDP growth rate was 15%, 8.8% in 2012, and 7.1% in 2013. In 2014, the real GDP of Ghana was 6.9% as indicated in the Government's 2015 fiscal policy statement. The macroeconomic environment of Ghana has been positive over the past few years, but in recent times, the economic environment has been challenged by continuing shortfalls in tax and nontax revenue, lower/declining national outputs, high stock of public debt, and the consequential depreciation of the cedi. All these have inflated the cost of doing business in the country.

Ghana's government has recently implemented policies such as the removal of subsidies and expanding the scope of tax in order to increase the government's income and to reduce fiscal deficit in the medium to long terms. The removal of subsidies and the increase in tax will have implications on the cost of doing business in the country. Investors will naturally be demotivated to operate in the country since there will be high cost of engaging business in the country. Despite the policies which tend to be unfavorable in doing business in Ghana, Ghana was the sixth largest recipient of FDIs in Africa at the end of 2013 (World Investment Report 2014).

Investors brought into the country a total amount of 3.226 billion US dollars, or 5.6% of the total FDI inflows in Africa. In the third quarter of 2014, for instance, the GIPC recorded a total of about 56 new projects with an estimated initial transfer of 34.27 million US dollars. Of the 56 new projects registered during the third quarter of 2014, 43 (76.79%) were wholly-owned foreign enterprises valued at GH¢626.71 million, which is 14.4% of the total estimated value of projects registered. The remaining 13 (23.21%) were joint ventures between Ghanaians and foreign partners valued at GH¢3,725.

Inflation in 2014 sharply depreciated the local currency and also had pass-through effects in fuel and utility price adjustments. The inflation rate increased from 13.8% in the beginning of 2014 to 15.4% in the middle of the year and ended at 17% in November, 2014. The BoG MPC attributed the rise in inflation to nonfood and food inflation.

Energy also influences the cost of doing business in Ghana. Hydroelectricity is the main source of Ghana's power and it is generated at the Akosombo and Kpong power stations. Electricity in 2015 was unstable and unpredictable. Frequent power outages were common and are still present even now, though not very severe. The government has, however, been able to manage the situation for some time now and it has become comparatively better to do business now than in 2015.

From a regional perspective, the cost of doing business in the major cities is higher, with Accra and Kumasi taking the dominant cost of investment. Nevertheless, the major cities – Accra, Kumasi, Sekondi-Takoradi and Tamale – have huge markets for investors to tap, and have adequate infrastructural bases for business-oriented individuals. Traffic congestion is severe in Accra and Kumasi, though, and this makes it quite tedious to move goods and services. In regions such as the Eastern, Central, and Upper regions, Volta, and Brong Ahafo, the traffic situations are more favorable, and access to power is almost the same as the major cities; but the market for goods and services is comparatively lower. It is, therefore, important for a particular investor to know how and where to operate in Ghana in order to reap full profits to ensure their sustainability.

6.4.15 *Economic Transactions and Changes in Ghana*

Issues considered in this section are market-oriented structural reforms in Ghana, labor market production and rigidities, losses of human capital due to out-migration, and the informal economy.

6.4.16 *Market-Oriented Structural Reforms in Ghana*

Market-oriented structural reform in Ghana is mainly the ERP, which started in April 1983 with the first cedi devaluation; thereafter, a progressive movement toward a realistic and flexible exchange rate was sought. This program made it possible to improve price incentives in the economy and to improve the economic conditions of the country. The program was intended to realign the exchange rates and interest rates of the country and to reform and restore productive incentives for key export crops such as cocoa, timber, and minerals to improve production. The program also was intended to reduce the cumulative deficit, rehabilitate the country's economic and social infrastructure, and encourage private savings and investments, and restore fiscal and monetary discipline and to establish workers' priorities for the allocation of scare foreign resources.

The IMF supported the program with three successive stand-by arrangements totaling SDR 611 million. In November 1985, the government of Ghana presented to the Third Meeting of the Consultative Group for Ghana in Paris the policy framework for 1986–1988, which consisted of the second phase of the ERP. The funding for the second phase included the World Bank's US$ 130 million Structural Adjustment Program for 1987–1989, and the IMF's US$ 245.4 million Extended Fund Facility for 1987–1990. The main objectives of this program were, on the one hand, to consolidate gains made throughout the first three years of the ERP and, on the other, to institute a gradual process of structural adjustment aimed at accelerating growth, improving incentives, strengthening the capabilities of the ministries in policy planning so as to remove the remaining barriers to efficiency and growth. Meanwhile, the Extended Fund Facility set annual macroeconomic targets in terms of additional conditionalities, growth rates in GDP, domestic inflation, rate of velocity, and growth of broad money supply.

6.4.17 *Labor Market Protection and Rigidities in Ghana*

Ghana is dominated by a large pool of unskilled labor, with the majority of its workforce being youth between the ages of 15–24: 46.2% aged 25–44 years, 9.9% aged 45–64 years, and 13% aged 65 years and older. The private sector is the largest source of employment in the country, accounting for 93.1% of the economically active persons (private informal, 86.1% and private formal, 7.0%). The public sector, which is the second largest employer, accounts for only 6.3%. The year 2013 experienced massive labor agitations from doctors, pharmacists, and teachers pressing home the demand for payment of salary arrears from government. This has largely been attributed to the implementation of the Single Spine Salary Structure policy (Okudzeto et al. 2014). Generally, labor regulations and policies remain favorable for businesses. Despite the country's positive labor management relationships, labor disagreement emanating from wage policies in Ghana and its inflation stricken climate seldom occurs. Most employers in Ghana deem it advantageous to maintain open lines of discussion on wage fixing and other forms of rewards as well as motivation (US Dept. of State 2015).

6.4.18 *Labor Laws and Employment in Ghana*

Ghana has relevant labor laws that regulate activities relating to employment. These labor laws are enshrined in the Constitution of Ghana and include the Labor Act of 2003 (Art 651), the Labor Regulations Act of 2007 (LI 1833), the Persons with Disability Act 2006 (Act 715), the Workmen's Compensation Act 1987 (PNDCL 187), Factories Offices and Shops Act 1970 (Act 328), the National Pensions Act 2008 (Act 766), and the Internal Revenue Act 2000 (Act 592). Sector-specific laws as well as regulations are also applicable (Djangmah 2015).

Under the Labor Law, the Chief Labor Officer sets Collective Bargaining Agreements (CBA) in lieu of the Trade Union Congress (TUC). This change limited the TUC's influence, since the prior CBA provisions implicitly compelled all unions to be part of TUC. Again, the National Labor Commission, charged with the responsibility to resolve labor and industrial related disputes, and the Tripartite Committee that sets the minimum wage is given legal authority (US Dept. of State 2015).

The Ghanaian Constitution has made provision for the general regulatory framework for labor. Every person is guaranteed the right to work satisfactorily under safe and healthy environment with right to get equal remuneration for equal work by the constitution. Employees are provided the guarantee to take rest, leisure, and reasonable limitation of working hours, as well as holiday periods (including public holidays) with pay (UHY, Djangmah 2015).

6.4.19 Labor Contract and Agreements in Ghana

All employment contracts for a period of six months or more must be in writing. The rights and obligations of the parties must be expressed in clear terms. A written statement of the particulars of the contract of employment must be provided to the employee within two months of employment in a prescribed form. The statement of particulars must be endorsed by both parties concerned [the employer and the employee (UHY, Djangmah 2015)].

Child labor in Ghana is considered to be a critical problem. Children in Ghana are engaged in the worst forms of child labor in agriculture, including cocoa farming, fishing, and small-scale gold mining activities (US Dept. States 2015)

6.4.20 Labor Union

The Constitution further provides the guarantee for the right to freedom of association. This includes the right to form or join trade unions or other national or international associations, for the protection of their interests. Employees have the right to join trade unions of their choice; there is no minimum or maximum threshold. Therefore, any number of employees may join or form a union of their choice at any time. The Constitution prohibits forced labor (Djangmah 2015).

The rigidities in the protection has been that, despite the presence of various protection nets for Ghana's labor market, there are still numerous workers who are maltreated and feel insecure in their places of works. For instance, despite the legal guarantees for trade unions in Ghana, only about 37.5% of the working age population are members of trade unions as at 2008 (GLSS, 2008).

6.4.21 Losses of Human Capital Due to Out-Migration

Ghanaian migration has increasingly become extra-regional since the decline of Nigeria as a major destination for Ghanaian migrants in the 1980s. Although the majority of Ghanaian emigrants (71%) still stay within West Africa, a growing proportion is migrating to a diverse range of countries outside the region (DRC 2007). According to 2008 Ministry of Foreign Affairs estimates, Ghanaian migrants can be found in more than 33 countries around the world. After West African countries, the most important countries of destination for Ghanaian emigrants are the US (7.3%) and the UK (5.9%) (DRC 2007).

An estimate of the Ghanaian emigrant population ranges from 1.5 million to 3 million (Black et al. 2003). Since the 1990s, skilled migration from Ghana, especially to developed countries in the North, has been accelerating. Ghana has the highest emigration rates for the highly skilled employees (46%) in Western Africa (Docquier and Marfouk 2006). The medical professions are particularly affected by emigration. It is estimated that more than 56% of doctors and 24% of nurses trained in Ghana are working abroad (Clemens and Pettersson 2007). The overall skill level of Ghanaian emigrants is relatively high. According to some estimates, 33.8% of emigrants from Ghana living in Organization for Economic Cooperation and Development countries possessed medium skills, while 27.6% had high skills. Only 3% of Ghanaian emigrants had no skills. Many Ghanaians acquire their skills at foreign universities. The latest available figures suggest that almost 8% of Ghanaian university students studied abroad in 2006. Although this marks a decrease from 2004, when 11.8% of Ghanaian students studied abroad, the proportion of Ghanaians enrolled in foreign universities is still small. Public scholarship programs may unintentionally encourage this trend by providing support only to students and academic staff that study abroad. While many Ghanaians leave for more far-reaching destinations, many of them also return either temporarily or permanently to Ghana.

The proportion of Ghanaians among persons who arrived in Ghana from 2000 to 2007 steadily increased from 18.6 to 34.6%. Of the 1,090,972 Ghanaians who left Ghana from 2000 to 2007, only 153,632 did not return within that period. Departure statistics show that the majority of resident Ghanaians leave for commercial activities, followed by spouses and child dependents (Quartey 2006). An important result of growing emigration is the dramatic increase in official remittance flows.

The BoG estimates that remittances to Ghana increased from US$476 million in 1999 to US$1.5 billion in 2005. This trend has been affected by the economic downturn in the developed world. The BoG reports a 7.3% decrease in remittances in the first quarter of 2009 compared to the same period in 2008 (US$1.9 billion).

In relation to economically motivated migration, forced migration from Ghana is insignificant and has been declining over the past decade. The number of Ghanaian asylum seekers and recognized refugees under the UN High Commissioner for Refugees' protection has decreased from 15,879 in 2003 to only 6,717 in 2007. Although emigration has been increasing at a faster rate than immigration since 1990, Ghana continues to be an important country of destination. According to recent census-based estimates, the migrant population, that is, foreign-born population, still constitutes 7.6% of Ghana's total population in 2005. The net migration rate (per thousand persons) for 2000–2005 was positive at 0.1 compared to the –0.6 recorded in the previous five-year period.

6.4.22 *Development Implications of Migration for the Origin Countries*

Migration is a decision that impacts the welfare of the household, the home community, and in the end the whole economy in various ways (Abdih et al. 2009). The welfare implications of migration on the origin country are most often, though not always, sizable and positive. The main channels through which migration alleviates poverty are increased incomes from remittances, ability to smooth consumption, access to finance for starting a new business, as well as tapping on to the knowledge and resources provided by the international community of the migrant diaspora. Beside pure monetary gains, migration allows for higher investment in healthcare and education. Yet, not all impacts are positive: exploitation of migrants by unscrupulous recruiters or employers is reportedly widespread; separation from family can be stressful for migrants; and large-scale immigration can pose serious challenges to a nation's identity and sovereignty.

6.4.23 Informal Economy

Since the discovery of the concept, "informal sector," in Africa, it has not lent itself to a comprehensive and universally accepted definition. A number of attempts to define the concept have resulted in diverse definitions. Nabi and Drine (2009) states that, attempts to measure the shadow economy (i.e., informal sector) first faced the problem of defining it. There are varied definitions of the concept in the existing literature, some of which are presented as follows:

(i) "All economic activities that contribute to the officially calculated gross national product but currently unregistered" (Feige 1989).
(ii) "Market-based production of goods and services, whether legal or illegal, that escapes detection in the official estimates of the gross domestic product" (Smith 1994).
(iii) "Unregulated economic enterprises or activities" (Hart, 1970).

According to Farrell et al. (2000), the informal sector is associated with certain characteristics that have been classified into four main categories. These include the employees (characteristics of the people engaged in the informal sector); enterprise (characteristics of the activities in the informal sector); habitat (characteristics of the informal sector land and housing); and credit (characteristics of the informal credit markets).

The development of the informal economy in Ghana is the result of a gradual process that has increased the pace during the last decade. The dominant economic model after independence in 1957 and the establishment of the Republic in 1960 was a state-led development. It was believed that the influence of the State will support economic development and social justice in a favorable way. However, the economic truth after the Nkrumah era was not in favor of the country. The external debt rose dramatically from £20 million in 1957 to £400 million in 1966 (Ministry of Education 1991). The idea to overcome the postcolonial struggle with a focus on public sector employment failed.

The structures laid down in the first decade of independence influenced the economic development of the decades to come. The economic crisis of the global south hit Ghana in the early 1970s and the negative effects were very harsh. Between 1970 and 1982 GDP per capita declined by almost 20% and across sector growth dropped depending on produce between 40% (cocoa) and 80% (rice) (Hutchful 2002).

There was obviously a very distinct need for structural change. After the economic downfall and the conviction of the government that external intervention in local markets is inevitable, the IMF imposed its ERP on Ghana, whose policy was to tackle the multiple dimensions of the economic crisis. The idea was that the externally developed policy plan for the Ghanaian state and economy would help reduce the inflation through the devaluation of the cedi and foster internal economic growth through long-term planning and private sector development. Part of the plan was to cut state spending and reduce public employment. Between 1960 and 1991 almost 150,000 public workers lost their jobs. Others were shifted into different jobs or pushed into early retirement (Gockel and Vormawor 2004). With the renunciation of the state-centered economy, the private sector came into the focus. By encouraging private sector development, poverty reduction and internal growth were supposed to happen (Obeng-Odoom 2012).

Historically, it is not the informal economy that should be growing. The prediction of scholars as well as economic professionals in the 1980s and 1990s was that with the establishment of the ERP, the growth of the formal and the decline of the informal economy would be certain. However, the opposite is the case. Total formal employment fell dramatically due to the negative influence of new established structures by the ERP. Gockel (1998) states that between 1985 and 1991 almost 280,000 jobs were lost during a six-year period, accounting for a decrease of almost 60%.

The number of economically active persons grew as well due to a high increase in population, reinforcing the pressure on the labor market. The lowest level of resistance came from the informal economy due to its under-organized character. According to data from the Ghana Statistics Service, the share of the informal economy of the total labor force grew from 80% in 2000 to 86.1% in 2010, which makes it by far the largest employer in the country (GSS 2012). Representatives of the TUC speak of more than 90%. Not only is the informal economy absorbing labor force from the public sector when there are budgetary cuts like in the 1980s, but it also absorbs the majority of graduates from universities and high schools. (Enrollment in tertiary institutions was at 261,962 in 2011/2012; Ministry of Education 2013.) The TUC estimates that 250,000 graduates enter the labor market every year, out of which 5,000 find employment in the formal economy. Due to the net hiring freeze in the public sector, the share of people seeking employment in the informal economy is staggering at 98% (TUC 2009).

6.4.24 *The Role of the Informal Sector in Ghana*

Most small-scale enterprises operate in the informal sector, making contributions to national development. The informal sector is rapidly growing and expected to expand its productive capacity so as to make more contribution to the overall national GDP. The contribution of the informal sector to the growth and development of economy includes the production of goods and services, job creation, and skills acquisition (ISSER 2003).

Since the discovery of the informal sector, it has made significant contribution to socio-economic growth of Ghana. According to ISSER (2003), a critical look at the operations of the informal sector vis-à-vis the economy's growth pattern demonstrates the significant contribution that it makes to national development. Some contributions of the informal sector worthy of specific mention follow.

6.4.25 *Contribution to National Output*

Collectively, the operators in the informal sector produce diverse goods and services that added up to the national output. Certain goods and services are better provided by the informal sector than the formal sector. According to ISSER (2003), the role of the informal sector in the domestic economy is demonstrated in the wide variety of goods and service produced by the sector. Based on the value-added estimates from the JASPA (1989) survey, it was established that the sector accounts for about 22% of real GDP, with the contribution of rural informal activity outstripping that of the urban sector. In the nonagricultural sector, contribution of trade and commerce is the largest accounting for 52%, followed by industry with 28%, services 12%, and transport 8% (The Institute of Statistical, Social and Economic Research (ISSER), the State of the Ghanaian Economy in 2003). The rural informal sector plays a critical role in the agriculture sector to feed the nation. Without the informal sector there would have been gross under provision of the raw foodstuffs.

6.4.26 *Job Creation and Income Distribution*

As stated earlier, one of the main causes of the informal sector is the paucity of job opportunities in the formal sector. The informal sector in Ghana provides an avenue for unlimited job opportunities. Hence, those people who are unable to secure formal jobs tend to seek solace in the informal sector. In the ISSER's (2003) report, it is stated that "the main source of employment is the informal sector". The sector provides employment opportunities for at least 80% of the labor. The sector as of 2,000 provided jobs for about 6.7 million people.

6.4.27 *Skills Acquisition in Training*

Another area in which the informal sector contributes immensely is in the area of the training of the labor force in the acquisition of artisanal skills. This is achieved through the traditional apprenticeship system. Though this is not a perfect system for training manpower for industrial employment because of the inadequacy of the methods used in training, through this function the informal sector plays an important role in the development of the indigenous entrepreneurship particularly in artisan activities in both the urban and rural areas in Ghana (Yankson 1989).

Successful industrialization must have an indigenous base. The expansion of the small enterprise sector will help develop the experienced managerial and entrepreneurial class that is needed as a basis for more efficient indigenous instrument and management of large-scale industries (Bruton 1990). Although some informal sector enterprises fail in the first five years of operation, some do survive and grow from being informal to formal and becoming big time businesses employing hundreds and thousands of workers.

6.4.28 *The Important Role in Increasing the Pace of Innovation*

Small and very large firms make a disproportionate contribution to innovation, while the number and importance of innovations vary by industry, according to a study by Smith (1994). Smith observed that failure rates among small firms are often higher because, in incurring extra risk, they play an important role in establishing promising ideas which can be nurtured into competitive products and processes. Sometimes many of these innovative companies also disappear, not because they succeed and are purchased by large companies which can market the products more effectively. There is thus a useful interaction between small and large companies as the small firms provide the means of increasing the motivation for the innovation and hence the pace of change which all firms can build on.

6.5 The Commercial System

6.5.1 Free Trade Blocs, Bilateral Treaties in Ghana

Ghana cooperates with all countries around the globe. Ghana is a member-state of the UN, the Commonwealth group, the ECOWAS, the AU, and several others. In bilateral terms, Ghana cooperates with countries in Europe, Asia, and the Middle East, North America, and other countries in Africa as well as the world. International trade is the avenue Ghana uses to generate foreign exchange to promote growth and development. Despite Ghana's peaceful trade relationship with all countries, some blocks to international trade exist which affect Ghana's engagement in international trade. Usually, the block takes the form of developed nations quoting a price tag for Ghana's products in the international market. The need for Ghana to add value to its raw state export materials is needed to overcome most of the blocs to trade around the globe (US Dept. of State 2015)

Ghana initiated an interim Economic Partnership Agreement with the EU at the end of 2007, but has not yet signed the agreement. Ghana maintains good relations with its traditional trading partners and donors, especially the US and the UK, both of which have a large Ghanaian diaspora. In addition, Ghana has good relations with many emerging countries, backed by funding for various projects (ADB & ADF 2012–2016).

6.5.2 EPZ of Ghana

Ghana's legislature enacted the country's free zone in July 1995, which created one of the world's most attractive incentive packages for hassle-free business operations for exporting firms. These incentives serve to amplify business in what is already a center for international business. The EPZ can be defined simply as an enclave or a designated area where processing activities undertaken within them occur "outside" the customs territory of the country, insofar as the jurisdiction of normal customs provisions is concerned. This means that all raw materials required for production in an EPZ may be imported duty-free and without regard to quantitative restrictions applying within the domestic market. Conversely, goods may be exported from EPZ without payment of taxes and sales duties. The economic activities occurring within the EPZs have been primarily garment production and assembling of electronic and light electrical goods. In recent times, however, the development of food processing activities, production of optical goods, watches, leather footwear, clothing, furniture and toys, and others including services have been prominent activities in the EPZs.

In Ghana, it is important to distinguish between EPZs and what is popularly known as Free Ports. While the EPZs are essentially productive in function, the Free Ports are basically commercial in nature. In a duty-free port, which is also known as Free Trade Zone or Commercial Free Zone, merchandise may be moved in and out of the designated area free of customs duty, stored in warehouses for varying periods, opened for inspection, and repacked for reexport and transshipment. The EPZs have undeniably improved the exportation of goods and services by Ghana and has imparted positively on the country's foreign exchange.

6.5.3 Investor – State Dispute Settlement in Ghana

Investors in Ghana have over the years entered into disputes with the government, especially at periods in which economic conditions have been slowed down by the government through its activities. The increase in tax and removal of subsidies as well as the frequent power outages were some concerns raised by investors against the government. The government in its quest to improve private participation and to improve FDI has tried to settle the issues raised by investors by putting in place measures to encourage their participation and contributions to the growth of the country.

Ghana has a good record in terms of state governance and relatively dependable legal framework that provides dispute settlement process benefiting foreign investors compared to other economies in the subregion (US Dept. of State 2015).

When there is dispute between the government of Ghana and an investor relating to business, every available effort should be made through friendly discussion to ensure a peaceful settlement.

Any disagreement which is not peacefully resolved through mutual discussion may be submitted at the option of the aggrieved party to arbitration as follows:

In accordance with the UNCITRAL Rules, or in the case of a foreign investor, within the framework of any bilateral or multilateral agreement on investment protection to which the government and the country of which the investor is a national are parties, or

In accordance with any other national or international machinery for the settlement of investment disputes that is agreed to by the parties,

With respect to any dispute, when there is disagreement between the investor and the government of the Republic of Ghana as to the method of dispute settlement to be adopted, the choice of the investor will prevail (Djangmah 2015)

6.5.4 *Future Economic Trends in Ghana*

The economy of Ghana is likely to witness a positive impact in 2016 through a slight improvement in its power supply, increased crude oil production, and cedi stabilization against the major foreign currencies. As part of Ghana's medium-term framework, an average GDP growth between 2015 and 2017 is expected to hit at least 6.8% with 8% inflation with a band of ±2%. By 2017, Ghana's overall budget deficit is targeted at 3.5% with gross foreign reserves covering not less than four months of imports of goods and services (PWC 2015).

According to PWC 2015 highlights on the summary budget of Ghana, the future trend of the economy can be seen in the projections of the various sectors between 2015 and 2017. The agricultural sector is expected to record 2.9% growth of GDP in 2015 as against 3.7% for 2016 and 4.3% in 2017. The average GDP for the sectors is pegged at 3.6%. Industry is expected to witness 5.2% GDP growth in 2015 compared with 11.5 and 17.6% growth for 2016 and 2017, respectively. An average GDP growth for industry is expected to be at 11.4%. 3.9% growth in services is expected for 2015 followed by 6.4% for 2016 and 7.7% in 2017. 6% average GDP is expected for the service industry. Overall GDP growth excluding oil for 2015, 2016, and 2017 is expected to record 2.7, 4.9, and 5.5%, respectively, with an average of 4.4%. Overall GDP growth including oil for 2015, 2016, and 2017 is expected to be 3.9, 6.9, and 9.6%, in that order, with an average growth of 6.8% (PWC 2015 and 2015 budget statement). Table 6.1 indicates the projected future economic trend of Ghana in relation to GDP growth.

Considering Ghana government operations for the budget between 2015 and 2017, there is a suggestion that government expects to increase

Table 6.1 The trend of Ghana's future GDP contributions 2015–2017

Sectors	*Years Projected*			*Average (%)*
	2015	*2016*	*2017*	
Agriculture	2.9%	3.7%	4.3%	3.6
Industry	5.2%	11.3%	17.6%	11.4
Service	3.9%	6.4%	7.7%	6
Overall GDP excluding oil	2.7%	4.9%	5.5%	4.4
Overall GDP including oil	3.9%	6.9%	9.6%	6.8

Source: PWC 2015 Summary Budget Highlights on Ghana

the debt stock in 2015 with Ghc 12.8 billion (gross). It is worth noting that excessive increases in domestic borrowings have the impact, making it very difficult for the private sector to access credit. This has an additional consequence of increasing interest rates and cost of doing business.

Potential risks expected in Ghana include weakening consumer sentiments, a slowdown in the pace of credit expansion, bearish conditions in the international commodities market, and to some extent continued tightness in both monetary and fiscal policies (Bank of Ghana Monetary Policy Report 2016).

As the government continues to meet competing demands for improved public service delivery, investment in education, health, and infrastructure, there is an equal need for serious public spending reform that looks at other innovative and equitable methods of mobilizing revenue as well as judicious prioritization of public spending (PWC 2015).

On the contrary, it seems highly not likely for the government to demonstrate the political will and fiscal discipline to meet IMF loan facility conditionalities, especially when considering the just impending 2016 elections. The country has a history of greatly increasing budget deficits during election years. The government faces a critical challenge in how it plans to reduce the wage bill from the current expenditure, which is one of the conditions of IMF loan facility (Theo Acheampong and Alex Barkers-Okwan 2015b).

6.5.5 *Natural Resources Nationalism*

Ghana is a member of the UN Framework Convention on Climate Change and is associated with the Copenhagen Accord of December 18, 2009. The country instituted the National Environment Policy in

November 2012 with an objective of using and maintaining natural resources in a sustainable manner (KPMG 2014)

In Ghana, the National Climate Change Policy Framework (NCCPF, 2011) aims at ensuring a low carbon economy, effectively adapting to climate change and social development. The country has the objective to generate 10% of its energy via renewable resources by 2020. There are many environmental challenges Ghana is faced with, including land degradation, coastal erosion, pollution of rivers and lagoons, especially due to recent illegal mining activities, deforestation, desertification, and waste management (Okudzeto et al. 2014)

The cost of Ghana's environmental degradation is approximated to be 10% of its GDP. More than 80% of disasters in Ghana are noted to be climate-related. The forestry sector, which provides a livelihood for approximately 2.5 million people, is in particular being depleted as 70% of Ghana's land is prone to soil erosion and over 50% of Ghana's forest is turned into agricultural land (Okudzeto et al. 2014).

Ghana's discovery of oil and gas in 2007 offered new opportunities for raising the country's energy capacity and increasing resource-related revenues. Ghana's Petroleum Management Act (2011) is considered fair and balanced, assisted by the Public Interest and Accountability Committee to ensure compliance with the law. The Extractive Industries Transparency Initiative reports showed that Ghana's revenues from natural resources have marginally increased between 2011 and 2013. Government revenues from natural resources in 2013 are estimated at 8.3% of domestic revenue, of which revenues from oil and gas was GHS 1.6 billion and mining GHS 389.17 billion, including 4.977 million barrels of oil in-kind (Okudzeto et al. 2014).

The Ghana EPA requires all investors whose activities will have an effect on the environment to provide periodic report on the environmental impact assessment of their business activities (KPMG 2014)

6.5.6 *The Debate About Investment Incentives in Ghana*

Investment incentives have faced an important criticism, which is that at some point they have to be paid for somehow. That is, whether companies receive grants or tax reductions. This revenue effect must be offset, either through tax increases on other tax payers, borrowing, or program cuts (Gberegbe 2007).

While the evidence is thin, there is some reason to believe that incentives have an impact on the technological choices of investors. At the very least, it is possible to identify cases in which the availability of incentives has led investments to be more capital-intensive than they would have been otherwise. For example, Schneider (2005) stressed that subsidies falling as a percentage of investment but rising in terms of cost per job showed that, for assembly plants, the automobile industry had reached the point where it was substituting capital for labor. That is, a given amount of dollars was attracting more capital and gaining fewer jobs. This undermines the argument that incentives are "creating" jobs. It should be noted that this is a different situation from that of a government targeting high value-added jobs by trying to attract pharmaceutical, biotech, microchip, and other high-tech firms.

In the case of Ghana, the physical location of business entities is not of much necessity. In contrast, government uses tax incentive framework as a means to lure and encourage business establishments. Again, import substitution restrictions are absent. Local labor requirements hold that any investment in trading enterprise must employ at least 20 Ghanaians, while the issuance of visa/work permits to foreign staff depends solely on the size of the business entity (U.S. Department of State 2015).

There are slight diversities in investment incentives depending on the regulations under which investors operate in Ghana. For instance, all investments under the Free Zone Act enjoy a ten-year corporate tax incentive, while investment under the GIPC regulations does not automatically enjoy tax exemption. This means that even tax incentives in Ghana differ depending on the sector of investment operations (U.S. Department of State 2015).

The GIPC law permits import and tax holidays for plant inputs, machinery and parts that are imported for the purpose of the investment. The government of Ghana recently imposed a 5% import duty on some items that were formally zero-rated, to conform to the ECOWAS common external tariff (U.S. Department of State 2015).

The Ghanaian tax system is replete with tax concessions that considerably reduce the effective tax rate. The minimum incentives are specified in the GIPC law and are not applied in an ad hoc or arbitrary manner. Once an investor has been registered under the GIPC law, the investor is entitled to the incentives provided by law. The government has discretion to grant an investor additional customs duty exemptions and tax incentives beyond the minimum stated in the law (U.S. Department of State 2015).

The law also guarantees an investor all the tax incentives provided for under Ghanaian law. For example, rental income from commercial and residential property is exempt from tax for the first five years after construction. Similarly, income from a company selling or leasing out premises is exempt from tax for the first five years of operation. Rural banks and cattle ranching are exempt from income tax for ten years and pay 8% thereafter (U.S. Department of State 2015).

The corporate tax rate is 25%, and this applies to all sectors except income from nontraditional exports (8% tax rate) and oil and gas exploration companies (35% tax rate). Some sectors have temporary tax exemptions (U.S. Department of State 2015).

These sectors include free zone enterprises and developers (0% for the first 10 years and 8% thereafter); real estate development and rental (0% for the first five years and 25% thereafter); agroprocessing companies (0% for the first five years, after which the tax rate ranges from 0 to 25% depending on the location of the company in Ghana), and waste processing companies. Tax rebates are also offered in the form of incentives based on location. A capital allowance in the form of accelerated depreciation is applicable in all sectors except banking, finance, commerce, insurance, mining, and petroleum. There are no restrictions on the issuance of work and residence permits to free zone investors and employees (U.S. Department of State 2015).

6.6 Conclusion

This chapter has provided ample documentary evidence of the market and economic overview of Ghana. Important variables such as monetary policy and the economic and commercial systems of Ghana have been considered thoroughly. This work provides a framework for conducting business in Ghana. It illustrates the areas that have very promising investment prospects and those that are trailing against macroeconomic benchmarks.

The study has also shown that the economy of Ghana currently seems risky and unfriendly to business investment. This seemingly gloomy picture, together with the slow pace of growth, is tied with many economic constraints such as high inflation, persistent increasing public debt, continued increased budget deficits, increased interest rates, poor electricity supply, unemployment, a high cost of living, high sociopolitical tension due to the IMF loan facility conditionalities as well as the impending 2016 elections and more, which the country is confronted with. Based on the above developments, the government is advised to ensure the use of prudent measures as well as strict financial discipline in its borrowings and expenditures. Revenues generated from mineral proceeds and other state resources such as human and natural must be prudently utilized to ensure economic freedom for the citizens.

References

Abdih, Y., R. Chami, M. Gapen, and A. Mati 2009. "Fiscal Sustainability in Remittance-Dependent Economies." IMF Working Paper WP/09/190, International Monetary Fund.

Acheampong, Theo, and Alex Barker-Okwan 2015. African Economist LLC (2015) Ghana: Economic Policy & 2015 Outlook Report, Ghana Secures IMF Program but Difficult Times Lie Ahead of 2016 Elections.

Acheampong, Theo and Alex Barkers-Okwan. 2015b. Ghana: Economic Policy & 2015 Outlook Report - in depth analysis and precision, Africa Economics LLC. http://www.africa-ecoonomics.com/file/2013/10/Ghana-andthe-IMF_Africa-Economics-Report_Final.pdf.

Adams, Samuel, and John Agbemade 2012. "Financial Liberalization and Banking Sector Performance in Ghana." *African Journal of Business Management* 6(47): 11598–11608, November 28, 2012.

ADB and ADF 2012-2016-Republic of Ghana Country Strategy Paper (2012-2016), African Development Bank, African Development Fund, http://www.afdb.org/fileadmin/uuploads/afdb/Documents/Project-and-Operations/Ghana520-520CPS%202012%20-%202016.pdf

Ahiawodzi, A. K. 2007. "Sectoral Analysis of Credit Mobilization In Ghana." *Journal of Business Research*, 1(1&2): 41–48.

Amato, J.D. and Gerlach, S.(2002)."Inflation Targeting in Emerging Market and Transition Economies: Lessons After a Decade." *European Economic Review* 46: 781–790.

Amidu, Mohammed 2006. "The Link Between Monetary Policy and Banks' Lending Behavior: The Ghanaian Case." *Banks and Bank Systems* 1(4): 38–48.

Bank of Ghana. 2015. Monetary Policy Report. 6(1). Real Sector Developments.

Bank of Ghana Monetary Policy Report. 2016. vol. 6, No. 1/2016.

Bank of Ghana Monetary Policy Report. Inflation Outlook and Analysis-Volume 4 No.1/2015, https://bog.gov.gh/privatecontent/MPC_Press_Releases/Inflation%20Outlook%20and%20Analysis%20Report%20-%20February%202015.pdf

Bank of Ghana Monetary Policy Report Inflation Report. 2016. vol. 4, No. 1/2016.

Black, R., Tiemoko, R. and Waddington, C. 2003. International Migration, Remittances and Poverty: The Case of Ghana and Cote d'Ivoire. Brighton: Sussex Centre for Migration Research, University of Sussex.

Bruton, H. 1990. "Broad Based Growth." Paper presented at a Workshop on Research Priorities for Policy Reforms Supporting Broad-Based Growth and Democracy, Washington DC, USAID.

Clemens, M., and G. Pettersson 2007. New Data on African Health Professionals Abroad. Working Paper No. 95, Center for Global Development, Washington DC.

Development Research Centre (DRC). 2007. University of Sussex Global Migrant Origin.

Nabi, Mahmoud S., and Imed Drine. 2009. "External debet, informal economy and growth." *Economics Bulletin* 29: 1695–1707.

Djangmah, Henry 2015. Doing Business in Ghana Uhy Voscon Chartered Accountants Ghana. www.uhy.com and UHY.

Docquier, F., and A. Marfouk 2006. "International Migration by Educational Attainment (1990–2000)." In *International Migration, Remittances and Development*, edited by C. Ozden and M. Schiff. New York: Palgrave Macmillan.

Farrell G., Roman J. and Matthew F. 2000. "Conceptualizing Shadow Economy." *Journal of International Affairs* 53(2): 393.

Feige, E. L. 1989. *The Underground Economies. Tax Evasion and Information Distribution*. Cambridge, New York: Cambridge University Press.

Gberegbe, F.B. 2007. *Tax Administration in Nigeria-Concepts and Practice*. Lagos: Fredsbary Printers and publishers.

Ghana Banking Survey. 2008. Raising the bar:increase in the minimum capital requirements, and implications for the industry, Ghana Association of Bankers, Price Waterhouse Coopers, http://www.pwc.com/gh/en/pdf/ghana-banking-survey-2008.pdf

Ghana Statistical Service. 2008. Ghana LIving Standards Survey (GLSS), Round 6 http://www.statsghana.gov.gh/glss6.html

Ghana Statistical Service. 2012."2010: Population&Housing Census –Summary Report of Final Results." Accra. p.79.www.statsghana.gov.gh/docfiles/2010phc/Census2010_Summary_report_of_reresults.pdf. Date:15th November, 2015.

Ghana Statistics Service. 2013. "2000 Population and Housing Census (PHC)." Available: http://www.statsghana.gov.gh/nada/index.php/catalog. Accessed on January 15, 2016.

Ghana Tourism Board. 2015. https://ghanafinancialmarket.wordpress.com/2016/06/ghana-tourist-boardcontributes-ghs10-5-billion-us2-7-billion-to-gdp-representing-7-8-the-gdp-in-2015/

Gockel, A. F. 1998. "Urban Informal Sector in Ghana: Features and Implications for Unionization." Paper presented within the Framework of the GTUC/ICFTU-AFRO.

Gockel, A. F., and D. Vormawor 2004. Friedrich Ebert Stiftung Trade Union Country Reports: The Case of Ghana, Wash.

Gordon, Peter, and Lanlan Wang 2004. "Does Economic Performance Correlate with Big Government?." *Econ Journal Watch* 1(2): 192–221.

Hart, J. Keith. 1970. "Small-scale Entrepreneurs in Ghana and Development Planning." *The Journal of Development* 6(4): 104.

Hutchful, E. 2002. *Ghana's Adjustment Experience: The Paradox of Reform.* Geneva: UN Research Institute of Social Development.

International Monetary Fund (IMF). 2008. "Foreign Direct Investment Report on Emerging Economies." IMF.

JASPA/ILO. 1989. *From Redeployment to Sustained Employment Generation: Challenges for Ghana's Programme of Economic Recovery and Development.* Addis Ababa: Job and Skills Programme for Africa (JASPA).

KPMG. 2014. "Cutting Through Complexities." Ghana Country Mining Guide.

KPMG. 2015. Doing Business in Ghana, Accra-Ghana.

KPMG cutting through complexity, Transparency Report for Financial Year 2012/2013, http://assets.kpmg.com/content/dam/kpmg/pdf/2016/07/131223KPMG_Ac_Transp_Report_FY12-13.pdf13

Ministry of Education. 1991. *History for Senior Secondary School.* Republic of Ghana: Accra.

Ministry of Education. 2013. Republic of Ghana, http://www.moe.gov.gh/assets/media/socs/FinalEducationSectorReport-2013.pdf

Ministry of Finance. 2016. Review of the Budget and Economic Policy and Supplementary Estimates of Ghana. July 25.

National Population Council. 2011. Ghana Population Stabilization Report, Republic of Ghana Country Strategy Paper 2012–2016, African Development Bank and African Development Fund.

NCCPF. 2011. Policy Brief NAMAs and the Ghana Shared Growth and Development Agenda 2010-2013, http://www.ecn.nl/docs/library/report/2011/o11019.pdf

Obeng-Odoom, F. 2012. "Neoliberalism and the Urban Economy in Ghana: Urban Employment, Inequality, and Poverty." *Growth and Change* 43: 1.

Okudzeto, Eline et al. 2014. Ghana 2014, Africa Economic Outlook AfDB, OECD, UNDP 2014, Ghana 2014 s www.africaneconomicoutlook.org.

PWC. (2015). Ghana 2015 Budget Highlights.

Quartey, J. K. 2006. "Forthcoming Key Determinants of Migration among Health Professionals in Ghana." Sussex DRC Working Paper.

Quatey, Peter, and Gloria Afful Mensah. 2014. "Financial and Monetary Policies in Ghana: A Review of Recent Trends." *Science Direct Review of Development Finance* 4: 115–125. www.sciencedirect.com.

Schiele, H. 2008. "Location, Location: The Geography of Industry Clusters." *Journal of Business Strategy* 29: 29–36.

Schneider, F. 2005. Shadow Economies of 145 Countries All Over the World: What Do We Really Know? Working Paper No. 4. Durham, UK: Durham University.

Smith, P. 1994. "Assessing the Size of the Underground Economy: The Canadian Statistical Perspectives." *Canadian Economic Observer* 7(5): 16–33. Canadian Economic Observer, Cat. No.11-010 Ghana Free Zones Act 1995 Act (504).

Stevenson, J. 2007. *Operations Management* (9th edition). Boston, MA: McGraw-Hill.

Taylor, S. J. 2005. *Asset Price Dynamics, Volatility and Prediction.* Princeton, NJ: Princeton University Press.

The Institute of Statistical, Social and Economic Research (ISSER), the State of the Ghanaian Economy in 2003, p.193.

TUC. 2009. Trade Union Congress, Union of Informal Workers Association, http://www.uniwa.org/?page_id=24

U.S. Department of State. 2015.Investment Climate Statement, June.

World Investment Report. 2014. Investing in the SDGs: An Action Plan, United Nations Conference on Trade and Development.

Yankson, Paul W.K. and Monique Bertrand. 1989. Challenges of Urbanization in Ghana, in The Mobile City of Accra: Urban Families, Housing and Residential Practices, CODESRIA 2012, for Developement of Social Sciences Research in Africa, DAKAR, Senegal, Africa.

CHAPTER 7

Establishing Business in Ghana

7.1 Introduction

Africa has been changing rapidly. It is now closely connected to the international economy. Its transformation has presented attractive opportunities that cannot be neglected or denied. During the last decade, business people, entrepreneurs, multinational businesses, and politicians have been advocating business development in Africa. With its abundant natural resources and its large consumer markets, Africa is a continent ready for investment and business development. Agreeably, it is not all African countries that are suitable for these business ventures. On the contrary, many countries in the sub-Saharan region and of course South Africa provide many business ventures and investment opportunities. Ghana is one of the sub-Saharan countries that is now ready, able, and eager to accommodate foreign and domestic business development. Reports from a variety of sources, that is, IMF, World Bank, Euro Monitor, confirm the fact that Ghana is a shining star just waiting for business ventures to set up shop in its economy. Therefore we must ask specifically an important question on why businesses should invest in Ghana. It can be answered by reviewing the positive business environment that Ghana offers.

J.E. Spillan, D.O. King, *Doing Business In Ghana*,
DOI 10.1007/978-3-319-54771-8_7

7.2 Background

Ghana is a country that manifests a great deal of political stability and has numerous opportunities for future business development and growth. The pro-business reforms that are being implemented by the Ghanaian government strengthen the business climate and set up a platform from which economic expansion can be launched. The existence of trade zones and the favorable laws promoting foreign direct investment (FDI) makes the business environment fertile for establishing a business in Ghana.

Ghana has a market orientation (MO) approach to business development. By creating markets and business space for entrepreneurs to work in, develop their products in, and sell their goods to Ghanaian nationals is a very promising circumstance. Additionally, the ability for businesses to expand their market penetration to other regional areas also offers very promising opportunities for business entrepreneurs.

Ghana offers tax incentives to encourage business investment in most parts of the country. Ghana has a young population which translates into a workforce that in most cases are eager to work and buy goods and services that are home grown and also produced by foreign companies, that is, Joint Ventures and wholly owned enterprises and other business structures. Some of the investment of foreign companies requires the employment of Ghanaian nationals. For example, a wholly owned non-Ghanaian enterprise requires a minimum investment of $300,000 with the commitment to employ 10 Ghanaian workers or more in its operations (Business Monitor International 2015). This is a win–win situation. Both Ghana and the foreign corporation win in this arrangement.

As one reviews the business situation in Ghana, it is clear that Ghana is continuously creating/establishing pro-business reforms. This is good news for the world business community. It demonstrates a major business opportunity in untapped markets. It also offers a path or gateway to other African country markets or other African regional markets. Knowing this gives established business people and entrepreneurs the capability to plan their strategies for establishment of business ventures and for allocation of resources to productive market ventures.

7.3 Investment in New Venture Business: Financial Issues, Financial Markets, Business Start-Up, Financing Alternatives, Exchange Rates, Projecting Cash Flows, and Risk Analysis

A major priority of the Ghanaian government is to attract more foreign investment. It is considered a major part of the government's plan to strengthen the Ghanaian economy. The policies have been established to create and enable investment throughout the country (Business opportunities in Ghana 2013).

One of the important pieces of legislation and policy development was the GIPC or the GIPC Act. This is a global policy that affects all investment throughout Ghana. It affects all business investment except mining, oil, mining, gas, and the free zones. This Act has allowed for easier compliance and adherence to the procedures for investing in Ghana. While there needs to be accepted policies and procedures for investment, there also needs to be sufficient money resources to fund and sustain the investment. In the absence of appropriate and sufficient finances, most investments will collapse and in many cases die (Business opportunities in Ghana 2013).

7.3.1 Financial Issues

Financial System in Ghana: Access to financing remains a major challenge for local companies. Commercial bank rates in some cases are as high as 25%. Overall banking in Ghana is the major financial force. Complementing this well-organized banking structure is the financial services industry, which is well regulated, well capitalized, and profitable. One of the weaknesses of the financial system relates to its internal risk management system. Essentially it has not kept pace with the rapidly growing and changing private sector. Without some reform and attention it will encounter more significant challenges.

Starting a business just about anywhere in the world requires attention to details. Financial details are critically important in any business, and indeed, they are important in Ghanaian businesses. Access to capital is important and crucial to new ventures. It is the one resource that cannot be missing and cannot be taken for granted. To get money in Ghana, a firm must prove that it has a very good idea, a very good business plan, and that the business is sustainable (Revamping Entrepreneurship in Ghana: Insiders Perception, 2014). The risk capital market in Ghana is underdeveloped and most banks avoid lending to risky or untested businesses. As such, start-up funding is a major challenge for Ghanaian start-ups. The primary reason for this scarcity of funding is due to Ghanaian business people's lack of understanding of how businesses operate. Really knowing what a business model means and how business models are funded is critical to any businesses success (Business News 2014). Additionally, there are few real established funding vehicles that are targeted for new ventures. This issue is exacerbated because banks, trade institutions, and other financial entities are not always in full support of new venture business development. This seems to be paradoxical because all the government and literature seems to indicate that Ghana has been promoting FDI constantly over the last few years. One would think that homegrown business ventures are just as important as FDI.

7.3.2 Exchange Rates

Ghana has liberalized its exchange rates so that now it has a floating exchange regime where the BoG can intervene and resolve any short-term fluctuations and augment its reserves. The government has installed a computerized interbank market for foreign exchange. The Foreign Exchange Act does not have any restrictions on payment for goods and services being imported to Ghana. Both residential and nonresidents are allowed to have exchange accounts with local banks (Business Opportunities 2013).

Even though the large banks and private funding entities are not excited about funding new ventures because of the high risk involved, there are organizations that do promote and engage in providing funding for new ventures. Some organizations that exist in Ghana that promote business development and assistance including financial help are:

(a) GROFIN – this is an SME finance/business loan company. This company processes business loans for SMEs. Specializes in financing and supporting small and growing businesses (grofin.com 2016).
(b) Ghana start-up capital fund is an initiative of the TANOE or the African network of entrepreneurs. It is set up to help entrepreneurs build/develop sustainable businesses. Some of its functions are to provide equity investment in entrepreneurial start-up businesses,

establish and financially support skill development, and capacity building centers (www.mensah.ekow.worldpress.com2011/06/Ghana-start-up-capital-fund/).

Funding in Ghana: Looking to fund your business in Ghana: We've got you covered with some helpful tips www.yecommunity.com/en/countries/Ghana/funding.

(a) Ghana start-up funding is a private sector entity, which promotes entrepreneurship and assists by producing revenues for entrepreneurs and provides skill development.
(b) Crowd funding – this is where entrepreneurs using the internet generate small amounts of funding from a large group of people who have money to invest. Some examples of crowd funding are: start some good, farmable, get me fund, Kickstart, indiegogo.
(c) Angel investments – wealthy investors take interest in a start-up and provide funding for this new venture.
(d) DASU capital Ghana limited – as a growth and capital fund manager it provides funds to new ventures. Started in 2009.
(e) GOLD venture capital limited (CVCL-owned by Gold Coast Securities limited and venture capital trust fund).
(f) Ghana growth funding company – a private equity investment firm that provides funding.
(g) Ghana angel investors: list of entrepreneurs and investors.

7.3.3 Risk Analysis

Some of the major or concerning risks that exist while doing business in Ghana are as follows:

Public debt risk: While Ghana seems presently capable of meeting its current debt obligations toward public debt, future risk beyond the present time horizons are possible if the government does not control the fiscal spending situation. Additionally, if there is no long-term investment growth then as the external debt grows the risk gets larger with currency depreciation and it is compounded.

Currency risk: While the present currency situation remains good with the cedi remaining strong, however the large fiscal debt in Ghana puts pressure on the cedi. Additionally, the fluctuation of oil prices put other elements of risk as demand for foreign currency for fuel imports are reduced.

Banking sector risk: With the increased allocation of private sector credit and rising interest rates and the possibility of tightening credit conditions and the slower growth implies that some challenges could lie ahead.

Political risks:: There always exists the possibility that some form of political risk may arise. The wrong candidate for election is presented to the people and because of various issues they elect a candidate that takes the country in the wrong direction or allies the country with other internal or external forces that cause strife and corruption among the elected officials.

Property risks: Property rights are not well protected in Ghana. Corruption exists because no consistent adherence to the rule of law exists.

7.4 Financing Alternatives (Including Microfinance)

7.4.1 Microfinance

The purpose of Microfinance Institution (MFI) is to create organizations that provide and deliver financial services to the poor. Since the poor are generally excluded from the financial services sector, it seems appropriate to develop the microfinance entities as a means of meeting the needs of the poor. A microfinance organization can become part of the formal financial system in order to access the capital markets to lend to people who need financial assistance. The idea of microfinance is not new in Ghana. Generally, it has been housed in the structures of self-help groups or organizations. In Ghana, the microfinance sector has thrived due to different financial policies that have been put in place. The microfiancé entities provide small amounts of funding through a variety of products, which are targeted at low-income people. The products include loans, savings, insurances, and transfer services (Asiama 2007).

Major example of this is the Ghana Microfinance Institution Network. This organization provides the policy structure and support for sustaining the MFI industry in Ghana (Asiama and Osei 2007).

Microfinance has become a leading global strategy for reducing poverty and transforming poor communities into productive communities through economic development, entrepreneurship, and small business development (Asiama and Osei 2007).

7.5 Agencies and Licensing

Smart regulation ensures that standards are met while making compliance easy and accessible to all. Coherent and transparent rules, efficient processes, and adequate allocation of resources are especially important in sectors where safety is at stake. Construction is one of them. In an effort to ensure building safety while keeping compliance costs reasonable, governments around the world have worked on consolidating permitting requirements.

Ensuring formal property rights is fundamental. Effective administration of land is part of that. If formal property transfer is too costly or complicated, formal titles might go informal again. And where property is informal or poorly administered, it has little chance of being accepted as collateral for loans – limiting access to finance (Doing Business Smarter Regulations for SMEs 2013).

Formal registration of companies has many immediate benefits for the companies and for business owners and employees. Legal entities can outlive their founders. Resources are pooled as several shareholders join forces to start a company. Formally registered companies have access to services and institutions from courts to banks as well as to new markets. And their employees can benefit from protections provided by the law. An additional benefit comes with limited liability companies. These limit the financial liability of company owners to their investments, so personal assets of the owners are not put at risk. Where governments make registration easy, more entrepreneurs start businesses in the formal sector, creating more good jobs and generating more revenue for the government.

Regulation of construction is critical to protect the public. As such, it needs to be efficient, in order to avoid excessive constraints on a sector that plays an important part in every economy. Where complying with building regulations is excessively costly in time and money, many builders opt out. In some cases they may pay bribes to pass inspections or simply build illegally, leading to hazardous construction that puts public safety at risk. Where compliance is simple, straightforward, and inexpensive, everyone is better off. This is why licensing and agency regulations are necessary.

7.6 Physical Infrastructure and Supply Chain Management

As mentioned in earlier chapters, Ghana has some important weaknesses in its infrastructure, speed and movement of goods, and tracking and tracing of goods. Overall, however, it is improving and getting better when compared to other countries in the region. The transportation infrastructure needs improvement in order meet the needs of the growing needs of the middle class. Interestingly, most of the transport infrastructure is being sponsored by Chinese Corporations. China will continue to be a major player in the region.

The Ghanaian government continues to look for private partners for financing infrastructure and development of infrastructure improvements.

Because Ghana's infrastructure is at the heart of its ability to move goods, its ability to integrate various regions of the country and to allow for the linkage to transport goods to customers and suppliers, it is imperative that it be improved and upgraded (Apenteng 2013).

A review of some of the major distribution infrastructure will provide a perspective on how Ghana moves its goods and connects suppliers and customers. As mentioned in Chapter 3, infrastructure is a continuing issue that has an impact on the way business is done in Ghana. The following discussion of the various infrastructure sectors provides insight on what the state of the infrastructure is and what entrepreneurs and managers have to think about as they move goods and services around the country and to worldwide markets through the international trade.

Ports: Tema at the capitol and Takoradi to the west.

Ghana has two major ports that allow large quantities of goods be imported to Ghana. Because of the increased activities of these ports, Ghana has had to modernize them and elevate their capabilities to a level that would meet the needs of ships and cargo vessels entering the ports. Tema and Takoradi serve about 90% of the movement of goods. Takoradi generally serves the gas and oil production industries. Tema services Accra, the capital of Ghana while also providing access to land-locked countries of Burkina Faso, Niger, and Mali. Servicing these three countries has significantly increased the traffic through this port. In some cases it has caused large backups of ships waiting in the port. (Africa gearing up, 2013). This has created concerns about pirate attacks and capacity gaps in the facilities at the port.

Fig. 7.1 Photo 1 – Port of Tema – Supply Chain Entry
Source: Author's photo

There are plans in place to resolve the congestion problems. While there are other ports in the region, Ghana's political stability and solid economic growth has made Ghana the gateway to the region.

Figure 7.1 shows the Port of Tema with cargo ships waiting for entry to the port in order to unload goods and load for continued sail to worldwide ports (Fig. 7.2).

This figure shows the cargo/freight in the Port of Tema waiting to be loaded or unloaded and sent to its final destination. Another example of the busy import/export activity that exist in Ghana's Port at Tema, Ghana.

Air transport: Ghana has eight airports and as such has a small transport market. Ghana's major airport market is international with most of the movement inter-Africa or international. While Ghana has encountered serious security and safety issues, the passenger numbers have been increasing significantly (Apenteng 2013).

Rail: Ghana has a poorly serviced and maintained network of rail transportation. The amount of freight transportation is less than 2%. Because of the weakness in rail transport, some sectors of the country's economy are not being developed as ambitiously as they could be, that is,

Fig. 7.2 Photo 2 – Container Ship – Port of Tema – Supply Chain Process
Source: Author's photos, 2010

mining. Repeatedly, there have been plans to upgrade rail transport but essentially nothing has been done (Apenteng 2013).

Roads: Roads are essentially the most important means of transportation in Ghana and most important means of transporting goods. Roads provide transport for 95% of the freight and 98% of the passengers. While roads are the major means of transportation, several problems continue to plague the network of roads. First, is the road condition. Most roads need improvement and upgrading. Second, there needs to be more connecting roads to various parts of the country. This would help both freight and passenger transport. Third, is the congestion. Because of the lace of connectivity and increasing number of vehicles on the road makes urban centers congestion a major issue (Africa gearing up 2013).

7.7 Negotiation Patterns and Partners

Negotiation is a wider concept than bargaining. Negotiation encompasses the processes that take place before the bargaining where the rules are established. Bargaining is more limited in which revisions can be made immediately (Ocran 1985).

The first step of negotiation process is informational gathering or preparation stage. To do business in Ghana or with the people in Ghana, the profile, objective and information provided to them must be clear of and find what they want.

The second step is to build relationship through face-to-face conversation. In this step, the manager has to consider whether the culture is task oriented or relationship oriented. Since Ghana has relationship-oriented culture, building a good relationship before doing business is very important.

The third step of the process is information or data gathering. This step is related to uncertainty avoidance. As mentioned above, Ghana has low uncertainty avoidance culture. Therefore, the people in Ghana require less information and giving too much information can piss them off. The fourth step of the process is persuasion. This step is related to communication. Ghana is a high context culture.

It is important that the negotiator and negotiating team have a good attitude and smile; the seller usually enjoys bartering as much the customer. If you're in a hurry or not prepared to have a bit of a chat with the seller, don't bother; the friendlier you are, the sweeter your bartering experience will be.

Haggling can be frustrating if you aren't familiar with it. Be assured that at the Centre of National Culture also known as the "Arts Centre" in Accra the customer can nearly always begin negotiations at half of the initial quoted price. A good strategy is to ask for the objects "last price." The seller will reduce the first price a bit once you ask – it's your game from that point on. Simple guidelines are to be fair, to consider the value of the object, and to buy from one vendor with a wide variety of goods, if buying more than one item, the shopkeeper will generally agree to a far better price and you're in for a bargain. (How to haggle 2016?).

Most companies are hierarchical and as such, the ultimate decision-making often rests with the CEO.

Decisions are reached slowly. If you try to rush things, you will give offense and risk your business relationship. Getting decisions from government officials can be even more protracted. Intercultural adaptability is essential. Ghanaians have a difficult time disagreeing, so do not assume that things are going well simply because no one is challenging what you say. Avoid showing anger. Controlling your temper is imperative in this culture. Ghanaians often request last-minute concessions at the close of negotiations (Interanational Management Guides 2015).

7.8 Corporate Social Responsibilities

Corporate social responsibility (CSR) is a concern in Ghana and has been incorporated into some of the company's philosophy of business and in day-to-day operations. This idea is not foreign to developing countries. Many of the traditional expectations of businesses are different today than they were decades ago and they are constantly changing. The notion that businesses are set up to just earn a profit, hire people, and pay taxes is not at the essence of business operations in contemporary environments. Companies today are being required to act responsibly and be accountable. Should companies be solely responsible to its shareholders or should its responsibility be much wider or responsible to a larger constituency? In Ghana CSR has been thought about and operationalized since 2001. The Tema Municipal Youth Coalition has been at the forefront of the CSR movement promoting corporate social and environmental responsibility. The CSR movement believes that profit maximization should not be the main goal of a company. The belief is that CSR is an important element that produces more efficient production of products and services. Additionally, CSR has increased the interest in asking the question: what is the proper role of business in society? This question has focused on promoting an increased sensitivity to and an awareness of environmental and ethical issues (Ofori 2010).

Ghanaian managers in many instances seem to understand that supporting the community through social programs is important. Most Ghanaian's appear to have a positive attitude about CSR, which has had an impact on both individual and corporate attitudes toward ethical values. While there are awareness of and practices of CSR in many Ghanaian companies, there is no comprehensive framework for CSR activities in Ghana. Moreover, there is no institutional organization that can monitor or regulate CSR activities such as reporting among corporations. CSR is necessary in Ghana because it is not possible for government alone to address all of the diverse needs that exist in the society (Ofori 2010).

7.9 Making a Choice

Business is all about decision-making. If a manager or owner or investor has the correct information and is in the right place, then making a choice is relatively easy. The unfortunate element of decision-making is that information, events, and environments change. Strategic thinking along with practical thinking are important dimensions when deciding whether to invest in a foreign environment. No matter what the situation is and no matter how much information one has, everything can change in a moment's notice and therefore one needs to have contingency or back up plans ready to implement if for whatever reason the initial plan cannot workout. History and experience has demonstrated quite clearly that there are real risks in entering any business. This is especially true in Ghana. While Ghana has a stable, fertile, and ready environment for business development, one has to be alert to the cultural dimensions that become intervening variables. Proper planning, organizing, and controlling will be critical elements for one to make a suitable choice. Being prepared for the positive and the negative consequences is an important dimension of making a choice. Nothing is guaranteed. It requires both hard work and smart work to survive in the Ghanaian business environment.

7.10 Setting Up a Business in Ghana

The government of Ghana has demonstrated a strong commitment to adopting proactive economic policies and initiatives with the aim of creating an environment conducive for doing business in Ghana (GIPC 2013). According to the World Bank Group survey on doing Business 2015 on sub-Saharan Africa, Ghana is a good environment for start-up businesses. Some of the issues to consider when setting up a business in Ghana can be seen below.

7.10.1 Domestic Legal Issues

There are certain domestic laws in Ghana that regulate the establishment of businesses in accordance with constitutional provisions. These laws include the following: The Companies Code, 1963 (Act 179), The Incorporated Private Partnership Act, 1962 (Act 152), and The Business Name Act, 1962 (Act 151).

An investor is able to conduct a resident business entity as a limited liability company (local company). The local company by shares can incorporate under the companies Act, 1963 (Act 179). A foreign investor has an equal privilege to partly or completely own a resident business entity in Ghana. A nonresident business entity – a business entity from outside the country which has its representative in Ghana only – has to submit required registration documents to the Registrar General's Department (RGD) for registration to be effected in the Register of External Companies. The agency responsible by law for the registration of all forms of company is the RGD (GIPC 2013).

7.10.2 Company Registration

An investor – Ghanaian or foreign – must obtain the legal permit to operate any manner of business activity in Ghana. The form of legal permit required depends on the kind of business an investor wishes to do, resident or foreign. The following are the registration processes an investor has to go through.

Resident Businesses, Entity Registration Requirement
The registration of a resident business entity involves the filing of proper documents of the company with the RGD, in order to obtain certificates of incorporation and start a business. The registration documentation requires the following information:

a. Company name;
b. Nature of the business operations of the company;
c. The first Directors (at least two), one of whom should be present in Ghana at all times;
d. Number of shares with which the company should be registered (shares of no par value);
e. Name and address of auditor;
f. Address of registered office and principal place of business;
g. Authorized number of shares; stated capital; issued shares; and
h. Name and address of subscribers/shareholders; and company secretary.

Foreign Company Registrations
A nonresident company (branch) is a corporate entity established outside Ghana but which has a representative and place of business in Ghana. Registration information and documents required for registering a non-resident company are as follows:

a. Name of company (name of head office entity)
b. Nature of business operations

c. Name and details of local manager
d. Authorized capital (for head office); issued capital (for head office)
e. Address of principal place of business in Ghana
f. Address of registered office in country of incorporation
g. Name and address of process agent
h. Memorandum and articles of association of the head office duly notarized by a notary public in the country of registration
i. A power of attorney executed in favor of the local manager, which must be notarized as well
j. Certificate of incorporation of the head office

7.10.3 Tax Identification Numbers

All the directors and the secretary of incorporated entities or the local managers of branches are required to register for tax identification number (TIN) prior to the registration of the company.

7.10.4 Legal/Regulatory Agencies for Registration

Aside from the registration of business organizations with the RGD, businesses are also expected to be registered with other regulatory agencies. This will be dependent on the industry under which the company will operate within Ghana. Such legally mandated agencies include the RGD, GIPC, Ghana Immigration Service (GIS), Ghana Revenue Authority (GRA), Environmental Protection Agency, Ghana Free Zones Board (GFZB), Petroleum Commission (PC), and MC.

7.10.5 Processes Involved in Business Registration

The most paramount action of an investor with an intention to set up a business in Ghana is to register with the RGD. The charge for registration is 0.5% of the company's stated business capital. The official processing period is between three and five days; the company then receives the certificate for the commencement of business operations.

Aside from certification and incorporation, business entities that have partial or complete ownership by non-Ghanaian should further register with the GIPC. Companies complete their registration procedures when the minimum equity requirements have been fully exhausted based on the following structure: the equity requirement can be sent to Ghana either by cash or kind (goods, plant and machines, vehicles, or other tangible assets). Cash can be transferred into the account of the incorporated business entity at a Ghanaian commercial bank. The bank should ensure a confirmation of transfer to the BoG, which later transmits information to GIPC. Equity in kind, in terms of documents such as bills of lading, invoices, and others, which have received confirmation by the Customs Division of GRA, should be delivered to the GIPC.

7.10.6 Ghana Investment Promotion Centre (GIPC)

The GIPC is a constitutionally mandated body under the GIPC Act charged with the responsibility to ensure the creation of an environment conducive to business and to regulate all business activities of local and nonresident investments in Ghana. GIPC regulates all business entities of all sectors of the economy with the exception of investments in the mining and petroleum sectors, which obtain licenses of operation from the MC and the Ministry of Mines and Energy. However, the GFZB and GSE are charged with overseeing the regulation of the activities of the EPZ and portfolio investments. The minimum capital required for an entity under the Act of GIPC is described below.

The capital requirement for a joint venture with a Ghanaian citizen is US$ 200,000 (in cash or tangible assets) as a contribution by the foreign partner. A Ghanaian citizen, the partner counterpart, shall contribute not less than 10% as a share in the joint venture. An enterprise that is completely owned by a foreign investor requires equity capital of US$ 500,000, either in cash or fixed assets (capital goods). An industry, which either partly or fully claims its ownership from a foreign investor, requires US$ 1,000,000 in either cash or fixed assets (capital goods). The minimum capital requirements vary for certain companies in other sectors. Some require Ghc 500 (approximately US$ 208) for private entities and Ghc 2,000 (approximately US $ 833) for public entities. It must be stressed that all these companies are made to make the payment of the GIPC capital requirement. A foreign business entity is exempted from foreign equity capital (PWC 2013).

7.10.7 GFZB and Act

The GFZB is the regulatory body charged with the responsibility to address issues regarding registration and licensing of companies that want to operate as free zone entities. Business entities that do not operate in mining, petroleum, and timber have to get permit for operations from GFZB to carry out activities as a free zone. Meeting the requirements for qualification as a free zone, an investor should be able to at least export 70% of its total goods or services (products) to a foreign country. The company gets the permit to operate as a free zone after the entity has fulfilled all registrations with the relevant authorities such as GRA, GIPC, etc. The Free Zone Act is applied by the GFZB in giving permits to investors not only to operate but also to enjoy a ten-year tax exemption, after which the entity will be required to pay corporate tax at the highest rate of 8% of its taxable profits. The GIPC monitors all investments in Ghana; however, the Free Zone Act regulates business entities that export 70% of their goods and services after being registered as free zone companies.

Minerals Commission

The Minerals Commission (MC) is a government regulatory body founded under the 1992 Constitution, as well as from the Mineral Commission Act of 1993 (Act 450), for the minerals sector. The MC regulates, manages, and implements measures regarding the use of the mineral resources in Ghana. The commission ensures industry players' full compliance with mineral and mining laws. All minerals and mining industry investors are expected to register with the RGD before obtaining a license of operation in the minerals sector from the MC. The registration permits industry investors some privileges, such as exemption from import duties, as well as filling a quota of foreign investors entitled to visas to work as foreign staff.

Environmental Protection Agency

This is a legally established body charged with the responsibility of issuing licenses to investors to operate in environmentally sensitive areas in the country. Industries operating in the country are expected to prepare and submit environmental impact assessment reports.

Petroleum Commission

All industry players in the upstream oil and gas sector are expected to register with the PC and honor the payment of required registration fees. The commission gives recommendations to the Minister of Energy sector on national policies connected to petroleum activities. Apart from performing certain roles such as monitoring, supervising, inspecting, and auditing all petroleum activities, the commission also receives applications and issues licenses for specific business operations in the petroleum field as stated by petroleum laws and regulations. Furthermore, the commission promotes local content and Ghanaian participation in the petroleum operations as demonstrated by the Petroleum Exploration and Production Law of 1984 (PNDCL 84), as well as other laws and regulations to ensure national development.

Ghana National Petroleum Corporation (GNPC)

This was founded by the GNPC Act of 1983 (PNDCL 64). The GNPC, a state-owned enterprise, is a legally mandated body endowed with the responsibility of exploring, developing, producing, and disposing of petroleum. The PNPC 84 forms the regulatory framework for governing the contractual agreements between the state, the PNPC, and the entities concerned in upstream petroleum activities. The GNPC was founded with the following aims: speeding up and promoting activities that explore petroleum and ensure an immediate discovery of large quantities of petroleum for production: appraising the existing petroleum discoveries to ensure that the production supply meets national demands; and ensuring that Ghana gets the maximum benefits from the development of its petroleum resources. In addition to the training and development of human capacity in the field of petroleum, the corporation also exists to make sure that modern technology is available for operations in the petroleum industry. Last but not least, the corporation oversees all petroleum operations to make sure they are done in a proper manner to prevent any negative effects on the environment and resources.

Ghana Revenue Authority

The administration of all tax laws falls under the agency of the GRA; however, revenue collection is conducted under the auspices of the IRS, the value-added tax service, and the customs Exercise and Preventive Service. These bodies conduct their functions as independent agencies with a Revenue Governing Board monitoring and supervising their operations. Recently, these tax-collecting agencies have been fused together into one mandated body known as the GRA. There are three divisions in the GRA. They are Domestic Tax Revenue Division, the Customs Division, and the Support Division. The responsibility of collecting customs and excise duties rests with the Customs Division, while the Domestic Tax Revenue Division is responsible for the collection of income tax, value-added tax, and national insurance levies. The GRA runs all internal operations, such as finance and administration, legal, and human resources. The Commissioner-General receives reports from each of the three divisional heads, who are also Commissioners managing the affairs of each division.

Ghana Immigration Service (GIS)
A legally mandated body, the GIS, issues work and residence permits. The body is in charge of reentry visas and the extension of visitors' permits, as well as providing arrival visas for visitors to Ghana who are in a situation where a Ghanaian Embassy or consulate is absent abroad.

Visitor's Permit
When foreign visitors fulfill all the necessary entry visa requirements, they may be given visitors' permits to enter and temporarily stay in Ghana for a period not exceeding two months (or 60 days), or three months (or 90 days) for ECOWAS nationals. A visitor's permit for residence is granted based on the condition that the visitor concerned will not engage in any profession or occupation except the one specified in the permit of residence, for reward.

Entry visas are issued from Ghana's diplomatic missions abroad. The application documents and timelines are dependent upon the requirements of the missions concerned. In the case of an applicant from a country where Ghana has no mission or consulate, emergency visas may be issued via immediate application to the Director of Immigration upon arrival in Ghana. This visa is issued in the form of a letter, and a copy is forwarded to the visitors to enable them to travel from their country. This visa is then endorsed to demonstrate authentication on arrival in the visitor's passport.

National Communication Authority
This agency registers investments, which deal in importing telecommunication equipment, such as servers, cellular phones, fax machines, cordless phones, and radio equipment.

Social Security and National Insurance Trust
Every employer is required by law to register with Social Security and National Insurance Trust and make social security for its employees.

Importance of the Framework
A framework that regulates the registration processes of all businesses currently exists. All necessary requirements for business registration are clearly specified in the framework to ensure easy and smooth incorporation.

Challenges of the Framework
The system has a lot of bottlenecks relating to registration and they include the following:

Unnecessary Bureaucracies and Delays
Bureaucracy causes too many delays in the system. A situation in which a foreign investor has to register at least twice, first with the Registrar General, and then again with the GIPC before obtaining licenses for operation as specified by the Acts, delays the process of doing business. Often, this registration is followed by registration with another agency related to the mining or agriculture sectors, causing further delays. This process may be too long, bureaucratic, and cumbersome for investors.

Bribery and Corruption
As a result of unnecessary delays, the system may breed corruption since resident and foreign investors may have to pay their way, through in cash or kind or both, in order to receive quicker services from the RGD, thus breeding corruption.

Over Centralization of the Framework
The process is too centralized. Investors in Ghana have their applications sent to Accra before approval licenses for operation are issued, causing bottlenecks and delayed results. There are no mechanisms that allow investors to register their businesses and pay the required fees of incorporation online, in the comfort of their homes; instead they must essentially queue up at the premises of, or otherwise directly contact, the RGD.

Inadequate Equipment, Logistics, and Infrastructure

Modern equipment/logistics and infrastructure is lacking and inadequate to effectively and efficiently carry out the registration process. The RGD does not have the infrastructure, logistics, and equipment throughout various regional and district capitals that would be required to bring the registration process to the investors' doorsteps.

Illiteracy

Most Ghanaian investors are technologically illiterate and do not have the necessary technical expertise in the use of computers and internet. Therefore, registering their companies online may be difficult.

Checking Illegal Businesses

The system lacks mechanisms for checking on businesses to ensure that they operate within the parameters for which their licenses were issued. Most businesses operate illegally outside the parameters they have been licensed to undertake. Sometimes the information that investors provide regarding the location and address of businesses is falsified and the system are unable to recognize fraud.

Registrar General Department and Internal Revenue Services

The system used by the RGD has insufficient links with the IRS for reporting all activities, dates of commencement, and due dates for paying the taxes. Getting a TIN from the RGD is difficult, making business registration very cumbersome.

Suggestions for the Registration Framework

- State-of-the-art modern technology should be introduced into the registration process. This involves the use of computers and other logistics that will facilitate online registration.
- Human resource capacity building should be encouraged to give the system a new image.
- A high-quality database system for online registration should be introduced. This centralized database system should be able to receive applications and connect all registrations to the required agency responsible for specific process.

- There should be provision for several outlets of the RGD in the regional and district capitals so that investors in the hinterlands of the country can have smooth and quick access.

7.11 Discussion

Anyone interested in doing business in Ghana needs to be fully aware of the pitfalls that exist and the unexpected issues that are always below the surface. Yes, being prepared is an absolute necessity. One can be prepared by doing the proper market research, the proper business plan development, and a good analysis of the culture and how it impacts the development and managing of a business in Ghana. The first two elements, market research and business plan development, are generally routine. However, the cultural analysis can be tricky, complicated but fun. It is one analysis that many companies entering a foreign market fail to do. As such, knowing how to analyze the culture is an important skill that a manager entering Ghana must know. Culture is a critical factor that can make or break the business. So having all the information about the business environment without the understanding of the culture is problematic. Doing a solid analysis of the culture, its impact on the business, and how it can constrain or promote the business is a need to know.

Finding a Ghanaian partner who has a good sense of what is happening in the country and how business is conducted is a viable path to business development and success in Ghana. There are partners who are willing to collaborate and initiate the synergy necessary to get a business going and sustained. The key to this path is offering some incentive to the Ghanaian partner. The "what is in it for me" concept is very important in this environment and a critical dimension for luring a partner to join the business.

Developing a business is hard work, so the incentive needs to be substantive and appropriate to the situation.

Because Ghana is such a stable environment with lots of people who are eager to become entrepreneurs, the chances of business development are many. The critical element once the business is going is making it sustainable. That is much more difficult because it means constant creative ideas that will outmaneuver the competition and offer the consuming public products and services that the need and want. Having a Ghanaian partner who is acutely aware of the Ghanaian culture and the Ghanaian consumer needs is key to making the business venture a reality and a success.

Finally, starting a business in Ghana requires a level of patience, persistence, and smart work. Those who stay with the process and have the business competencies (i.e., management, finance, and marketing) necessary to successfully operate a business will eventually achieve its goals. Those of faint of heart will fall by the way side and eventually fad away.

7.12 Conclusion

Ghana has lots of business opportunities. Having the opportunities and actually doing business in Ghana are two different things. The opportunities are available to anyone who is interested. The ability to develop and sustain a business in Ghana takes a lot of energy, skill, and constant flow of creative ideas. While the economy and the general economy is a market-oriented business environment, it is the subtle business attributes that are not evident at first glance nor after a short time in business. Many business people who enter and set up business many time say "I did not realize __________." As such, future business owners, entrepreneurs, or collaborators in Ghana need to have a thorough understanding of what they are actually getting involved in before they make the venture.

Yes, there are unknowns but the ability to reduce the number of unknowns will make the business more prosperous and life easier. Is Ghana a place to establish a business, I would say yes. This yes is contingent on the idea that the entrepreneur has a full knowledge of what he/she is getting into and has analyzed and planned the successful exit strategy if things begin to go wrong. Almost all entrepreneurial ventures are risky no matter where they may be. As such, studying and preparing for all eventualities are the best path to being successful in the Ghanaian business environment.

References

Africa Gearing Up. 2013. "Future Prospects in Africa for the Transportation & Logistics Industry." Price, Waterhouse, Cooper(PWC), pp. 1–89, http://www.pwc.com/gx/en/industries/transportationlogistics/publications/africa-infrastructure-investment/africa-infrastructure-report.html

Apenteng, Magdalene. 2013. "Voice of the Market." *World Finance*. http://www.Worldfinance.com/inward-investment/middle-east-and-africa/ghana.steps-up-infrastructure-investment-programme, accessed 2/24/16.

Asiama, Johnson, P., and Victor Osei. 2007."MicroFinance in Ghana: An Overview." Research Department Bank of Ghana and Research Department, Bank of Ghana. http://www.economicswebinstitute.org/essays/microfinance ghana.htm.

Business Monitor International Ltd. 2015. www.buisnessmonitor.com.

Business News. 2014. http://www.Ghana.web.com/Ghana,%20homepage/business/addressing-Ghanas-startup-funding-challenges-32580.

Business Opportunities in Ghana. 2013. U.S. and Foreign Commercial Service Aid U.S. Department of State.

Doing Business Smarter Regulations for SMEs, 2013. 10th edition, The International Bank for Reconstruction and Development/The World Bank 1818 H Street NW, Washington, DC 20433Telephone: 202-473-1000; Internet: www.worldbank.org

Ghana Investment Promotion Centre. 2013. http://gipcghana.com/pres-and-media/downloads/category/11-2013.html

Gofin. 2016. www.grofin.com. "How to Haggle and Barter." Ghanaian Style. http://www.timeout.com/accra/shopping/how-to-get-the-right-price-haggling-and-bartering-ghanaian-style.

Interanational Management Guides. 2015. Ghana Management Guide, Intercultural Management-Being a manager in Ghana, Commisceo Global (CG). Http://www.commisceo-global.com/management-guides/ghanamanagement-guide.

Nunoo, Isaac (2014). "Revamping Entrepreneurship in Ghana: Insiders Perception" https://www.modernghana.com/news/549385/1/revamping-entrepreneurship-in-ghana-the-pe.html

Ocran, T.M. 1985. "The Process and Outcome of Negotiations with Multinational Corporations: A Conceptual Framework for Analysis." *Akron Law Review* 18(3): 406–434.

Ofori, Daniel 2010. "Executive and Managerial Attitudes on Social Responsibility and Ethics in Ghana: Some Initial and Exploratory Insights." *Global Partnership Management Journal* 1(1–2): 14–21.

Price Waterhouse Cooper(PWC). 2013. Ghana Banking Survey-harnessing the SME potential, https://www.scribd.com/document/287708166/Ghana-Banking-Survey-2013-PWc

CHAPTER 8

Commercialization

The Marketing Process

8.1 Introduction

One of the major problems of low-income countries is scarcity of products and services. Identifying the goods and services that people want and need, many times, is a major challenge. One of the main reasons for such shortages is because companies cannot make the profit levels they need to achieve company goals. This problem exists because of several major issues:

a. Low per-capita income among the country's citizens,
b. High inflation,
c. Major income distribution inequality,
d. Increased taxation on imported goods,
e. Fragmented communication and distribution channels,
f. Inadequate distribution and logistics infrastructure (Keegan 2014).

Even though these obstacles exist, there are still many marketing opportunities available for those companies that competently research the opportunities and strategically enter viable markets in these lesser-developed countries. These markets, if managed properly, can be profit centers and opportunities for innovation. Because emerging market consumers have different needs and requirements that

J.E. Spillan, D.O. King, *Doing Business In Ghana*,
DOI 10.1007/978-3-319-54771-8_8

necessitate companies to adapt products and services to fit the consumer needs, using appropriate marketing communication techniques can help marketers to expand these new adaptions. These techniques can provide an effective means of getting consumers to accept products and services that are beneficial to their needs. Marketers in emerging markets and lesser-developed countries must think about the following principles when entering and sustaining a business in these countries:

a. Affordability – since per-capita income is so low, present products and services that are affordable yet meet the quality and effectiveness standards must be provided.
b. Accessibility – making products and services available where low-income customers live and when they are available. This approach gives the marketer the chance to put the products in reach of the customer.
c. Availability – the low-income people shop when they have cash. Marketers who make products and services available can take advantage of different locations where the low-income consumers reside (Keegan 2014).

8.2 Background

Despite the recent slowdown, the outlook for Ghana's economy is bright. Ghana's economy is well diversified, with several sectors contributing to the country's GDP.

Ghana will continue to be one of the largest producers of gold in the world. Presently, gold can explain more than 40% of its exports. Additionally, the country's oil resources will power the economy since other commodities are not as "in demand" as oil. Ever since the unearthing of precious hydrocarbon in 2007, oil income has influenced, to a greater degree, Ghana's economic prosperity. As such, it has made Ghana a net oil exporter. It is estimated that Ghana's production of oil will rise to 200,000 barrels a day by 2019. Again, the country started gas commercialization in 2015. Ghana Gas runs the Sinopec Petroleum facility, built by China. Understanding its very recent start, a robust growth potential is anticipated. Although prices for gold, oil, and gas have shown recent declines and are projected to remain at a lower level than they have in recent years, these commodities will still be amongst the main drivers of Ghana.

Ghana's agricultural sector has caused GDP to decline between the years of 2008 to 2013. This is a loss of almost 10% of its share of the economy. Nevertheless, agriculture will continue to be a major pillar of the country's economy as well as the main sector of employment. Cocoa is the primary agricultural product, with Ghana earning the title of second largest cocoa grower in the world.

Trade has been, and is, a significant cause for Ghana's economic growth. Since Ghana is a member of the ECOWAS and AEC, it is well connected to trading partners. Furthermore, the government's eliminating or reducing import quotas, tariffs, and requirements over the past 20 years has provided the fuel for increased economic growth. Overall, Ghanaian trade increased from US$17.4 billion in 2010 to US$29.3 billion in 2013. This constituted a growth rate of 19.0% (CAGR) (Africa Asset Management 2020).

In 2013, the major trading partner of Ghana was the EU (30.5%), followed by China (18.1%). However, intra-African trade is very important as well. The list of Ghana's top ten trading partners includes Nigeria (8.6%), Ivory Coast (4.7%), and South Africa (3.3%). In May 2013 the GSE introduced the Ghana Alternative Market (GAX) to allow SMEs with potential for growth to access funds (Africa Asset Management 2020).

Ghana's initial oil discovery occurred in 2007. The IMF estimates that commercial oil production of Ghanaian oil could generate US$1 bn per year once it attains full capacity. The consequence of this situation allowed the Ghanaian government to introduce the Petroleum Revenue Management Act in 2001. This Act created the Ghana Petroleum Funds. The fund is made up of two financial statements having different economic purposes. The one account is termed the Ghana Stabilization Fund (GSF), which operates as a fiscal buffer for shortfalls in public expenditure. The second account is entitled the Ghana Heritage Fund. This account is used to collect savings for the next generation. Both of these accounts were formally established with combined seed capital of US $69.2 million in November 2011. The BoG manages these funds and provides quarterly reports to the Ministry of Finance and Economic Planning. The rules governing these funds say that no money can be drawn from the GSF until 2026. At that time, only the accrued interest can be withdrawn. In spite of this, a worsening economic situation is presently placing the funds under political pressure. As such, the government may need to revise its revenue allocation policies (Africa Asset Management 2020).

Investors view Ghana as the most promising entry to West Africa. The country's political stability, economic liberalism, natural resources, and diverse economy contribute to its attractiveness. When compared to its African neighboring countries, Ghana provides a less constraining business environment and better macroeconomic policies. FDI flourished in past years. As a consequence, Ghana has become the center for FDI in West Africa. Ghana's positive economic outlook and diversified economic sectors will make the country an attractive place for investors. This circumstance will provide plenty of investment opportunities.

Ghana has a mature financial sector, stable democracy, and strong legal framework, all ingredients for strong growth of its fund industry. The total Assets under Management (AUM) amount has increased steadily. While it showed a slight drop, it was followed by a sizable recovery after the global financial crisis. While the largest proportion of AUM is managed for institutional investors, there are 40,000 retail investors. This suggests that as Ghana's economy grows, the retail fund sector will begin to accelerate. It is forecast that AUM will reach 0.92 bn by 2020 (Africa Asset Management 2020).

8.2.1 The Marketing Management Function in Ghana

Marketing is a key business function. It is this activity that is responsible for satisfying the customer and keeping the rest of the organizational network informed about the customer so that superior value is delivered. Companies make long-term assurances to customers in order to maintain their relationship. They accomplish this task by offering and giving quality products, service, and innovation. Accordingly, implementing a MO strategy has become a criterion for success and profitability.

Academics and practitioners in a similar way have broadly noted that a market-oriented corporate strategy has been fundamental to achieving superior company performance. As such, MO in both manufacturing and service industries has attracted significant interest in the marketing literature (Kohli and Jaworski 1990; Han et al. 1998). The MO approach represents the implementation of the marketing concept and embodies a firm's predisposition toward delivering superior value to its customers on a continuous basis (Slater and Narver 1994). Essentially, MO denotes an organization-wide generation of market intelligence through Decision

Support Systems, Marketing Information Systems, and marketing research efforts. It focuses on the dissemination of the intelligence across company departments, and promotes the organization-wide responsiveness to the changes taking place in the firm's environment (Kohli and Jaworski 1990).

As has been seen in the study of globalization, country cultures are different, consumers' desires are constantly changing, and new approaches are needed to satisfy the consumers' needs. One way to achieve a competitive edge in the global market is by developing a marketing strategy that consistently provides the consumer with a high-quality product and service satisfaction. Studying the MO of companies can help marketers develop insights into what is needed to satisfy the consumer in their diverse markets (Fig. 8.1).

Retail outlets with well-established marketing plans have been and are still functioning well in Ghana. This large store in Tema, Ghana provides a popular outlet for customers who are not interested in buying their goods at the informal market (Fig. 8.2).

Another view of the informal market from a less active side. Cars, taxis, and trucks are constantly moving around with people and goods, coming and going. This is the life of many marketers in Ghana.

Fig. 8.1 Mass market in central part of Ghanaian city

Source: Author's photo

Fig. 8.2 This is an example of a major section of the Central Open Informal Market

Source: Author's photo

8.3 Market Research

Marketing research aims at taking some of the risks out of marketing decisions by providing information that can form part or the entire basis of decision-making. It is applicable to all aspects of marketing-mix decisions and should be an integral part of the process of formulating marketing strategy (Earley, 2013) Gathering the right information necessary for analyzing the foreign markets may in some instances be a tedious task.

After evaluating and analyzing the foreign market and deciding which country is the new potential market, the decision of the product or service value is considered. The next step is to decide what entry modes will be suitable in this process. It is also an important aspect in the market evaluation process. The promotion and communication stage is vital to the organizations marketing strategy. In order to effectively execute these stages, managers need data and information to make decisions. This requires market intelligence. The role of market intelligence is to reduce the level of risk in decision-making. Though with market intelligence, the seller finds out what the customer needs and wants. Marketing research provides the insight into knowing what products are right for the market, which channels of distribution are most appropriate, how best to promote products, and what prices are acceptable to the market (Richardson 2015; Ammattikorkeakoulu and Yrkeshogskola 2009).

8.4 Where Are the Markets?

The Ghanaian retail sector managers have used a split market-oriented strategy. One segment is located at the Makola and Agbogloshi market places. One sees a lower end market segment existing in these locations. On the other end of the spectrum is the Accra Mall, which is considered a high-end market segment. The mid segment at this point seems to be unexplored. A firm that enters this retail segment will be driving the market segment rather than being driven by it. This segment is an important segment to explore because it is composed of middle-income customers who purchase profit-oriented products and services (Kuada and Hinson 2014).

Ghana has become a large market for dumped products from Europe and China. This has caused factory closures, unemployment, and poverty to expand. Ghanaians prefer imported products for a variety of reasons. Essentially, they have little interest in local goods. Such issues as product quality, price, and product availability are reasons for Ghanaian's preferring foreign goods. There is a belief that locally manufactured goods are inferior in quality and of higher price to foreign goods. Effective marketing management is essential in the process of building up a favorable image for any product. The absence of consumer orientation on the part of the producers has forced consumers to look for other alternatives. Ghanaian producers have to improve quality of goods and services they produce and offer. They need to attend to marketing in order to attract customers. Ghanaians have to change their attitudes toward local goods and support the industry by patronizing local goods (Addressing the Consumer Preferences 2013)

The influx of mobile phone has enhanced access across the world. The ability to communicate is more easily facilitated, because practically everybody needs a phone call, email, or tweet away. The virtual world is one full of opportunities, which might not be easily accessible in real life. The penetration of mobile in Africa has been on the rise, largely from the use of feature phones. Now smartphones are becoming more predominant. In fact, it is predicted that mobile data traffic is expected to have a 20-fold increase by 2019.

The 50% increase in mobile use across business and leisure travelers makes businesses like Jovago.com accessible across mobile platforms and browsers, easing the process of purchase for customers across continents (Gaitho 2015).

8.5 Regional Differences

Infrastructure deficiencies, including inadequate agri-business technology development infrastructure, weak capacities and skills shortages, productivity constraints, managing economic policy in a globalized economy, and weaknesses in the fiscal stances constitute the key challenges Ghana still faces in its development trajectory. Despite this, there are strengths and opportunities, which can be exploited toward placing the economy on a green growth path with increased jobs creation. These include its rich endowment of agricultural, oil, and mineral resources, recently improving confidence, deepening domestic and regional markets, taping the potential of the manufacturing sector and of remittances, getting the most of foreign aid, and maximizing the benefits from increased engagements with the major emerging economies of the BRICS. The Bank Group has traditionally played a key role in supporting Ghana's development efforts, and the current promising developments in the country offer an opportunity to continue this productive partnership.

8.5.1 Regional Integration and Trade

Ghana is an active member of key regional integration arrangements in West Africa and in the continent, including the AU, the ECOWAS, and the West African Monetary has reemphasized the country's objective to accelerate economic integration. Ghana also maintains a relatively open trade regime with the rest of the world. Its most favored nation Tariff Restrictiveness Index is 9%, below both the sub-Saharan African and low-income country group average of 11.3 and 11.6%, respectively. Ghana initiated an interim Economic Partnership Agreement with the EU at the end of 2007 but has not yet signed the agreement. Ghana maintains good relations with its traditional trading partners and donors especially the US and the UK, both of which have a large

Ghanaian diaspora. In addition, Ghana has good relations with many emerging countries, backed by funding for various projects (Republic of Ghana Country Strategy 2012).

With this in mind, it is well understood that Ghana has a fast growing consumer market. Local businesses and MNCs cannot afford to overlook the marketing opportunities that exist in Ghana. Both in the formal and the informal market, we find consumer needs in constant need of satisfaction. Goods and services, especially consumables, are necessary to keep the society healthy, moving, and sustainable. Regional differences do exist. The people who live in the Northern region have different cultural orientation and thus have some differences in the types of goods and services they desire. People who live in the Ashanti, Eastern, and Central regions seem to connect more with many Western styles and offerings. This appears to originate from the constant movement of goods that exist because of the large seaports and the international airport. The strong linkage to the Western countries is easily accessible and hence presents goods that may not be strongly desired by the consumers in the Northern regions (Fig. 8.3).

8.6 Other Marketing Information Needed to Do Business in Ghana

Marketing products and services require more than just getting close to the customer. It requires anticipating the customer's future needs and understanding the market so that the marketer can construct and reconstruct the value propositions that are attractive to the customer. Making marketing strategies and approaches attractive to customers is a critically important aspect of marketing in Ghana (Kuada and Hinson 2014).

Many times the customer does not have the exact information a marketer really needs to satisfy their desires. The customer lacks the imagination for product changes and thus do not have the proper information that would give the marketer sufficient motivation to create a product that would uniquely meet the customer's needs (Kuada and Hinson 2014).

When marketers think beyond the customers' immediate needs, they can create new markets that offer alternative value to customers. Much of this action is called value innovation that offers the customer, in many cases, a value proposition they cannot refuse (Kuada and Hinson 2014).

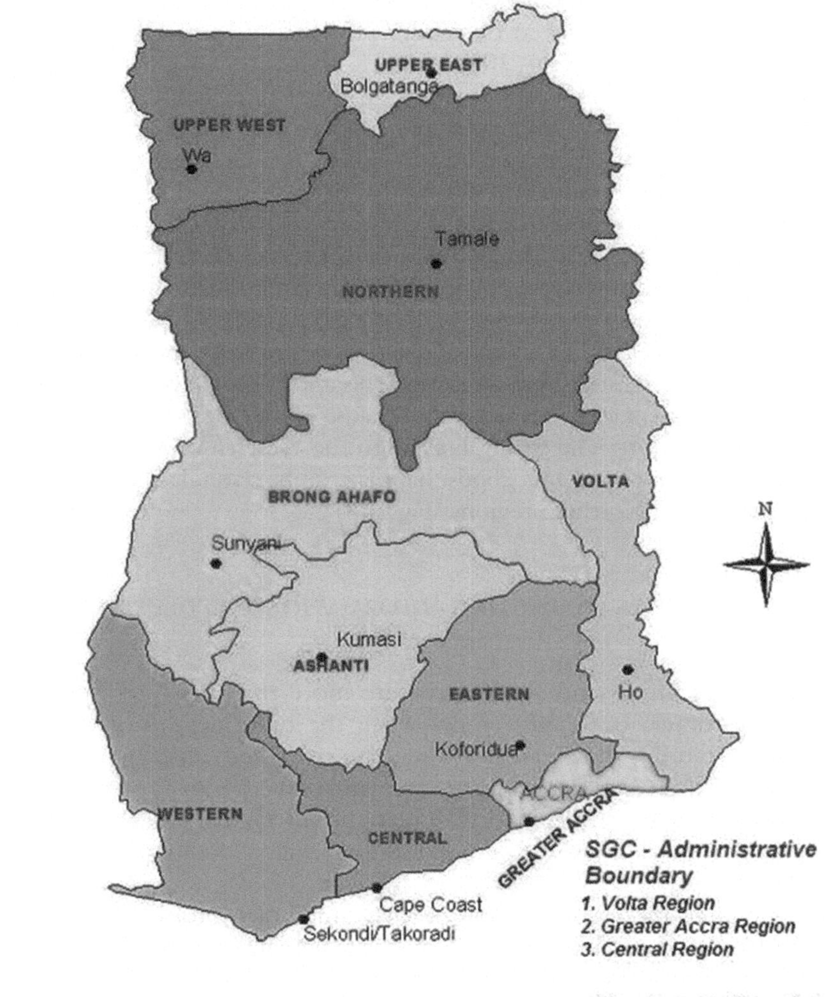

Fig. 8.3 Map of Ghana. The regional sectors of Ghana

Source: http://www.ghanaembassy.ru/about-ghana/regions-in-ghana2016

8.6.1 Ghana's Customer-Oriented Business Culture

The orientation toward customers' means that the employee of the firm, company, or business creates an environment where the customer is the primary focus. This type of culture is not always present in Ghana. The present business culture that exists in Ghana becomes an obstacle to an effective execution of market-oriented behavior. Ghanaians have to change the culture on non-MO to a MO. This turnaround takes education and training among business owners, managers, and their employees (Kuada and Hinson 2014).

Some of the most popular irritations that Ghanaian customers have encountered in their shopping and buying activities:

a. Employees failing to show up to appointments;
b. Poorly informed employees do not have good answers to customer questions;
c. Employees on personal phone calls while customers wait to be served;
d. Talking down to customers;
e. Robotics.

All of the items presented above have major impact on whether Ghanaian business people effectively and efficiently implement marketing strategies. Knowing upfront that they affect business operations, marketing, and selling activities give managers the chance to address these disruptions/distractions before they negatively affect the marketing of goods and services (Kuada and Hinson 2014: 44).

Ghanaian culture has changed significantly over the years. Some of the changes that are now appearing in the customer orientation approaches in the market place are:

a. Tendency of Ghanaians to accept an individualistic and opportunistic attitude
b. Disregard for collective rules and codes of conduct as being the norm.

Successful Ghanaian service providers are those that create something new and at the same time respond effectively to the declared needs of their customers. To develop marketing strategy in this particular case study also involves an analysis of other potential competitors and the potential target group. Other relevant determinants like trade barriers, price localization, local expertise, and export and import subsidies will not be discussed in this research study. A company's marketing strategy is often the key to whether a product/service succeeds or fails in every market. Below are some reasons why marketing efforts fail in Ghana:

- Same marketing strategy used elsewhere will not fit in Ghana;
- Ghana has 70 ethnic groups with different tastes, desires and demands;
- Loss of unique appeal;
- Not understanding the 4 Ps of marketing in Ghana;
- Not staying current with current events affecting consumers.

Making sure that a successful marketing program is developed and implemented in Ghana begins with competent planning. This requires not just observations but methodical study of the regions and the people who reside in these communities. The first step in planning is to survey the country environment and find out what are the outstanding/obvious concerns and needs.

8.7 Planning

Planning requires data and information about many direct and indirect activities that affect the ability to properly implement a marketing strategy. Marketing strategies are frequently well-structured methods of delivering goods and services to a target markets and distributing them there according to the marketing plans. Standard Bank's report on the middle class in Africa indicates that Nigeria will add 7.6 million middle-class households by 2025, while Ghana will add 1.6 million. Knowing this information will have an impact on how expansive the marketing strategy and campaign will be. How marketers reach these new middle-class consumers becomes a major task. With the digital society being more intense with social media controlling just about all of our thoughts, marketers need to look at non-traditional ways of connecting with customers. E-marketing holds a number of benefits such as a wide market reach. Problems with it relate to the exchange of information, especially financial transactions and pricing information. There is a concern that the marketing concept will be adopted by some parts of the system but not others. The conflict may occur when the marketing concept people (meeting the needs of the consumer) interfere with the agricultural or manufacturing sectors that are production-oriented. When this conflict occurs, then there are partial resolution and the MO, which puts the consumer first. In the agricultural arena, three primary actors – the farmer, intermediaries, the processors and the consumer – exist. All have their self-interest at stake and in some cases do not care about the MO process even though it would be very important to all the stakeholders. Marketing is about creating a customer. Marketing is about establishing and maintaining long-term relationships with customers (Africa Asset Management 2020). E-commerce is still developing in Ghana. One reason is because of the limited existence and strength of the Internet – still widely under-developed. Since the privatization of the telecommunication industry, there has been more reliability and better transmission infrastructure created. Rural communities still are far behind the urban areas. Since the privatization there has been a major improvement. This effort may lead to greater and more efficient use of E-commerce in the future for Ghanaians.

To say the Internet offers tremendous opportunities for marketers, it presents a new way of conducting marketing and approaching consumer markets (Rahman 2003; Lichtenthal and Eliaz 2003) (Table 8.1).

8.7.1 Equipment Needs

Ghana has major thermal power plant construction and upgrade needed. A company, which can complete this work, can enter the market and achieve lots of opportunities. Additionally, the existence of oil and gas production has shown moderate growth and other auxiliary service opportunities. Mining is a major part of the Ghanaian economy – goods and services to this sector are a major marketing opportunity. Ghanaian

Table 8.1 Ghana's Internet usage and population growth

Year	*Users*	*Population*
2000	30,000	18,881,600
2006	401,300	21, 801,662
2008	880,000	23,382,848
2009	997,000	23,887,812

Source: Internet World Statistics, 2010

construction industry has demonstrated sustained growth with major needs for goods and services. Construction equipment is going to continue to be a major market opportunity.

8.8 The Marketing Mix: Global Marketing

What products, branding, packaging are appropriate and needed? What are the pricing policies, promotion and advertising approaches, channels, and distributions networks?

Contemporary global environment of intense competition requires a high level of marketing skills for all types of organizations. Historically, marketing contained in a silo arrangement bus has changed dramatically over time to become a major part of each employee's daily activities. The marketing mix concept has become an important tool that enables marketing managers to develop marketing strategies that strengthen the organization's competitive position and generates many attributes that are beneficial to the organization. These tools are used to gratify customers and company objectives. There are various models, theories, and approaches of analyzing a market, discussed under different perspectives, but with the same objective. The decision to take when analyzing foreign markets will automatically result from the company's marketing plans (Gameti and Preko 2014).

The core of any marketing effort revolves around the 4Ps of marketing. They are the components that drive any marketing strategy and any marketing campaign. This next section discusses these marketing components and how (Fig. 8.4).

8.8.1 Product Strategy

A product can be described as anything that can be offered to a market for attention, acquisition, use, or consumption that might satisfy a want or need (Kotler and Armstrong 2010). The key benefit or purpose for which a consumer buys a product varies from consumer to consumer.

According to Kotler, Armstrong, Wong, and Saunders (2008), price is the amount of money charged for a product or service, or the total values that consumers exchange for the benefits of having or using the product or service. Determining pricing strategy is a delicate task. It requires that you assess customer demand and analyze cost in order to choose a price that will create customer satisfaction and yield a satisfactory level of profit

Fig. 8.4 The marketing mix circular flow
Source: Author's creation, 2016

(Markim 1982). The objectives of pricing are for market survival, sales growth, profitability, competitive pricing, and quality and image enhancement (Kotler and Armstrong 2001).

A great many Ghanaians are interested in new products, different products, and products that are of high quality with a reasonable price. Marketers in Ghana need to find equilibrium where the product is satisfying while reasonably priced. This also has major impact in regional marketing because the needs and desires are so much different. Product strategy development for the Ghanaian market is challenging but exciting.

8.8.2 Place (Channel) Strategy

Distribution is delivering the desired product and service to the customer on time and desired place. There is an overall strategy about distribution. This is to direct and help distributors provide their goods and services to consumers (Gilaninia, Taleghani, and Azizi 2013). A distribution channel function is to move goods and service from producers to consumers.

Armstrong and Kotler (1999) have indicated that, in general, there are two main channel strategies: the "pull" and the "push" strategies. The pull strategy according to them is when the producer directs its marketing activities toward final consumers to induce them to buy the product. This approach they say, intends to encourage customers to "pull" products through the channel network.

Selling – face-to-face contact is the preferred approach in transacting business. It is the most effective way to build long-term relationships.

In Ghana, the informal trade has enjoyed dominance over the years. Informal trade is estimated to capture around 90% of the Ghanaian market. This market has seen high patronage from companies and Ghanaian consumers for all forms of transaction.

Presently, the influx of big shopping malls in the urban centers such as Accra, the capital of Ghana is slowly bringing a paradigm shift toward the patronage in the retailed markets. Ghana's retailed platform has local and foreign participants. Examples of the retailed markets in Ghana include Melcom, Palace, Maxmart, Shoprite, Accra Mall, West Hills Mall, and Marinas Mall, the Junction, and Oxford Street Mall and the upcoming ones (kpmg.com/Africa). Additionally, technology advancement has introduced into the Ghanaian market landscape what is known as online trade, locally referred to as Tonaton.com. On this platform companies and consumers have alternative market to transact businesses online.

Ghanaians have seen that the convenience which one-stop-shopping offers cannot be overemphasized, and therefore have developed a taste for shopping at the super markets. The increasing population of foreigners in Ghana could probably be responsible for the gradual attitudinal trade shift. Due to the fragmented nature of the Ghanaian retailed market, fresh industry players should consider the keen competition; ensure quick penetration and sustenance in the market (kpmg.com/Africa 2014).

8.8.3 Promotion Strategy

Promotion is all the communication tools that can deliver the message to the intended audience. Roosta et al. (2007) posited that promotion basically is a set of activities to inform, persuade, and influence existing and potential customers (Roosta et al. 2007). On the other hand, Kotler et al. (2002) defines promotion as the activities a company performs in order to communicate to its existing and potential customers. Promotion can be divided into four groups that each group has different dimensions: advertising, sales promotion, public relations, and personal selling. Melcom is an example of a company that has strategically positioned its products. Melcom provides customers with more than 40,000 low-cost products and offers everything a customer needs to maintain their homes (Asiedu 2015).

Promotion and communication efforts in marketing strategy are directed at accomplishing brand awareness, brand loyalty, and increase in market share. The increase in market share is characterized by effective advertising, secured channels of distribution, retail outlets, other forms of communication, and other promotion variables. Marketing communication and promotion specialist in every organization are faced with the demanding issues of how to communicate and promote the organization's brand name to its clients or consumers (Shimp 1996: 10). Seeing that products and services do not market themselves, it is a key factor, for any organization seeking to create brand awareness or rekindle the consumer brand loyalty, to assign time and resources in its marketing strategy, in terms of promotion and communication. Using the traditional methods of communication like radio, television, and billboards, Ghanaian business people promote their products vigorously, using festivals, conferences, and sophisticated brochures and Internet messages. Tourism is an example of an industry that is constantly trying new communication methods to attract customers. ICT has become a major asset in many Ghanaian businesses (Ammattikorkeakoulu and Yrkeshogskola 2009).

8.9 Pricing

The pricing strategy suggests that there are five main segments, which need consideration: Firm, Environment, Distribution Channels, Competition, and Customers. One of the segments is the Firm, which contains: corporate objectives, costs, and marketing programs and product assortment. In this segment, the authors suggest that the cost should be evaluated widely in such a way that it would include costs such as the product production costs and also the marketing costs such as market penetration costs in different areas. The marketing program includes taking into consideration the marketing unit targets about how the products are positioned in the markets. For example, are the products unique or standard ones. In the product assortment the products price relationship to other products prices from the same product line are considered.

Pricing strategy is the reasoned choice from a set of alternative prices (or price schedules) that aim at profit maximization within a planning period in response to a given scenario described pricing strategy as the interdisciplinary bridge through all business functions: the final determination of value is in the mind of the buyer, while good pricing aims at enhancing the worth of the product so that the value is increased regardless of the price. Understanding of the value of the product to the business of the buyer is necessary, while the current competitive situation and expectation of future competitor behavior has to be taken into account.

Pricing decision is a crucial decision every organization has to make, because this will eventually affect their corporate objectives, either directly or indirectly. For every business entity, irrespective of their line of business and objective, cost minimization and profit maximization is a general factor to be considered and for non-profit making organizations, there will always be the need to reduce cost at all means and to maximize output. A business whether small or big, simple or complex, private or public, is created to provide competitive prices (Kankam-Kwarteng et al. 2016).

In Ghana, product pricing plays significant role in marketing. It determines whether a company can penetrate, sustain itself, and maximize profit in the market, considering all factors of production. Ghanaians prefer high-quality products with moderate and affordable pricing on the market. Ghanaian consumers usually complain if desired products are priced high. They therefore shift to purchase other products that are of equal quality but affordable pricing (Frimpong 2013). In order to penetrate the Ghanaian market, fresh products of high quality should be affordable using pricing advantage to enter the competitive market landscape.

8.10 Marketing Strategies

Customer service is a marketing activity that needs all employees to place the customer at the center of the firm's decision-making process. Many times company or firm rules require employees to respond to customer complaints or concerns in a specified timeframe. Since these rules lead to a more intense customer focus, employees need to think about the details of these requirements and thus provide superior customer service (Kuada and Hinson 2014).

Rules and guidelines are really important in Ghana because many Ghanaian employees are fearful of taking action, which leads to mistakes. Their belief is that it is much easier to work according to specified rules than to be incorrect in their customer responses (Kuada and Hinson 2014).

Well-recognized companies such as Toyota are emphasizing customer satisfaction as the foundation of their marketing strategies. Toyota of Ghana is a company that wants its customers to see the company as customer focused (Kuada and Hinson 2014).

Companies in Ghana have taken on a variety of MO attributes. This means that some companies are market driving, which means they believe the customer, knows exactly what he/she wants. As such, the market research does not always show or predict what the customer wants or desires. This approach also assures that customers like companies that present new products and services that will add value to their operation. Companies such as Google, Facebook, or Starbucks illustrate companies, which have successfully implemented market-driving strategies. In Ghana Databank Group is an example of a company that has successfully responded to the market with market-driving strategies. Market-driving companies are companies that teach customers about the goods and services they want rather than giving them what they want. The effort with this strategy is to develop sustainable competitive edge (Kuada and Hinson 2014).

There are several marketing strategies an organization employs in order to enter a market for the first time and to retain its consumer base. A marketing strategy can also serve as a marketing plan for the organization. They both go hand-in-hand and help yield effective results.

There are various reasons underlying why companies, whether small or medium size companies or even the giant multinationals, decide to expand their business internationally. As globalization and increase in trade continue, there has been growing concerns among many individuals, labor groups, businesses, and governmental bodies regarding the effectiveness and the fairness of freer trade, the costs as well as benefits to the nation or regions and finally the behavior of international business and their social and environmental impacts (Albaum and Duerr 2008: 63).

8.11 Marketing and the Informal Markets in Ghana

The informal markets comprise a major economic sector of the Ghanaian economy. It is at these locations that many rural and urban residents do a great deal of their shopping. Consumers rely heavily on the informal market for a variety of products from food, household goods, and clothing for their families. Walking around the informal market area one would see a variety of items used in many different aspects of Ghanaian life.

The informal sector in Ghana dates back to early colonial times. This sector is comprised of a variety of different types of labor such as agricultural labor, buyers, repairers, transporters, vendors, and distribution agents among others. Over time, the informal sector has expanded both in rural and in urban areas of Ghana. It is estimated that the informal sector composes 80% of the workforce (Osei-Boateng and Ampratwum 2011). This sector has expanded due to (a) restricting the Ghanaian economy and (b) inability of the economy to create sufficient jobs for employees. The importation of foreign goods has caused the formal sector to lose ground in terms of job creation. Additionally, the absence of social protections, that is, unemployment benefits has motivated people to move to the informal sector as a means of survival. In general, the informal sector is comprised of proprietary entities, which consists of micro businesses and small vendor enterprises. These businesses are made up of wholesalers, retailers, artisans, food processors, traders, and craft workers. In Ghana 75% of the agricultural workforce is informal, while 43% of the urban workforce is informal (Osei-Boateng and Ampratwum 2011 and Madichie and Hinson, 2013).

A large majority of Ghanaian workers are stuck in poverty since wages earned in the informal sector is insufficient to move them above the poverty line. Because the workers in this sector do not have sophisticated skills or technology, their level of production is significantly affected. Additionally, the working conditions are below standards and expose the workers, their children and families to unhealthy working conditions (Osei-Boateng and Ampratwum 2011) Figure 8.5 depicts what an informal market looks like in Tema, Ghana. It is very similar to other informal markets in developing countries in other parts of the world. (Fig. 8.5).

In contrast to the formal market establishment pictured in the previous photo, throughout Ghana visitors see the informal market flourishing. It is a main location where a great deal of business is transacted seven days a week. All kinds of products and goods are presented and sold. The methods of buying

Fig. 8.5 Informal Market in Tema, Ghana

Source: Author's photo

and selling are traditional bargaining approach where a price is initially set by the vendor but is subject to negotiation. This approach to marketing has been around for centuries and continues in a vibrant way in Ghana. This market is in Tema, Ghana.

8.12 Discussion

Marketing and the distribution of goods and services are at the core of any country's sustainability. Ghana is no different. While there has been a belief that low-income countries have had problems acquiring products and services needed for its population, Ghana seems to be an exception to the rule. Overall Ghana is able to obtain just about all the products it needs. While it may be somewhat difficult to get products to all parts or regions of the country due to infrastructure challenges, eventually citizens are able to acquire just about all the goods they want. Because Ghana's economy has been growing, there have been investment opportunities for businesses, which have brought in a large array of products and services. An example of this is the mobile phone industry. Even though Ghana is considered a poor country, with substantial poverty, its citizens have been able to acquire cell phones. This opportunity has created a multiplier effect because with a cell phone a person can call other people, share their excitement about products and services, and as a result provide the catalyst for more selling and marketing activity. Ghana's growing middle class has also provided a push for marketing and selling. The Ghanaians' desire for goods from Europe and North America and their desire to shop online for goods is also a major indicator that marketing is alive and well in Ghana.

One major factor that has afforded Ghanaians' the access to products is its strong readily available seaport. The Bay of Guinea just south of Accra, the capital and Tema one of Ghana's major cities provides a gateway to the rest of the world and a powerful import and export arrangement. The existence of this infrastructure allows goods to be shipped in and out of Ghana easily and to and from all parts of the world. The seaport provides a major mechanism that allows marketers from Ghana and all over the world to do business in Ghana. Supply chain strength is a key component of the marketing function. Ghana's easy accessible, barrier-free seaport is a huge asset that fuels the consumption function in Ghana.

The other part of Ghana's market infrastructure relates to its informal market. These markets are as old as civilization. They have changed slightly but for many Ghanaians they are the only place to buy their goods and services. The traditions are strong and the products and services that the Ghanaians obtain at the informal markets are convenient, price appropriate, and reliable. Ghanaians can trust the informal vendors because they have been doing business with them for years.

In summary, we can say that the market and marketing environment that exists in Ghana has real possibilities. While Ghana is classified as a developing country, its progression and its steps toward comprehensive development have been substantial. Ghana still has a long way to go to make its economy a solid business environment, but its signs/signals over the last decade show that it has great potential and is headed in the right direction. It has major challenges such as its infrastructure, and its conditions of poverty, yet it has major indicators that point in the right direction. Time will tell whether it can continue on a path toward solid economic development and marketing success over the near term and hopefully over the long term.

8.13 Conclusion

Marketing is a critical part of Ghana's growth process. When people buy goods and services it creates a multiplier effect and provides the catalyst for business creation and economic development. As more people find jobs because of economic development, more consumption exists and one thing leads to another. Ghana has a fertile economic infrastructure for marketing to exist. The Ghanaian people need goods and services, and as we have seen over the last decade, the free market has flourished and generated the economic growth that has attracted worldwide attention. Marketing of goods and services is at the core of business sustainability and business development. Without the ability to sell products, services, and ideas, the market economy does not work. Ghana has all the factors of production (land, labor, and capital). It just needs to make sound business decisions and implement progressive growth policies. It needs to strengthen its free market system so that progress can be made both in the short and long term. In all of these activities, marketing is a critical function that must be efficiently and effectively applied to the development process. Once Ghanaian business people and policy makers truly believe in this idea, then they can continue to promote business development, increase job availability, and create a much better quality of life. This will require energy, ambition, and smart decision-making. Based on Ghana's history, they can do it and be a competitive player in the global economic environment.

References

Addressing the Consumer Preference for Foreign Goods, Feature Article. 2013. http://www.ghanaweb.com//GhanaHomePage/NewsArchives/Addressing-the-consumer-preference-for-foreign-goods-276309.

Africa Asset Management 2020-www.amafrica2020.com.

Albaum, Gerald, S. Gerald Albaum, and Edwin Duerr 2008. *International Marketing and Export Management*. Pearson: New York.

Ammattikorkeakoulu, Vaasan, and Vasa Yrkeshogskola. 2009. "Mwaawaaru Laaru Sarah Marketing Strategy in Terms of Promotion and Communication for Energy Drinks in Ghana. Case Company: Sinebrychoff Brewery." *Business Economics and Tourism*, pp. 1–100.

Armstrong, Gary and Philip Kolter. 1999. *Marketing: An Introduction*. New Jersey: Prentice-Hall.

Asiedu, Elvis. 2015. “A Critical Assessment of the Strategic Position of Melcom Within the Retail Industry in Ghana.” *Journal of Entrepreneurship and Organization Management* 4(2): 2–7.

Earley, Dan. 2013. Proctor & Gamble- Organization 2005- https://prezi.com/mqp–iervb2e/procter-gamble/

Frimpong, Charles Yeboah. 2013. Addressing the Consumer Preference for Foreign Goods. *GhanaWeb.* http://www.ghanaweb.com/GhanaHomePage/NewsArchive/Addressing-the-consumer-preference-for-foreign-goods-276309.

Gaitho, Lillian. 2015. “Infographic-Mobile Revolution in Africa.” http://africainternetgroup.pr.co/100040-infographic-mobile-revolution-in-africa, April 16, 2015.

Gameti, Daniel, and Alexander Preko. 2014. “Evaluation of the Contributions of Marketing to the Development of the Banking Sector in Ghana.” *European Journal of Business and Management* 6(34): 370–77.

Gilaninia, Shahram, Mohammad Taleghani, and Nadia Azizi. 2013. “Marketing Mix and Consumer Behavior.” *Kuwait Chapter of Arabian Journa of Business and Management Review* 2(12): 53–58.

Han, J.K., N. Kim, and R.K. Srivastava. 1998. “Market Orientation and Organizational Performance: Is Innovation a Missing Link?” *Journal of Marketing* 62 October: 30–45.

Internet World Statistics (2010). http://www.internetworldstats.com/africa.htm.

Kankam-Kwarteng, Collins, Jacob Donkor, and Stephen Acheampong 2016. “Determinants of Wood Prices: Analysis of Wood Retailers in Kumasi.” *Open Journal of Business and Management* 4: 36–44.

Keegan, Warren J. 2014. *Global Marketing Management.* Boston: Pearson.

Kohli, Ajay K., and Bernard J. Jaworski. 1990. “Market Orientation: The Construct, Research Propositions, and Managerial Implications.” *Journal of Marketing* 54 (April): 1–18.

Kolter, P., and Armstrong, G. 2001. *Principles of Marketing*, 9th edition. New Jersey: Prentice Hall.

Kolter, Philip, and Gary M. Armstrong. 2010. *Principles of Marketing.* New Jersey: Prentice Hall.

Kolter, Philip, Armstrong, Gary, John Saunders, and Veronica Wong. 2002. *Principles of Marketing.* New Jersey: Prentice-Hall.

Kolter, Philip, Gary Armstrong, Veronica Wong, and John Saunders. 2008. *Principles of Marketing.* New York: Financial Times Prentice Hall.

Kpmg.com/Africa. 2014. Sector Report: Fast-Moving Consumer Goods in Africa. http://www.kpmg.com/Africa/en/IssuesAndInsights/Articles-Publications/General-Industries-Publications/Documents/Fast-moving%20Consumer%20Goods%20in%20Africa.pdf.

Kuada, John, and Robert Hinson. 2014. *Service Marketing in Ghana: A Customer Relationship Management Approach.* London: Adonis & Abbey.

Lichtenthal, J. D., and S. Eliaz 2003. "Internet Integration in Business Marketing Tactics." *Industrial Marketing Management* 32: 3–13.

Madichie, Nnamdi, O., and Robert Hinson. 2013. "Doing Business in Ghana's Informal Sector – Auntie Muni and the Waakye Kitchen." *African Journal of Business and Economic Research* 8(2&3): 39–50.

Markin, R. 1982. *Marketing: Strategy and Management.* Wiley & Sons.

Osei-Boateng, Clara, and Edward Ampratwum (2011). "The Informal Sector in Ghana," Friedrich, Ebert and Stiftung, pp.4–40.

Rahman, Z. 2003. "Internet-Based Supply Chain Management: Using the Internet to Revolutionize Your Business." *International Journal of Information Management* 23: 493–505.

Republic of Ghana Country Strategy Paper, 2012–2016, African Development Bank and African Development fund, Country Operations Department – West 1 Region – April (2012). World Stats http://www.internetworldstats.com/af/gh.htm University of Applied Sciences

Richardson, Rich. 2015. Agricultural and Food e-Marketing in Ghana and Why? http://www.akuafoadanfo.com. http://www.linkedin.com/pulse/Agriculture-Food-e-marketing-ghana-why-rich-richardson.

Roosta, A. Ebrahimi, A., and D.Venous. 2007. *Marketing Managment.* Publication of Smat.

Shimp, T.A. 1996. *Advertising, Promotion, and Supplemental Aspects of Integrated Marketing Communications.* Tennessee: South-Western Publishing.

Slater, Stanley F., and John C. Narver 1994. "Does Competitive Environment Moderate the Market Orientation – Performance Relationship?." *Journal of Marketing* 58 (January): 46–55.

CHAPTER 9

Conclusion

9.1 Summary of Current Business Environment

Ghana is a country in the western part of Africa. It shares borders with Burkina Faso, Cote d'Ivoire, Togo, and the Gulf of Guinea. Lake Volta, the largest artificial lake in the world, can be found entirely in Ghana. As a low middle-income country, its population is estimated at 26,786,598 million with an annual growth rate of 2.35%. Ghana is endowed with human, oil, agricultural, and mineral resources. Ghana occupies a land area of 239,000 sq. km and exists as West Africa's second largest economy next to Nigeria. Since its independence in 1957, the country has experienced economic fluctuations. Sometimes, it would seem the country had no hope of future achievement. The Ghanaian people and leadership deserve the credit for making remarkable progress.

Ghana is blessed with an uninterrupted peaceful political environment over a decade compared to the economies in the subregion. This places the country in an excellent position in terms of investments and entrepreneurial activities. As part of the global web, Ghana is not excluded from the effects of global social, political, cultural, technological, and economic activities. Globalization and other trade blocs such as EU and AU have made both positive and negative impacts on several aspects of Ghana's economy through integration. Ghana has well-established democratic political structures and clearly defined legal systems that regulate all

J.E. Spillan, D.O. King, *Doing Business In Ghana*,
DOI 10.1007/978-3-319-54771-8_9

political and business activities. Ghana is globally recognized as one of the Gems of Africa.

Culturally, Ghanaians are noted for their hospitality, peace-loving attitude, and interest in promoting and ensuring national unity in the midst of diversity. The Ghanaian national culture evolves from the common integration of a collection of varied traditions, customs values, and practices of many ethnic groups. Interestingly, it is obvious that the Ghanaian and his religion are highly inseparable and that religion permeates all spheres of his endeavors. In understanding the cultural climate of Ghana and deciding to set up businesses, companies, firms, and other small businesses are to endeavor in tailoring their operations in accordance with the received cultural knowledge in order to maximize performance and profit.

On the economic front, Ghana is supported by the informal and formal forces. The informal sector is also known as the private sector. The informal sector is dominated by an estimate of 90% businesses. Enterprises in the informal sector are largely SMEs which have the capacity to employ at least 20 people. The sector which is massively agricultural inclined is the largest primary employer in Ghana, and responsible for generating export. Surprisingly, the agricultural sector provides a minimal support to the GDP of Ghana.

The service sector remains a higher supportive engine of economic growth in Ghana. Largely, businesses in this sector involves buying and selling of goods and services as well as ideas. There is a free and open market business climate which attracts people from all part of the continent to engage in diverse forms of business activities and generate economic development for Ghana. This calls for policy and business development structures to be strongly established and constantly reformed or updated to keep pace with the rapid globalization process. Ghana has all the factors of production (land, labor, and capital).

Building a stronger economy and ensuring a good business environment, the government of Ghana has been very active in its efforts. Ghana is well positioned twice among the top ten global reformers' ranking conducted by the World Bank Doing Business team. The country is considered as one of the best destinations for investment in Africa with lower risk but higher returns (World Bank group flagship report 2015 and 2016 & US Dept. of State 2015). The country is rated "B" and a good investment environment (according to globaledge.com). There is the development of PPP regulatory framework being developed by the government of Ghana to whip up confidence in the business environment, and control fiscal commitments. The government seeks to improve SMEs access to the capital market.

On the contrary, Ghana's current economy seems risky and unfriendly to business investment. This seemingly gloomy picture together with the slow pace of growth is tied with many economic constraints such as infrastructural weaknesses, poor access to technology, high inflation, persistent increasing public debt, continued increased budget deficit, increased interest rate, poor electricity supply, unemployment, high cost of living, high socio-political tension due to the IMF loan facility conditionalities as well as the impending 2016 elections and more which the country is confronted with.

Based on the above developments, the government is advised to ensure the use of prudent measures as well as strict financial discipline in its borrowings and expenditure. Revenues generated from mineral proceeds and other state resources such as human and natural must be prudently utilized to ensure economic freedom for the citizens. This will boost investment confidence in Ghana. In a nutshell, doing business in Ghana presents such a promising future returns on investment despite the high level of risk that could be encountered.

9.2 Identifying the Countries with the Best Environments for Doing Business

Economic activity requires workable or reasonable rules that encourage business start-ups and growth and avoid creating misrepresentations in the marketplace. Ease of doing business or the absence of obstacles confronting business is critical to successful economic development. According to the most recent World Bank Doing Business publication (2016), Ghana ranks 114th among 189 countries that were surveyed regarding ease of doing business. This means Ghana has some major work to do to achieve a level of ease of doing business that is favorable and would attract businesses to Ghana readily. On the major scale that was evaluated, Ghana was competitive on only two items that of getting credit and protecting minority investors.

Ghana has the wherewithal to meet many of the factors that make it easier to do business. It is a matter of will and putting various priorities in order. It also means proper allocation of resources (Doing Business 2016).

Ghana has lots of major possibilities for the future. Some of the goals have been outlined by the National Development Planning Commission. These goals include the following:

a. "Build an industrialized, inclusive and resilient economy,
b. Create an equitable healthy and disciplined society,
c. Build safe, well-planned and sustainable communities,
d. Build effective, efficient and dynamic institutions,
e. Strengthen Ghana's role in international affairs".
(*Source:* Ghana: A History of Our Future 2016, page 1)

By 2057, Ghana plans to be listed with and among the high-income countries of the world. It is planning on having an industrialized, diversified, and export-oriented economy that is robust and determined by entrepreneurship among the Ghanaian people. It will promote and develop high value services with a vigorous and globally competitive manufacturing sector. It will additionally have an effective and efficient agricultural segment that is not only skilled enough to provide food for Ghana but also to export to global markets (Ghana: A History of Our Future 2016).

The government along with the private sector will develop the economic infrastructure with modern transportation system that will be connected with all the major capitals both by road and rail systems. The society will create modern energy delivery systems and significantly upgrade the sanitation and sewage structures so that the average citizens around the country can be proud to use these new arrangements. The supply chain sector will be rearranged and restructured in order to transport, package, and house and distribute goods in a timely and efficient manner that will allow Ghana to be competitive in the world economy (Ghana: A History of Our Future 2016).

From a social and human development point of view, the Ghanaian people will develop a social and civic framework that will meet the recreational, fine arts, and athletic needs of the Ghanaian people (Ghana: A History of Our Future 2016).

Finally, focus will be on the issues of externalities such as air and water pollution and the preservation of water, land, forests, and biodiversity as prescribed from Ghana's green economy policies (Ghana: A History of Our Future 2016).

These are ambitious goals. One would say how could a poor country such as Ghana achieve all of these enthusiastic goals. This is a good question but it should not be thought of from a negative perspective. Ghanaians are thoughtful, intelligent, and young people. Given the chance, which they are carving out now – 2016 – they will beagle to achieve these goals. Will it be easy, not at all? Can it be done, certainly? Barging any major catastrophic event, politically, financially, or physically (natural disaster), Ghana is on a path to meeting all of the goals mentioned in the aforementioned listing.

9.3 Themes for Further Exploration

The content of this book has been quite extensive, addressing important issues in connection with economic, social, cultural, and political climates that relate with doing business in Ghana. The knowledge and content of this study can assists investors and academics in making informed decision and choices.

However, there are few thematic areas that are missing, hence the need for further exploration. These sensitive areas that failed to be captured by the lens of the researchers include taxation, sanitation, and health-related issues, water and sewerage, social intervention programs, security issues, media, political parties, and elections and citizenry. If the above limitations are catered for in the next study, the result will be highly comprehensive to demonstrate detailed doing business in Ghana phenomenon.

References

Doing Business. 2016. 13th Edition. Measuring Regulatory Quality and Efficiency, World Bank Flagship Report Comparing Business Regulation for Domestic Firms in 189 Economies. http://www.doingbusiness.org/~/media/GIAWB/Doing%20Business/Documents/Annual-Reports/English/DB16-Full-Report.pdf.

Ghana: A History of Our Future. 2016. https://s3.amazonaws.com/ndpc-static/CATCHES/PUBLICATIONS/2016/04/01/Final+-+Vision+Statement+-+Ghana's+Future+History.pdf, pp.1–8.

Ghana, US Dept. of State. 2015. https://www.state.gov/p/af/ci/gh

Index

J.E. Spillan, D.O. King, *Doing Business In Ghana*,
DOI 10.1007/978-3-319-54771-8